The NEW ENCYCLOPEDIA *of* SOUTHERN CULTURE

VOLUME 2 : GEOGRAPHY

Volumes to appear in
The New Encyclopedia of Southern Culture
are:

The NEW

ENCYCLOPEDIA *of* SOUTHERN CULTURE

CHARLES REAGAN WILSON General Editor

JAMES G. THOMAS JR. Managing Editor

ANN J. ABADIE Associate Editor

VOLUME 2

Geography

RICHARD PILLSBURY Volume Editor

Sponsored by

THE CENTER FOR THE STUDY OF SOUTHERN CULTURE

at the University of Mississippi

THE UNIVERSITY OF NORTH CAROLINA PRESS

Chapel Hill

This book was published with the
assistance of the Anniversary Endowment Fund
of the University of North Carolina Press.
Designed by Richard Hendel
Set in Minion types by Tseng Information Systems, Inc.
Manufactured in the United States of America
The paper in this book meets the guidelines for permanence and
durability of the Committee on Production Guidelines for Book
Longevity of the Council on Library Resources.
Library of Congress Cataloging-in-Publication Data
The new encyclopedia of Southern culture / Charles Reagan
Wilson, general editor ; James G. Thomas Jr., managing editor ;
Ann J. Abadie, associate editor.
p. cm.
Rev. ed. of: Encyclopedia of Southern culture. 1991.
"Sponsored by The Center for the Study of Southern
Culture at the University of Mississippi."
Includes bibliographical references and index.
Contents: — v. 2. Geography.
ISBN-13: 978-0-8078-3013-0 (cloth : v. 2 : alk. paper)
ISBN-10: 0-8078-3013-5 (cloth : v. 2 : alk. paper)
ISBN-13: 978-0-8078-5681-9 (pbk. : v. 2 : alk. paper)
ISBN-10: 0-8078-5681-9 (pbk. : v. 2 : alk. paper)
1. Southern States—Civilization—Encyclopedias. 2. Southern
States—Encyclopedias. I. Wilson, Charles Reagan. II. Thomas,
James G. III. Abadie, Ann J. IV. University of Mississippi.
Center for the Study of Southern Culture. V. Encyclopedia of
Southern culture.
F209.N47 2006
975.003—dc22
2005024807
The *Encyclopedia of Southern Culture*, sponsored by the Center for
the Study of Southern Culture at the University of Mississippi, was
published by the University of North Carolina Press in 1989.

cloth   10   09   08   07   06   5   4   3   2   1
paper   10   09   08   07   06   5   4   3   2   1

Tell about the South. What it's like there.

What do they do there. Why do they live there.

Why do they live at all.

WILLIAM FAULKNER

Absalom, Absalom!

CONTENTS

In 1989, years of planning and hard work came to fruition when the University of North Carolina Press joined the Center for the Study of Southern Culture at the University of Mississippi to publish the *Encyclopedia of Southern Culture*. While all those involved in writing, reviewing, editing, and producing the volume believed it would be received as a vital contribution to our understanding of the American South, no one could have anticipated fully the widespread acclaim it would receive from reviewers and other commentators. But the *Encyclopedia* was indeed celebrated, not only by scholars but also by popular audiences with a deep, abiding interest in the region. At a time when some people talked of the "vanishing South," the book helped remind a national audience that the region was alive and well, and it has continued to shape national perceptions of the South through the work of its many users—journalists, scholars, teachers, students, and general readers.

As the introduction to the *Encyclopedia* noted, its conceptualization and organization reflected a cultural approach to the South. It highlighted such issues as the core zones and margins of southern culture, the boundaries where "the South" overlapped with other cultures, the role of history in contemporary culture, and the centrality of regional consciousness, symbolism, and mythology. By 1989 scholars had moved beyond the idea of cultures as real, tangible entities, viewing them instead as abstractions. The *Encyclopedia*'s editors and contributors thus included a full range of social indicators, trait groupings, literary concepts, and historical evidence typically used in regional studies, carefully working to address the distinctive and characteristic traits that made the American South a particular place. The introduction to the *Encyclopedia* concluded that the fundamental uniqueness of southern culture was reflected in the volume's composite portrait of the South. We asked contributors to consider aspects that were unique to the region but also those that suggested its internal diversity. The volume was not a reference book of southern history, which explained something of the design of entries. There were fewer essays on colonial and antebellum history than on the postbellum and modern periods, befitting our conception of the volume as one trying not only to chart the cultural landscape of the South but also to illuminate the contemporary era.

When C. Vann Woodward reviewed the *Encyclopedia* in the *New York Review of Books*, he concluded his review by noting "the continued liveliness of interest in the South and its seeming inexhaustibility as a field of study." Research on the South, he wrote, furnishes "proof of the value of the *Encyclopedia* as a scholarly undertaking as well as suggesting future needs for revision or supplement to keep up with ongoing scholarship." The decade and a half since the publication of the *Encyclopedia of Southern Culture* have certainly suggested that Woodward was correct. The American South has undergone significant changes that make for a different context for the study of the region. The South has undergone social, economic, political, intellectual, and literary transformations, creating the need for a new edition of the *Encyclopedia* that will remain relevant to a changing region. Globalization has become a major issue, seen in the South through the appearance of Japanese automobile factories, Hispanic workers who have immigrated from Latin America or Cuba, and a new prominence for Asian and Middle Eastern religions that were hardly present in the 1980s South. The African American return migration to the South, which started in the 1970s, dramatically increased in the 1990s, as countless books simultaneously appeared asserting powerfully the claims of African Americans as formative influences on southern culture. Politically, southerners from both parties have played crucial leadership roles in national politics, and the Republican Party has dominated a near-solid South in national elections. Meanwhile, new forms of music, like hip-hop, have emerged with distinct southern expressions, and the term "dirty South" has taken on new musical meanings not thought of in 1989. New genres of writing by creative southerners, such as gay and lesbian literature and "white trash" writing, extend the southern literary tradition.

Meanwhile, as Woodward foresaw, scholars have continued their engagement with the history and culture of the South since the publication of the *Encyclopedia*, raising new scholarly issues and opening new areas of study. Historians have moved beyond their earlier preoccupation with social history to write new cultural history as well. They have used the categories of race, social class, and gender to illuminate the diversity of the South, rather than a unified "mind of the South." Previously underexplored areas within the field of southern historical studies, such as the colonial era, are now seen as formative periods of the region's character, with the South's positioning within a larger Atlantic world a productive new area of study. Cultural memory has become a major topic in the exploration of how the social construction of "the South" benefited some social groups and exploited others. Scholars in many disciplines have made the southern identity a major topic, and they have used a variety of methodologies to suggest what that identity has meant to different social groups. Literary critics have adapted cultural theories to the South and have raised the issue of postsouthern literature to a major category of concern as well as exploring the links between the literature of the American South and that of the Caribbean. Anthropologists have used different theoretical formulations from literary critics, providing models for their fieldwork in southern communities. In the past 30 years anthropologists have set increasing numbers of their ethnographic studies in the South, with many of them now exploring topics specifically linked to southern cultural issues. Scholars now place the Native American story, from prehistory to the contemporary era, as a central part of southern history. Comparative and interdisciplinary approaches to the South have encouraged scholars to look at such issues as the borders and boundaries of the South, specific places and spaces with distinct identities within the American South, and the global and transnational Souths, linking the American South with many formerly colonial societies around the world.

The first edition of the *Encyclopedia of Southern Culture* anticipated many of these approaches and indeed stimulated the growth of Southern Studies as a distinct interdisciplinary field. The Center for the Study of Southern Culture has worked for more than a quarter century to encourage research and teaching about the American South. Its academic programs have produced graduates who have gone on to write interdisciplinary studies of the South, while others have staffed the cultural institutions of the region and in turn encouraged those institutions to document and present the South's culture to broad public audiences. The center's conferences and publications have continued its long tradition of promoting understanding of the history, literature, and music of the South, with new initiatives focused on southern foodways, the future of the South, and the global Souths, expressing the center's mission to bring the best current scholarship to broad public audiences. Its documentary studies projects build oral and visual archives, and the New Directions in Southern Studies book series, published by the University of North Carolina Press, offers an important venue for innovative scholarship.

Since the *Encyclopedia of Southern Culture* appeared, the field of Southern Studies has dramatically developed, with an extensive network now of academic and research institutions whose projects focus specifically on the interdisciplinary study of the South. The Center for the Study of the American South at the University of North Carolina at Chapel Hill, led by Director Harry Watson and Associate Director and *Encyclopedia* coeditor William Ferris, publishes the lively journal *Southern Cultures* and is now at the organizational center of many other Southern Studies projects. The Institute for Southern Studies at the University of South Carolina, the Southern Intellectual History Circle, the Society for the Study of Southern Literature, the Southern Studies Forum of the European American Studies Association, the new Deep South Regional Humanities Center at Tulane University, and the South Atlantic Humanities Center (at the Virginia Foundation for the Humanities, the University of Virginia, and Virginia Polytechnic Institute and State University) express the recent expansion of interest in regional study.

Observers of the American South have had much to absorb, given the rapid pace of recent change. The institutional framework for studying the South is broader and deeper than ever, yet the relationship between the older verities of regional study and new realities remains unclear. Given the extent of changes in the American South and in Southern Studies since the publication of the *Encyclopedia of Southern Culture*, the need for a new edition of that work is clear. Therefore, the Center for the Study of Southern Culture has once again joined the University of North Carolina Press to produce *The New Encyclopedia of Southern Culture*. As readers of the original edition will quickly see, *The New Encyclopedia* follows many of the scholarly principles and editorial conventions established in the original, but with one key difference; rather than being published in a single hardback volume, *The New Encyclopedia* is presented in a series of shorter individual volumes that build on the 24 original subject categories used in the *Encyclopedia* and adapt them to new scholarly developments. Some earlier *Encyclopedia* categories have been reconceptualized in light of new academic interests. For example, the subject section originally titled "Women's Life" is reconceived as a new volume, *Gender*, and the original "Black Life" section is more broadly interpreted as a volume on race. These changes reflect new analytical concerns that place the study of women and blacks in broader cultural systems, reflecting the emergence of, among other topics, the study of male culture and of whiteness. Both volumes draw as well from the rich recent scholarship on women's life and black life. In addition, topics with some thematic coherence are combined in a volume, such as *Law and Politics* and *Agriculture and Industry*. One new topic, *Foodways*, is the basis of a separate volume, reflecting its new prominence in the interdisciplinary study of southern culture.

Numerous individual topical volumes together make up *The New Encyclopedia of Southern Culture* and extend the reach of the reference work to wider audiences. This approach should enhance the use of the *Encyclopedia* in academic courses and is intended to be convenient for readers with more focused interests within the larger context of southern culture. Readers will have handy access to one-volume, authoritative, and comprehensive scholarly treatments of the major areas of southern culture.

We have been fortunate that, in nearly all cases, subject consultants who offered crucial direction in shaping the topical sections for the original edition have agreed to join us in this new endeavor as volume editors. When new volume editors have been added, we have again looked for respected figures who can provide not only their own expertise but also strong networks of scholars to help develop relevant lists of topics and to serve as contributors in their areas. The reputations of all our volume editors as leading scholars in their areas encouraged the contributions of other scholars and added to *The New Encyclopedia*'s authority as a reference work.

The New Encyclopedia of Southern Culture builds on the strengths of articles in the original edition in several ways. For many existing articles, original authors agreed to update their contributions with new interpretations and theoretical perspectives, current statistics, new bibliographies, or simple factual developments that needed to be included. If the original contributor was unable to update an article, the editorial staff added new material or sent it to another scholar for assessment. In some cases, the general editor and volume editors selected a new contributor if an article seemed particularly dated and new work indicated the need for a fresh perspective. And importantly, where new developments have warranted treatment of topics not addressed in the original edition, volume editors have commissioned entirely new essays and articles that are published here for the first time.

The American South embodies a powerful historical and mythical presence, both a complex environmental and geographic landscape and a place of the imagination. Changes in the region's contemporary socioeconomic realities and new developments in scholarship have been incorporated in the conceptualization and approach of *The New Encyclopedia of Southern Culture*. Anthropologist Clifford Geertz has spoken of culture as context, and this encyclopedia looks at the American South as a complex place that has served as the context for cultural expression. This volume provides information and perspective on the diversity of cultures in a geographic and imaginative place with a long history and distinctive character.

The *Encyclopedia of Southern Culture* was produced through major grants from the Program for Research Tools and Reference Works of the National Endowment for the Humanities, the Ford Foundation, the Atlantic-Richfield Foundation, and the Mary Doyle Trust. We are grateful as well to the individual donors to the Center for the Study of Southern Culture who have directly or indirectly supported work on *The New Encyclopedia of Southern Culture*. We thank the volume editors for their ideas in reimagining their subjects and the contributors of articles for their work in extending the usefulness of the book in new ways. We acknowledge the support and contributions of the faculty and staff at the Center for the Study of Southern Culture. Finally, we want especially to honor the work of William Ferris and Mary Hart on the *Encyclopedia of Southern Culture*. Bill, the founding director of the Center for the Study of Southern Culture, was coeditor, and his good work recruiting authors, editing text, selecting images, and publicizing the volume among a wide network of people was, of course, invaluable. Despite the many changes in the new encyclopedia, Bill's influence remains. Mary "Sue" Hart was also an invaluable member of the original encyclopedia team, bringing the careful and precise eye of the librarian, and an iconoclastic spirit, to our work.

INTRODUCTION

The past 20 years have been some of the most tumultuous in the cultural history of the South. For almost a century and a half the region was largely cut off from the mainstream of cultural life in America. Few outsiders came to this economic backwater. For the first century few left. The region stewed upon its own history and cultural roots to create the most distinctive regional subculture in America. The 1930s brought the beginning of the great diaspora from the region; but the insular life within the region was intensified, if anything, by these movements. America's post–World War II economic expansion and regional realignments, however, did not ignore this region, and for the first time large numbers of outsiders started coming into the region, while local residents began leaving the family home place permanently in even larger numbers, not so often to go north or west as to move to larger towns and cities where new economic opportunities were to be found. The result was an entirely new southern demography that implicitly carried with it a new cultural geography of the region.

The changes were well under way in the 1980s, but the first edition of the *Encyclopedia of Southern Culture* could never have foretold how widespread, fast, and pervasive the region's cultural transformation would be. The nationalization of southern culture is obvious to all of us; less visible are the subtle changes wrought by an urbanizing society where "cultural heritage" is increasingly learned from books rather than from sitting on Granny's knee listening to tales of olden days. Taught cultural heritage inevitably collapses the individuality of each person's interpretation of everything from barbecue sauce to what is a proper house. Books, and most especially magazines like *Southern Living*, help us understand the past, but in the process they sanitize it, simplify it, and make it palatable to modern tastes.

The geography of southern culture has been especially affected by these changes. The in-migration of millions of "Yankees" and other Americans from outside the region, to cluster primarily in Florida, on the Carolina Coast, and in other attractive areas, changed not only those areas but surrounding communities as well, as these new arrivals search for the "Old South" of books and magazines. Immigrants from outside the United States also started coming in large numbers for the first time since the early 19th century. Hispanic immigrants are now living in virtually every county in the region, bringing with them their foods, their life attitudes, and their ways of doing things. Their impact on traditional southern culture is slight as of yet, but as they have children and those children intermarry with traditional southerners we are going to see a "salsaization" of our region's culture, to say nothing of the effect of the tens of thousands of Vietnamese, Chinese, and Eastern Europeans, and others who less pervasively, but no less importantly, are appearing across the region.

Geography is about where things are and why they are there. The "geography," the where and why, of southern culture has been turned topsy-turvy over the past 30 years. The traditional distribution of traits and characteristics found things originating on the Atlantic Coast and migrating westward within the framework of two great internal regions: the Lowland South and the Upland South. The postmodern era has almost completely overridden this traditional pattern. Cities have exploded in size and importance in the region, in itself a reversal of the traditional antiurban bias of the region. Atlanta with its four-plus million residents (as well as Charlotte, Orlando, Miami, New Orleans, and Dallas) now dominates the areas around it, introducing new ideas and subtly changing old ones. These cities have become the centers of innovations in new ways of life. There are eddies of resistance to this massive nationalization and homogenization of the region's culture, but they are becoming increasingly difficult to find.

The new *Geography* volume of *The New Encyclopedia of Southern Culture* attempts to cast these changes within the context of traditional southern culture. This volume is the most complete look at the spatial character of southern culture ever published. The hope is that the discussions about the nature and spread of culture and change throughout the region will not only provide a contextual setting for the discussions that follow in the later volumes but will also give our readers a better understanding of the "where" of this changing culture and some insight into how and why these spatial changes have been taking place over the past 30 years.

The NEW ENCYCLOPEDIA *of* SOUTHERN CULTURE

VOLUME 2 : GEOGRAPHY

LANDSCAPE, CULTURAL

The South stretches more than 1,200 miles westward from the Atlantic Ocean to create the largest of the American landscape regions. Isolated from the mainstream of American cultural and economic life through much of the 19th and most of the 20th centuries, the people of this sprawling region created a distinctive way of life and landscape. Though the South was recognized as a distinct American economic and political region from colonial times, its unique character did not mature until the 19th century. Colonial housing, town patterns, general material culture, and even diet were all largely transplanted from Europe and were much like those found in the northern colonies well into the early 19th century. The region's character as a distinct cultural entity began in earnest when the northern economy industrialized both economically and culturally. The South's continuing adherence to what were becoming relict traditional ways elsewhere in the nation created an increasingly visible cultural difference from other regions. The continuing dependence upon a monocultural agriculture (tobacco, cotton, rice, etc., depending on the subregion), the increasingly pervasive impact of tens of thousands of African-heritage residents not found elsewhere in the nation in large numbers, widespread poverty that curtailed social and technological advancement, and a crushing social and economic isolation after the Civil War all contributed to the elaboration and definition of this region's distinctive culture and landscape.

Widespread change began to be felt in the late 19th and early 20th centuries as textile milling, coal mining, and other industrial activities changed the economic order in some areas. Labor recruiters during World War I brought economic hope to thousands as they moved north to better jobs, but the final destruction of the plantation/sharecropper system during the Great Depression forced even more thousands off the land to seek opportunity elsewhere and to realize that other lifestyles existed. These realizations became even more apparent during and after World War II as hundreds of thousands of southerners were shipped out of the region, while millions of outsiders were introduced to the alluring qualities of the region as well. Substantive social change, however, did not take place until the civil rights movement freed both African- and European-heritage residents alike from the region's failed social system. The expanded external investment in the region that came as a result of this change brought the hoped-for economic and social growth and a new pace of cultural change.

This historic landscape and way of life are currently undergoing a pervasive transformation of character. Nationalization of the culture and landscape is most visible in the largest cities, where traditional life has virtually disappeared under the onslaught of growth and the swirl of in-migration. Even the most rural of residents have been introduced to McDonald's, video games, alien foods, *Southern Living*, manufactured homes, and *Star Wars*. Sitting on the porch in the evening, telling stories of the past, making music, and spooning is today something of the movies if not of the present.

Few pure traditional southern cultural landscapes remain today. Enhanced traditional landscapes, on the other hand, have become increasingly common. Rising education levels and disposable incomes, increased ennui with a seemingly rootless national society, the return of retiring expatriates, and the arrival of tens of thousands of "nouveau" southerners have heightened awareness of the importance of a sense of place and the positive qualities of this one. Southern traditional landscapes have become fashionable. Charleston, S.C., alone hosts seven million visitors a year searching for a sense of history—amply provided in its rebuilt, often reconstituted, and increasingly nonsouthern-owned historic district. Williamsburg, Savannah, New Orleans, and other cities have done likewise in search of both visitors and new residents.

Urban foraging by city dwellers in search of roots, even if just for the day, has encouraged the retention and resuscitation of folkways and landscapes that have not existed "in the wild" for a generation or more. Artists, craftspeople, and providers of traditional foods have all found new markets in these foraging shadows. As if all this were not enough, those who like "quaint" but not old "new towns" have created an ersatz world of genteel southern living that never existed, such as in Seaside and Centennial, Fla.

Geographically, the traditional southern cultural milieu extended northward from the Gulf of Mexico to just beyond the Potomac and Ohio rivers and westward from the Atlantic coast to central Texas. Transition zones, or spheres of influence, were found along the northern border, where the region intermixed with the Midwest, and on the western margins, where it mingled with the Hispanic Southwest. The western limits of the region have always been the most poorly defined because of decreasing population densities. The explosive in-migration of Hispanics in recent years has further blurred this line. The northern boundary has come under assault as well. The industrial Northeast and Midwest have moved southward in search of cheap labor, cheap land, low taxes, and state-offered development incentives. Kentucky, Tennessee, Alabama, and

Northeast
Expansion

Mexico,
Middle America

Mexico,
Middle America

Caribbean,
South America

Areas of Most Rapid
Nationalization

Major External
Change Force

MAP 1. *The Contemporary South*

South Carolina, for example, have all become sites for Japanese and European automobile manufacturing plants with promises of more in the future. Northern Virginia especially has been influenced by the expanding influence of the Washington, D.C., metropolitan economic region. Florida too is rapidly changing. The inundation of retirees and the Orlando phenomenon have increasingly made that state southern in location only.

All of the region's major cities, especially Atlanta, Dallas, Houston, Washington, D.C., and Raleigh-Durham, have become islands of national culture in a sea of decreasingly distinctive regional culture. Especially attractive rural areas, such as the Sea Island Coast and the southern Smoky Mountains, have been virtually transformed into nationalized islands of life as affluent retirees and second homeowners have purchased retreats in these areas. These nouveau southerners have often adopted and clung to the region's mythic past more tenaciously than have the residents who were born there.

Landscapes are mirrors of the lives of the past and present. The numbers of buildings, their locations, when they were built, their designs and floor plans, the ways that the surrounding areas are arranged, the crops in the fields, the commercial buildings and their services, along with a myriad of other details, tell the entire economic and cultural history of a place. Even culture without material form—foodways, language, and attitudes, for example—influences what is perceived in the landscape. The following discussion of the geography and history of the region is a guide to reading this landscape. The discussion begins with a characterization of the traditional past and its character, followed by an attempt to place that past within a contemporary context.

Shaping the Traditional Southern Landscape. The geography of the traditional South was strongly shaped by a combination of the physiography and early migration patterns. The physiography defined what could and could not happen; the migration patterns created the opportunities for those potentials to take place. Understanding both the land and how it came to be settled is important to understanding the evolution and character of the southern landscape.

Landforms. The physiography of the South may be divided into four great regions with portions of others found along the margins. The Appalachians are the largest single physiographic region and provide the initial basis for the separation into the Upland (Appalachia and its outliers) and the Lowland (Coastal Plain and adjacent areas). This general division into distinct areas is more than one of elevation; it is also one of cultural origins.

The southern Appalachians consist of five provinces. The Piedmont is a gently rolling erosional plain lying along the eastern edge of the Appalachians and is the only portion of these mountains that is a part of the Lowland South. Its western edge is marked by the Blue Ridge and Smoky Mountain ranges that contain some of the most rugged terrain on the eastern seaboard of the United States. The Blue Ridge stretches southward from New Jersey until it widens into a broad knot of infertile, crystalline rocks known as the Smoky Mountains in North Carolina, Tennessee, and northern Georgia. These formations created a barrier to westward migration and provided the initial basis for the creation of the Upland South.

A band of heavily folded sedimentary rocks forming an almost corrugated effect more than 50 miles wide in some areas is found directly to the west. The resulting alternating linear ridges and valleys provided a series of distinctive living environments that tended to isolate those who settled there. The valleys were floored with moderately good limestone and shale soils, but the flanking mountains were good for little more than livestock foraging and forest products.

The Appalachian Plateaus lie to the west of these areas. Few good agricultural soils are found here, except in two eroded domal areas, the Kentucky Bluegrass and the Nashville Basin. Early farmers took up these rugged lands because that was all they could obtain, and they settled into a life of subsistence farming supplemented by small amounts of tobacco and moonshine production. The Industrial Revolution brought development of a far different sort. Some of the world's finest bituminous coal deposits underlie large areas of the eastern margins of the Appalachian Plateaus. But often the owners did not realize the value of the wealth under their lands and sold the mineral rights for a fraction of the true value. The ensuing economic boom brought little economic benefit to most of these people and often made their lives more difficult. Unlike the Pennsylvania coalfields, however, these fields were mined primarily by the sons of the longtime residents, not by outsiders, as in western Pennsylvania and northern West Virginia.

The Ozark and Ouachita mountains are two hilly outliers of Appalachia lying just west of the Mississippi River, primarily in Arkansas and Missouri. Poor soils in the uplands, coupled with isolation from most markets, brought scant agricultural profit to the farmers who settled in them. In contrast, the Arkansas River valley, a band of rich agricultural lands separating the upland areas, was endowed with rich soils and easy access to markets. Cotton was the dominant early crop. Rice was introduced in the late 19th century, and the area soon became the largest rice-producing region in the United States. Corn, soybeans, and catfish farming now supplement rice as the primary crops.

A rolling area of low hills, isolation, and little economic value lies south of the Middle West and west of the true Appalachian Plateaus. These areas were excluded from the mainstream of economic development for generations. They continue even today to play only a small role in the evolution of the region's distinctive cultural heritage.

The Lowland South is composed primarily of the Piedmont and Coastal Plain physiographic provinces, as well as Florida. The Piedmont is a low granitic erosional surface with only a few low hills. Stone, Kennesaw, and Kings mountains, for example, are covered with a moderately thin layer of red clay soils. Piedmont soils did not make for productive agriculture, but they were available and handy. The eastern edge is marked by a series of falls and rapids along the streams that drain the Piedmont. This "fall line" created a break point for river navigation. Goods had to be unloaded and reloaded either onto wagons or onto smaller vessels above the falls. Mill operators of all types who sited mills on almost every stream that crossed the divide also quickly took advantage of the waterpower potential. A series of larger communities soon developed along the larger streams, including Baltimore, Washington, D.C., Richmond, Durham, Columbia, S.C., Augusta, and Columbus, Ga.

The Coastal Plain is composed of three main subareas. The Atlantic Coastal Plain is a flat alluvial area that slips into the Atlantic Ocean with little ceremony. The coast is composed almost entirely of large areas of swamp (flooded areas with trees) and marsh (flooded areas without trees), with scattered beach ridges creating islands of upland habitation sites. These ridge islands and their associated marshes provided a rich biotic environment for cypress swamps, fish breeding grounds, and the cultivation of rice. Charleston, Wilmington, and other cities are sited on river cut banks, on bluffs of varying heights, and as a result are several miles inland from the shoreline. The Gulf Coastal Plain is similar except that the angle of the beds' downward tilt is somewhat greater, with fewer swamps and marshes. These tilting beds also create a series of low ridges, or cuestas, parallel to the coast in the interior that provide the only relief between central Mississippi and Alabama and the coast.

The Mississippi Delta and Mississippi River valley slash through the western end of the Gulf Coastal Plain to make a natural pathway into the interior. The Mississippi River and its distributaries meander across most of south Louisiana in an area of marsh, mosquitoes, and more marsh. This isolated area was unsettled except for a few Acadians, colloquially Cajuns, who were descendants of French settlers from Canada and the Caribbean, a scattering of Creoles of diverse cultural heritage, African-heritage workers where sugar plantations existed, and a few Indians, known locally as Redbones. These people made their living cultivating sugar on the uplands and fishing and hunting along the natural levees of Bayou Lafourche, Terrebonne, and others. The discovery of oil after World War II changed all of this. Settlements unconnected physically or culturally with outside life were thrust into the mainstream, and the traditional ways soon began to erode.

"The Delta" region has not actually been the river delta for thousands of years and is located primarily in western Mississippi. The term was synonymous for whites with great plantations and lush lifestyles until the boll weevil and low cotton prices brought this romanticized life to an end. The diaspora of tens of thousands of African-heritage residents, along with many European-heritage poor, along the tracks of the Illinois Central Railroad during the 20th century, created some of the most evocative literature and music of the times. Chicago, St. Louis, and Kansas City all developed large enclaves of southerners, black and white, changing these cities forever as well. The arrival of these southern refugees in the North introduced barbecue, southern blues, real jazz, and the foundations of rock and roll to the remainder of the nation. The counter stream in recent years has had its impact on the original home areas as well. The Delta itself remained mired in poverty until recent stirrings of industrialization, a renewed cotton market, and catfish have begun to slow, but not stanch, the flow of out-migration of the region's young.

Florida has a completely separate geologic structure for most of its length. Composed of a limestone ridge flanked by coral sticking southward into the Gulf of Mexico, it was largely uninhabited until the 20th century. Florida played little role in the creation of the traditional southern landscape, except for the saw grass areas north of Ocala. South Florida remained mostly empty until Henry Flagler's railroad was completed in the 1890s and air-conditioning became economically viable after World War II. South Florida has never been a part of the cultural South and remains an independent cultural milieu to this day.

Migration Streams and Patterns. The European invasion of today's South began in the early 17th century with a series of tentative colonial intrusions along the Atlantic Coast. Chesapeake, Va., was the region's first cultural hearth. The Virginia planter culture thrived on the cultivation and export of tobacco. Large commercial farms, known here as plantations, were created early and quickly made their owners very wealthy. Virginia society was primarily British in origin, and the cultural landscape that evolved reflected its English origins. The demand for new lands in the Chesapeake area exceeded supply by the early 18th century. Settlement expanded westward onto the Piedmont to fill the demand and then again into the mountains (today's West Virginia remained a part of Virginia until 1861) and finally into the Ohio River valley in the late 18th century. Virginian influences are visible today throughout northern West Virginia, southwestern Pennsylvania, and southern Ohio, although they are becoming fainter with each passing year.

Many Virginians also moved southward along the Piedmont in search of new lands. Their initial destination was the Piedmont region of South Carolina and Georgia, since much of central North Carolina was already settled. The rise of cotton as an alternative commercial crop after the invention of the cotton gin in the late 18th century sent the sons and grandsons of these settlers across Georgia onto the Gulf Coastal Plain. The road along the eastern edge of the Piedmont was the largest and most important migration and transportation route in the eastern South.

MAP 2. *Source Areas and Routes of Traditional Southern Culture
(excluding direct European contact)*

The adjoining Cumberland, Shenandoah, and Tennessee valleys west of the Blue Ridge and Smoky mountains provided the second great migration artery in the eastern South. The difficult terrain of the Ridge and Valley Province, a series of alternating ridges and valleys extending from the St. Lawrence Valley in New York to the coastal plain of central Alabama, funneled settlers from Pennsylvania, Maryland, and New Jersey along this easier route to assure that the Upland South would be distinct from the Lowland South. The Cumberland Gap was the only east-west route for hundreds of miles, and most who started this route continued at least as far south as Tennessee before turning westward. Many more continued until they mingled with the westward-moving Virginians and Carolinians in Tennessee and Alabama in the northern Gulf Coast Lowland. Some Lowland settlers did cross the Blue Ridge to enter this southward-moving stream, but their numbers tended to be comparatively small.

Several lesser migration routes are also important in the eastern South. Many Carolinians moved up the Little Tennessee into southern Tennessee and then westward across northern Alabama and southern Tennessee all of the way to the Mississippi River valley. Others traveled the easier route southward around the south end of the mountains and then rejoined the mainstream in Tennessee. This new westward-moving stream created a distinctive landscape across southern Tennessee, northern Alabama, and Mississippi that is surprisingly "Carolinian" in its character.

Charleston, Savannah, Wilmington, and other coastal communities developed interior tributary areas but were never able to make a significant impact upon the Piedmont. The Pee Dee was an especially influential artery carrying Lowcountry culture into the southern margins of central North Carolina, but the breadth of influence did not extend far beyond the watershed. Similarly, Biloxi, Mobile, and other Gulf Coast cities maintained strong import/export linkages with the interior but were unable to have a significant impact upon the culture of their interior tributary areas.

The western South is dominated by the Mississippi River as the major artery moving both goods and cultural innovations back and forth along it and its tributaries. New Orleans was the primary transaction center for this vast area, but its own inherent cosmopolitan character was only deepened, not significantly altered, by the culture stream that passed its doorstep. The Natchez Trace connected the Upland to the western Lowland as well, giving those non-Acadian portions of central and northern Louisiana a decidedly Upland southern look, often with remarkably sharp boundaries between these settlements and those of the earlier Acadian settlers.

General Distinguishing Characteristics of the Region. The traditional cultural landscape received its distinctive face from a myriad of interacting lifestyles too numerous to explore here. This discussion focuses upon just six: agricultural practices, urban patterns, residential buildings, religious preferences, foodways, and language. These provide a comprehensive view into the geographic patterns of life within the region, though incomplete in defining the entirety of southern culture and its landscape. The discussion begins with an exploration of the overriding characteristics of the region before exploring the peculiarities of the various subregions.

Southern farms appear to be small island clearings in a sea of forest even today. Farmers in the region generally cleared smaller proportions of their arable land than farmers in other American regions did, and individual fields tended to be smaller, except on the great plantations. Although at least a part of the Texas cattle culture had its roots in South Carolina, cattle herding was never an important activity in most areas of the South. Fewer cattle meant fewer cleared pastures, which contributed to an "unsettled" look to the countryside. Hogs were quite important in most of the region and were commonly allowed to forage in the woods without restraint. Large tracts of cleared, open lands were neither needed nor created, then and now.

The agricultural landscape was thus dominated by forest rather than cleared land, in all but the most favored regions. An 1860 map of the ratio of improved land to unimproved land on farms shows concentrations of counties with more than half of their farmlands improved only in the tobacco areas of northern Virginia and adjacent Maryland and in the Kentucky Bluegrass. Bands of higher-than-average ratios follow the Shenandoah/Tennessee Valley corridor, the eastern/southern edge of the Piedmont, the Nashville Basin, and the Mississippi Delta.

The settlement pattern — the distribution of people, housing, and their social activities — went through four phases during the evolution of the contemporary landscape. The first phase was often described as desolate, or unsettled, by European travelers who were unfamiliar with the American landscape. Plantation areas had few small farmers prior to the Civil War, giving much of the region an empty look to those used to the agricultural villages and tightly farmed areas of Europe. Settlement that did exist was clustered around the plantation house. The end of the Civil War and slavery brought sharecropping. Tenant farmers contracted with landowners to farm bits of land for a share of the crop they harvested. The tenant often was a former slave who moved his home from the slave area at the plantation headquarters to his new plot or built a new home from local materials. Farms and farmhouses were thus decentralized and scattered throughout the previous plantation arable lands, most connected only by a rude road network. This pattern continued until hard-surface roads began to be constructed in the early 20th century. The promise of all-weather access convinced many sharecroppers and other small farmers to move their homes to the main roads. This revolutionized not only the distribution of houses but also accessibility to town and beyond. School attendance became simpler. Purchasing goods in town, rather than doing without or going to the nearby country store, became easier. Part-time or full-time employment off the farm became practical for the first time, allowing more cash to enter the farming economy.

Rural depopulation, the last phase, started during the Depression of the 1930s when many sharecroppers left and plantations started mechanizing farm operations. The cause-and-effect relationship of this process has been hotly debated among scholars trying to determine which was the instigator of the process. Rural depopulation increased dramatically after World War II as factory jobs became more available in the North. It turned into a flood after the civil rights movement demonstrated to even the most isolated farmers that there were rational alternatives to their traditional lifestyles both in and out of the region.

A strong antiurban bias has permeated southern life from the very beginning. There have always been fewer cities, and cities were smaller than in other regions of the United States. Most traditional southerners avoided urban places and moved to them only when it was no longer possible to make a living on the land. Even today millions remain in rural areas and commute long distances to avoid moving to town. Appalachia has the highest rate of rural nonfarm residents in the nation, and the remainder of the region is not far behind.

Traditional southern housing is distinctive in both construction preferences and floor-plan selection. The vast majority of all traditional southern houses were of frame construction with clapboard siding. Brick was used for residential construction during the colonial period in some coastal areas, where ships routinely used brick as ballast on their return trip to America to pick up new cargos of agricultural products. It was always an option for the construction of "great" houses such as Monticello. Brick residential construction began appearing again in the 1920s and has been used sporadically ever since. Few stone houses were ever built except in northern Virginia, there generally by southward-moving settlers from Pennsylvania, and in the Bluegrass and Nashville basins.

Southern house builders preferred to place their fireplaces and chimneys outside of the end walls, except in portions of North Carolina and in and around Charleston. Most homes were raised off the ground to reduce moisture accumulation beneath the house and to avoid flooding in coastal areas. People with Caribbean connections tended to build their houses an entire floor height off the ground in the belief that this lowered the threat of miasma (malaria). It also significantly reduced the threat of flooding during storms in coastal zones.

Church attendance and activities play a far more significant role in family and community life in the South than in other parts of the United States. Southern religious practices are distinguished by their conservative fundamentalist orientation rather than by denominational membership. Southerners tend to be more emotional and personal in their religious practices than are mainstream American Christians, and southerners are more likely to interpret the Bible literally. The Southern Baptist Convention is the largest single denominational body, and its distribution is often considered diagnostic of the region, though Methodists are more important in some areas.

The Methodist Church was the single most important denomination in the region during most of the 19th century. The factors underlying its decline are unclear, though its centralized rather than local control and its tendency to be perceived as less emotional in its worship services have often been cited. The higher educational requirements for clergy have also been suggested as a contributing factor in this region where education was generally less available for rural residents than elsewhere in the United States.

Thousands of independent and localized denominations are also found throughout the region. These churches are especially common in inner-city urban and isolated rural areas, but this regional preference has little to do with either poverty or lack of education. Large, independent, fundamentalist churches are also found in the most affluent neighborhoods of every large southern city, as well as in many suburban areas. The dominance of these independent churches appears to be an extension of the southern belief in individuality and independence rather than from more prosaic factors.

A strong belief in the rights of the individual and the localization of political power played a role in the rise of the Baptist denomination and is broadly reflected in the region's overall attitudes about politics, government, personal behavior, and life in general. The region has defended, literally to the death, its belief in the sanctity of states' rights, local decision making, and independent action, both before and after the civil rights movement of the 1960s. This attitude is reflected in the region's having the smallest counties in the nation, with 159 in Georgia alone. Southern county governments typically have more far-reaching authority than those in other states, and the state police forces typically have less power in local matters than is the norm nationally. The region also has had far higher rates of personal violence than elsewhere. Most southerners have traditionally believed that it is the individual's right and duty to resolve conflict personally when possible. The national rise of drug-related crimes and the general decay of the family and community structure in recent years have tended to obscure this historical pattern, though it still remains true.

Many writers have summarily dismissed southern food as fried, greasy, overcooked, and bland. Few foods are characteristic of the entire region, though southerners show a general preference for pork, fish, corn products, and certain vegetables, most notably okra, fried green tomatoes, pole beans, yams/sweet potatoes, various peas (e.g., black-eyed peas and butter beans), and cooked greens. Other elements that distinguish the traditional diet include the wide use of quick breads (primarily corn muffins and biscuits), grits, sweetened iced tea, and carbonated drinks, especially cola and fruit flavors. Many African-heritage southerners have mild to strong lactose intolerance, and sweet milk is consumed at much lower levels than the average in many of these communities.

A telling sight in many predominantly black schools is the sight of trash cans full of unconsumed federally mandated milk at the end of the lunch period. In contrast, buttermilk remained as a "standard" drink option on plate meals (a meat and two vegetables) at restaurants well into the 1960s.

Southerners traditionally ate the fewest restaurant meals in the nation, and the region had the fewest restaurants serving local patrons. Almost every county seat had a café or grill on the square to meet the needs of court patrons and local store owners, and most did almost all of their business serving breakfast and lunch. Otherwise only three types of commercial food establishments were found in any numbers: cafeteria/family-style restaurants, barbecue places, and fish camps. The South and Midwest are the two largest centers of cafeteria-style restaurants. They began appearing after the Chicago World's Fair in the late 19th century. The cafeteria/family-style restaurant dominated the mainstream restaurant business until the rise of fast food after World War II.

All great pit barbecue is found in rural settings, with the exception of Memphis and Kansas City. The vast majority of truly rural pits are open for business on only two or three days a week (Thursday, Friday, and Saturday), though most cater special events on other days. These places commonly sell more food as carryout than is/was consumed on the premises. True traditional southern barbecue consists of pork shoulders or butts slow cooked over hardwood charcoal on an outdoor grill with little or no basting. The debates about sauces, sides, types of hardwood, and even the proper construction of a grill are all secondary to these facts. It should be noted that the region's residents cannot even agree on how to properly spell barbecue (barbeque/bar-b-que), much less on which accouterments might be best.

Fish camps are the third type of restaurant found in many parts of the region, most commonly in the Lowland South. Southerners eat more fish than do residents of any other region; and African-heritage southerners eat even more fish than the region average. It is unimportant whether the species served is freshwater or saltwater as long as it is fried before serving. The name of this restaurant form is misleading—these places are neither camps nor located necessarily near fishing spots. Fish camps are small, rural freestanding restaurants serving fish that are locally obtained.

Finally, no discussion of the South could be complete without mention of the southern dialect. Speech patterns were once one of the most diagnostic subregional characteristics to establish a southerner's geographic origins. Well into the 20th century, a trained listener could place speakers to within 50 or 100 miles of their original homes after talking with them for a few minutes. Tele-

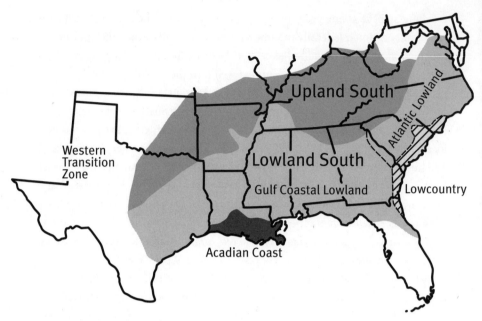

Western Transition Zone

Upland South

Atlantic Lowland

Lowland South

Gulf Coastal Lowland

Lowcountry

Acadian Coast

MAP 3. *Historic Southern Culture Areas*

vision, radio, and the invasion of incomers have all contributed to the loss of these subtle variations in southern regional speech.

Regions of the South. The South has never been a single, homogeneous place. Although it has been perceived as one of the nation's great regional entities since colonial times, the early difficulties of travel, the wide differences in physical environments, and the variety of cultural origins all but ensured that this place would become a patchwork of localized diversity. Essentially the region is broken into two great subregions, the Upland South and the Lowland South, but each of these regions has very distinct subregions within it. The following discussion examines each of the two main regions and something of the variations within them.

Lowland South Landscapes. The Lowland South is most commonly stereotyped by outsiders as a land of rolling plantations, languid plantation owners sitting on wide piazzas drinking mint juleps and talking of great books, and "darkies" working either happily or brutally oppressed (depending upon the political leanings of the viewer) in endless fields of cotton. Some areas did support this opulent lifestyle, but most areas could have been better described as smallish hardscrabble farms almost lost in the white heat of a sweltering summer sun as the owners and their help fought swarms of mosquitoes to plant, cultivate, and harvest the meager cotton crop for market.

The Lowland South encompassed the earliest settlement areas and as a result has the greatest degree of both geographic and structural variation within its boundaries. Three primary subregions can easily be identified within the Lowland South. Several smaller distinctive areas also exist, and a discussion of them will help better understand the whole.

The Atlantic Lowland. The Atlantic Lowland came into existence on the margins of the Chesapeake Bay as English colonists settled and began farming there in the early 17th century. These colonists created a commercial monoculture economy based on the production and export of tobacco. The heavy labor inputs demanded by tobacco cultivation limited the number of acres under cultivation at any one time and required some source of labor beyond the traditional family plus a hired helper or two. The labor problem was initially solved by the use of indentured servants from Europe, but these left to seek their fortunes as soon as their bond was completed. Some slaves of African ancestry were used from a very early period and eventually replaced all of the indentured servants for heavy field labor.

Lands were granted in large acreages even though only a small percentage of the land could be used at any given time because of the limitations of labor. Most of the farmland continued in forest throughout the colonial period. Few counties in the Virginia Tidewater had the majority of their farmlands improved for cultivation as late as 1860. The landscape was mostly one of oak and hickory forests, with narrow dirt tracks connecting the plantations, which were oriented to the rivers rather than to the land. It was not unusual for 18th-century road travelers to journey all day and see only a handful of homesteads. The difficulty and cost of overland shipping made planters prefer to ship directly from their own docks when possible, and only later, after sufficient farms without water access developed to create the demand for public facilities and the need to have tobacco graded before it was shipped, did commercial ports come into existence.

Towns represented gathering places for idlers, parasites, and troublemakers in the minds of the early planters and were to be discouraged whenever possible. The first towns were county seats. The first county seats were very small places. A neo–middle class of smaller farmers, artisans, and merchants eventually began to become more viable in the 18th century, prompting the growth of some larger centers. The gentry generally did not frequent these places. This antipathy was reflected in Virginia by the need for the House of Burgesses to mandate the survey of county seats to make sure that they came into existence at all. A century later some of those "towns" still consisted of little more than the county courthouse, a general store selling goods to people transacting business at the courthouse, and an inn for those who were forced to stay the night. Some still continue today with few additional structures.

The demand for a court, agrarian processing, and other urban services grew as the power of the gentry declined, especially in outlying areas where farm units tended to be smaller. The expanding settlement frontier brought a continuing demand for new counties and seats of county government. Many of these newly platted communities were envisioned to become fairly large places as the numbers of streets and building lots continued to increase. The typical early 19th-century county seat in the Lower South was located near the geographic center of the proposed county, preferably on an upland site. The rectilinear town plan was in vogue by this time, and most surveyed after 1820 had six or more streets in each direction and at least 25 building blocks. Early examples had 80 to 100 one-quarter- to one-half-acre building lots, 30 or more narrow frontage commercial lots facing the square, and 20 or so larger commercial lots at the rear of the small commercial lots. This practice of using widely differing sizes of lots in preplanned rectilinear towns is not typical of most American planned communities of the era but fit the needs of the region. The proceeds of the sale of these lots were used to pay for the development of the town and the construction of public buildings.

Early courthouses were of log or frame, but by the late 19th century most were two-story brick structures with a distinctive cross-hallway pattern. The courthouse typically was the largest building in town and was located in the center of an open square. Its rooms, halls, and steps were the stages for trials, sheriffs' sales, tax and permit payments, and gossip for the entire county. This public space was also used for other activities as well, including the site for the jail, public well, bandstand, and public memorials. Weekly farm markets were also commonly held along one or more sides of the square. The statue of a Confederate soldier in battle dress is an often-remarked-upon feature of the county courthouse, but these did not begin to appear in numbers until after 1890.

The square, the courthouse, and the facing businesses formed the core of these communities. The largest and most prestigious businesses in a moderate-sized example from the late 19th century typically included a hotel, four or five large general merchandise stores, a ladies' apparel shop or two, the bank, and a drugstore. Doctors', lawyers', and insurance offices were located on the second floors of these brick buildings. The post office, telegraph office, and livery and artisan shops were on the side streets.

Today these communities continue to look much as they did 100 years ago. The great 19th-century brick courthouse set in a grove of oaks on the square presents a sharp contrast to the plainer commercial buildings surrounding it. Some stores continue as always, but increasing numbers are boarded up or just sit empty. Antique shops and gift stores are about the only new businesses on the square, taking full advantage of the increasing average age of the population and its needs.

Southern towns have always appeared to be more bucolic than those in Pennsylvania and other nearby areas because of a preference for larger in-town residential building lots. Many wealthier plantation owners maintained homes in town in the local county seat or shipping center so that they could have a better developed social life than was possible among the widely scattered large holdings. Some towns, such as Camden, S.C., and Madison, Ga., have become the subject of magazine articles as their large, beautiful homes have increasingly become migration targets for incomers in search of that idyllic life of a better time long past.

Dispersed communities were the most common type of urban settlement throughout the entire South. These communities were not towns at all, but rural districts that were given names and performed urban functions without any apparent population agglomeration. Shake Rag, Dog Run, and Shady Oaks were once viable local centers with a church or two, one or more general stores, a blacksmith, and other artisan activities scattered across a small area. A combination of rural out-migration, paved roads, and large national retail chains building "big box" stores in central locations has conspired to make them superfluous in today's economic fabric. The church and the crossroads store may be the only functioning service activities, and increasingly they remain open more as symbols of stubbornness than because of viability.

The explosion of the railroad network across the South after the Civil War brought a third form of urban setting. Most county seats had rail access, but hundreds of communities were also established along railroad rights-of-way with freight depots, cotton warehouses, and gins. These communities looked little different from the railroad towns of the Dakotas and Kansas, except for the distinctive cotton gin structures. As such, they represented in many ways the first wave of nationalization of the southern cultural landscape.

The late 19th-century urban landscape was generally one of national, rather than regional, trends. New store buildings were of brick and used the same designs as those built throughout small-town America. Indeed, a careful examination of storefronts demonstrates that many used prefabricated cast iron facades or facade parts manufactured in the industrial Northeast. Few new houses were built during this period, but those that were tended to follow national designs rather than regional trends. Ornamented with a few "southern" details, these homes look as much a part of the regional fabric as those that evolved here. The pell-mell nationalization of the southern landscape may be seen as a modern phenomenon, but its roots lay in these late 19th-century market centers.

A drive down a small-town street or a country lane gives even the casual visitor an almost immediate sense of southernness. Many factors contribute to this, but few have more influence than the homes and outbuildings that one passes. The "look" of these structures, combined with their absolute and relative locations, governs much of the overall appearance of farmstead and townscape alike. House forms are defined by the arrangement, relative size, and function of rooms, along with facade elements. These apparently superficial elements have proven to be amazingly effective indicators of cultural origins because a society's allocation of home space reflects the very essence of family life and its perceived needs. Colors, materials, and facade design elements may change with the whims of society, but the internal allocation of space remains amazingly constant through time and across space within culture histories.

Few moderate-sized residential structures were built during the early plantation period in the Chesapeake, and fewer still have survived. The cottage, a single-room home, was the basic building unit in medieval English architecture. Cottages were rarely built in the Lowland South except as slave quarters and kitchen appendages to a larger house. The two-room expansion of this house, often called a hall-and-parlor, was the single most common small house in all of the Atlantic colonies. The Chesapeake version, the tidewater, usually was a story-and-a-half in height and had a peculiar side profile that distinguished it from other regional variations. Later versions were constructed with a central hall (after c. 1750), and a structural porch (porched tidewater) became an integral feature in many examples after that time as well. The porched tidewater was rarely found in the Gulf Coastal Lowland partially because the sleeping loft area is less functional and partially because of the popularity of the flattish roofline favoring the Greek Revival architectural style during the period of greatest population expansion and new home construction.

The two-story "I" house also evolved in England prior to the colonization of America and was commonly used throughout the entire Lowland South. This house became identified with the upper middle class and higher and appeared when the householder wished a larger or more pretentious house than the more prosaic tidewater. It was rarely used as the basis of a plantation house in Chesapeake Virginia. The smaller holdings and resources typical of much of

Greek revival house, near Eufala, Ala., 1975 (Richard Pillsbury, photographer)

western Virginia and the Carolinas made it an attractive foundation as a plantation house. Decorative piazzas, rear additions, larger rooms, and wider central hallways transformed this relatively prosaic house into an elaborate frontier showplace home.

Later Atlantic Lowland farms outside of the hearth area were usually small and cultivated a comparatively small portion of the land owned. Labor requirements were less as a result, and few slaves were kept. Not one county on the Piedmont averaged more than 20 slaves per farm unit in 1860, and more than half of the counties averaged fewer than 10 per farm unit.

Mild winters and limited livestock production reduced the need for large outbuildings for the storage of winter fodder. The largest farm buildings on most Atlantic Lowland farms were tobacco barns. North Carolina tobacco farmers flue-cured their crop, that is, they heated the fresh-picked leaves in an enclosed space to dry and stabilize the tobacco. The classic flue-cured tobacco barn was a frame or crude log cube, 12 to 20 feet on a side. A wide shed roof was constructed along one side for loading and unloading wagons protected from the weather. These began to be replaced in the 1960s by metal garagelike structures that reduced labor input by allowing farmers to pull a wagon of raw tobacco into the barn and cure it without additional handling.

Most tobacco farmers in northern Virginia and Maryland and even those few across the border in Pennsylvania air-cured their output. The tobacco was cured in great single-floor straight-gable barns, an adaptation of the English flat barn found in portions of upstate New York and in the Connecticut River valley, except that the main access doors were built in the gable ends of the structure. Alternate boards on the side were set so that they could either be propped away from the wall or swung away from the wall on hinges to allow a free flow of air through the barn when the weather was dry or closed during the rain. These barns are still common on the western shore of Maryland and in adjacent Pennsylvania, as well as in the upland tobacco-producing areas in Kentucky. (The minuscule tobacco production region along the Wisconsin and Minnesota border also uses a form of these structures.)

Log construction was rarely used in the Atlantic Lowland South and was of crude design when it was. Techniques of log construction and the houses typically constructed with logs will be discussed as a part of the Upland landscape, where they were the norm rather than the exception.

Dietary preferences reflect the Atlantic Lowland's prototypical heterogeneity in relationship to the remainder of the South. Both individual dishes and entire menus have a far greater variety over relatively short distances because they were evolving in this region, not imported completely formed. Brunswick stew recipes, for example, vary from Little Jimmy Mathews's original recipe, which was little more than squirrel stew, to a rich mixture of corn, tomatoes, chicken, lima beans, and other vegetables far to the south. Barbecue, Hoppin' John, and numerous other dishes exhibit this kind of variation as well.

Gulf Coastal Lowland. The transition into the Gulf Coastal Lowland landscape is gradual, but within a hundred miles of crossing the Savannah River, the observant westward-moving traveler knows that he or she has come into a different landscape region. The ratio of pine forest to cultivated lands has increased, and the farms and villages are visibly less economically well-off now and seemingly always in the past. The houses are similar, but they seem smaller and less well built, and the trailer in the woods looks so natural that it must have always been there.

In many respects the Gulf Coast Lowland is the definitive Lowland South landscape. Here is where the various southward-moving migration streams merged their disparate elements from the mountains, from the Atlantic Piedmont, and inland from the coast to form a single landscape. It is far from homogeneous, yet the regional variations take on a different character. Instead of the raw "work in progress" feel often evoked to the east, the landscape elements feel as if they represent the ends of their evolutionary cycles rather than the beginnings.

The Gulf Coastal Lowland was once the heart of the Cotton Belt, but the boll weevil, competing agricultural areas, and polyester began changing that after 1930. Large acreages of cultivated lands reverted to forest, others were converted to pasture, and the remainder have been used primarily for corn and soybeans. Trees became the most important agricultural crop in many areas, especially in southern Mississippi, Alabama, and Georgia.

The classic Gulf Coastal tenant farm dwelling is a small, two-room, frame, hall-and-parlor house with rusting galvanized metal roof and unpainted clapboard walls sitting in the weeds along a narrow macadam road. Two or three chairs sit on a drooping, attached porch that stretches across the front. The house stands in the midst of a hard-packed swept yard in the shade of a huge chinaberry tree. The attached rear kitchen is connected to the house with a wrap-around porch on the inside of the "L." A frame, single-crib barn with shed addition on one side sits behind the large family garden. Dried gourds to house purple martins hang from a line stretching across the garden from a pole to the barn. The small, raised, square, log corncrib and smokehouse to one side are shaded by massive live oaks that gave shade before this farm existed and will give shade long after it is gone. Small cornfields behind the barn can barely be seen through the hazy white heat of summer.

Gulf Coastal vernacular houses have lower-pitched rooflines than those of the Atlantic Lowland. Often cited as a contributing factor is the popularity of the Greek Revival architectural style that favored nearly flat Mediterranean-style roofs when much of the early settlement of this area took place. Another popular explanation is that high summer temperatures made the lofts impossible to use as sleeping quarters for much of the year. Central hallways are noticeably wider in all houses across the Gulf Coast. The hallway of a tidewater or an I house in Virginia commonly was eight feet wide. The Gulf Coast equivalent might have a twelve-foot-wide hallway. These widened spaces acted as breezeways to cool the homes. The homes were oriented to catch the prevailing breeze, and each end of the hall had double doors that could be thrown open during much of the summer. Dining tables were often placed in these spaces during summer months to provide a more agreeable dining environment.

The use of these wide "dogtrot" halls seemed to have begun in the southern Uplands but became standard through almost all of the Gulf Coast Lowland. Gulf Coastal houses also tended to be built with taller foundation pillars than those to the east. The detached kitchen was often moved closer to the house so that porches could tie the building units together to reduce the number of times family members had to go to ground level each day.

The most important vernacular house forms during the early period were large and small versions of the hall-and-parlor, the I house, and the dogtrot house. The southern pyramidal, shotgun, and frame saddlebag house forms were the most common new homes of the late 19th and early 20th centuries. The southern (Louisiana) bungalow was widely used after World War I. National styles dominated new construction after 1930. Two-unit modular homes, doublewides, probably are the single most commonly erected new house form in the region today.

The small size of many Gulf Coast farm units meant that many farmers used either an enlarged hall-and-parlor or I house as their "plantation" house. The hall-and-parlors were made more elegant with the addition of an oversized Greek Revival portico across the front, ornate brackets and returns on the eaves, and the placement of the kitchen as a catslide (shed) extension across the rear of the house to give it more bulk. I houses were also made more elaborate in much the same way, though two-story columned porches were especially popular, even if the columns had to be made locally and crudely.

Three houses rarely found in other areas are common to the Gulf Coast Lowland. The frame dogtrot house is the strangest of these because its origins are unclear. It began as two single-pen log units tied together with a floored breezeway, porch, and common roof somewhere in the Upland South. Isolated examples have been found as far north as Maryland, although the upper Tennessee River basin was apparently the earliest center for its widespread use. Log versions of the house are found in northern Alabama and Mississippi, but frame versions appear without apparent connection to the Upland South across the entire Gulf Coastal plain. Although it is an obvious environmental adaptation, unconnected appearances of full-blown house forms are extremely unusual.

The shotgun house originated in Africa, matured in the Caribbean, and first appeared in the United States in New Orleans and in other Caribbean settlement areas, though typically not on the Carolina rice coast. It was commonly used on sugar and cotton plantations as slave quarters, and large numbers are found in river towns along the Mississippi as far north as Louisville. Most Gulf Coast Lowland shotgun houses any distance away from the Mississippi River and its tributaries probably were not directly related to this tradition. Lumber companies specializing in precut and prefabricated houses sold thousands of shotgun house kits, and plans were sold in the late 19th and early 20th centuries to lumber, textile, and other company town proprietors as tenant and worker housing.

The southern pyramidal is the third house form initially unique to this area. It probably evolved during the mid-19th century from an earlier straight-gable

Shotgun house, Grosse Tete, La., 1964 (Richard Pillsbury, photographer)

house in the Savannah River area of Georgia. The oldest examples of this house have four rooms with a wide central hall. A high-peaked pyramidal roof with two chimneys placed a few feet on either side of its short roof ridge made the house quite distinctive visually. This was a favorite townhome of the upper middle class from Reconstruction to the Depression, although it is found in smaller numbers in rural areas as well. Some early versions were created by placing a common pyramidal roof over two saddlebag houses that had been moved close to each other. Prefabricated housing companies also marketed several other versions of this house for management and worker housing in company towns, and examples of these may be found all of the way west to the Pacific Ocean.

The saddlebag house, a simple two-room house with two doors sharing a common central chimney, is a log house form that was built of frame in the Gulf Coast region. Some Gulf Coast saddlebag houses were used as slave quarters, but most were built as tenant and worker houses after 1880. They were most often built as a company house with a shed or catslide kitchen on the back to house two worker families. A door has frequently been cut to connect the rooms in most single-family-occupied homes today. The vast majority were built from precut or prefabricated house kits, or modeled on these kits.

Frame single-crib barns with side-shed additions are the most visible outbuildings of the Gulf Coast. These structures evolved from the single-crib log barns of the Upland South. Some double-crib log barns are also found along the northern margins of the region, but they are not common. Several types of corncribs are also found. The most distinctive is of Cherokee (possibly Creek) origin and is a squarish log (or frame) crib raised a few feet off the ground.

The region's dietary patterns are also a simplified version of those found on the Atlantic Coastal Plain. The dominance of pork, chicken, corn, and yam products is almost complete. Game, including local fish, is even more important. It is not entirely by accident that commercial catfish farming began and continues to be centered here. The high consumption of colas, sweetened iced tea, buttermilk, hush puppies, greens, and peas also continues, though the presence of barbecue in many areas is less well pronounced.

The Atlantic Coastal Plain. The Atlantic Coastal Plain has always been a mosquito-infested boggy place of either endless stretches of salt grasses and indolent rivers or of virtually impenetrable cypress swamps, alligators, and even more mosquitoes. This was not an inviting landscape to the settlers—but a rich one for those who knew how to mine its wealth. Shrimp, crab, oysters, and fish teemed in the endless inlets to provide feasts for all. The cypress, live oak, and hickory could be cut and milled and shipped to build the finest of houses and ships. And even more importantly for the colonial planters, the soils could be coerced into yielding rice and indigo, sea island cotton and tea, and winter vegetables for northern markets. Success at these endeavors was dependent upon the importation of Africans from the Guinea Coast and the Caribbean to clear the lands, teach the planters how to cultivate rice, and even provide some of the rice seeds for the impending economic revolution.

Two quite different landscapes quickly emerged. Charleston, Wilmington, and Savannah all took on a cosmopolitan feel, with ships, people, and goods coming and going from seemingly every corner of the globe. Their look was more European than American well into the 19th century. Charleston still presents an almost medieval image of narrow, twisting streets lined cheek by jowl with houses crowding each other and the sidewalk. Great live oaks are scattered everywhere through the historic districts, twisting the often stone-paved sidewalks as they push their roots to the surface. Spanish moss hangs languidly from branches, and resurrection ferns give even their great arms a strangely serene look. Walls everywhere protect what little privacy remains. The city's famous gardens are only glimpsed through gaps in the brick walls, or through the wrought iron fronted hedges, or occasionally more easily through the wrought iron gates.

These may have been English colonies, but they attracted entrepreneurs from around the world. Charleston was especially diverse, with not only traditional English settlers, but also large numbers of French Huguenots, Germans, Irish, and the pervasive African-heritage slaves and freedmen. This cultural milieu was leavened with the second-largest Jewish community in the United States; about one-quarter of all American Jews lived in South Carolina at the time of the Revolution. Smaller numbers of planters resettled here from the Caribbean, most notably Barbados, and brought a Creolized version of European culture with them. The result was a basically English landscape with influences from the rest of the world.

The single most distinct urban house feature of the Lowcountry was the "Charleston single," a basic I house turned on end to the street. Most today have two-story porches that stretch down the side of the house, usually separated from the street by a wall. The main entrance with central hall remains in the same location as always but is now approached by means of stairs and usually a doorway at the street end of the porch. This house almost always has its fireplaces and chimney set on the side away from the main entrance. This "back" side never has the traditional balanced window arrangement of the standard I form but instead has minimal windows placed to provide maximum privacy from the house beside it, which probably would also be of a similar floor plan.

The sharp contrast between the urbanity of the region's cities and the rural areas was staggering. Palatial mansions with formal gardens and all of the other accouterments of English country homes were built up and down the rivers, but the heat, mosquitoes, and isolation drove the European owners to town or to more salubrious climes for at least part of the year. There was little settlement not directly connected with the plantations prior to the Civil War, and the plantation country was dominated by a population that was as much as 90 or 95 percent African heritage. The great houses and the other material culture were of the most cosmopolitan European design. Surviving smaller houses too were primarily English, though most likely there did exist purely African houses that were too humble to have been recorded or preserved.

The task work system employed in the Carolina Lowcountry gave the slaves working in the rice field far more time to hunt, fish, grow crops, practice artisan crafts, and remember their histories than did the slaves working the gang system elsewhere in the South. Gullah became the patois of the coast; the church services, at least in predominantly African membership churches, have strong overtones of the African past; local musical forms echo the Guinea Coast; and food preferences, until recently at least, often were more African than European.

The Upland South. The evolution of the Upland South began with the southward migration of Pennsylvanian settlers along the limestone valleys of the Ridge and Valley Province. They mixed with Virginians from the Piedmont moving up the Potomac and James rivers and Carolinian settlers entering by way of the Little Tennessee River. A cultural milieu soon evolved that was similar, yet strikingly different, from either hearth region. Complexity was added by the Cherokee nation, which stopped European expansion into its section of the southern Appalachians until the 1830s and contributed several cultural elements of its own. The Mississippi and Ohio rivers and the Natchez Trace played significant roles in later alterations but were not important to the initial creation phase.

Three types of centers dominate urban landscapes in the Upland South: industrial cities, county seats, and coal camps. The Industrial Revolution left its mark on the region's larger cities: grimy brick buildings, thriving chemical plants, abandoned factories, tortuous streets to serve sites never meant for urban living, and aged housing. In contrast, the region's county seats are marked by their typically bucolic settings, formal designs, and relative cleanliness. Southern Upland coal camps seem to have a more temporary feel than those on the northern Appalachian Plateau. A straggling line of asbestos-sided company houses ending at the tipple and mine entrance marks their location, though many houses and mines are abandoned, apparently to rust for eternity. The tipple looms over the village like a malevolent monster, made more so today by its abandonment as fixed location shaft mines are replaced by strip mining.

Traditional coal and agrarian landscapes have always maintained an uneasy coexistence. The cultural and economic divide between the miners and the farmers meant that little or no interaction would ever take place. This tradition has been made even more stark as agricultural abandonment has increasingly dominated the landscape. This is not land abandonment, but just the giving up of hope that a living can be wrested from this land in the age of corporate farming. The sense of place is too strong here for land abandonment to take place. Although few continue to make their living from the land, the need to be connected with distant forefathers is strong. Farming the back 40 has been replaced by a 40-mile drive to a factory or mine. Many did leave, only to discover the depth of their attachment to home. Their return is often marked by a new brick home with a view and grazing Angus cattle in the pasture.

The terrain of the Upland South favors the creation of many distinctive landscapes. A typical traditional farmstead of central West Virginia consisted of a log saddlebag or small frame I house, a single-crib log barn, a small house gar-

Cabin in eastern Kentucky mountains, 1940 (Marion Post Wolcott, photographer, Library of Congress [LC-USF-34-55745-D], Washington, D.C.)

den, a springhouse, a smokehouse, and several fields of corn or hay, all clustered in a small hollow. Larger houses, mechanization, and commercial agriculture appear where the land is better. The rolling limestone pastures, thoroughbreds behind their wooden fences, and mansions of the Kentucky Bluegrass form yet another landscape. So too do the estates, orchards, and poultry farms of the Shenandoah Valley, the dairy farms of the Ridge and Valley Province, and the horse farms of central Tennessee. The elegant restored plantation homes, enormous new horse barns, fields set out for fox hunting, and rider training facilities characterize Middleburg, Charlottesville, and other local centers.

Log houses of all forms and kinds are found throughout the region, although they are often covered by layers of asphalt, clapboard, vinyl, or aluminum siding. Early builders favored central European log construction featuring hewn logs, half dovetail corner timbering in the earlier and "V" corner notching in the later structures, and boards to cover the eaves. Group house raisings were one of the most important forces in the evolution of standardized construction and housing styles. Gangs of neighbors worked together to create virtually the same structure over and over again as the land became filled with settlers. Construction techniques were simplified over time. Logs continued to be used in the house and outbuilding construction until the 1930s, and isolated examples were built as late as the 1970s.

Religion based on the literal interpretation of the Bible, often emphasizing a passage or passages little noticed by mainstream denominations, is one of the best diagnostic features of the subregion. This is a region where serpent handling and other practices unknown in mainstream churches are found. The Baptist and Methodist churches may dominate the religious scene numerically, but the region's religious character stems from its unaffiliated churches and small denominations that stress fundamentalism. Most are uncounted in church membership surveys, but the larger denominations include the Church of God, Disciples of Christ, Assemblies of God, the Churches of Christ, and the Pentecostal and Holiness sects. The Presbyterian Church is strong in many areas because of the numerous early Scotch-Irish settlers.

Country music has recently undergone a dramatic nationalization, loosening its bonds to the region. Recording continues to be concentrated in Nashville, but country music has become as geographically free as any other American music form. Gospel music and general religious programming in the electronic media are far more diagnostic of the area than country music today.

Other Cultural Landscapes. The South includes some areas that are not a part of the mainstream regional landscape, including Acadian Louisiana, southern Florida, and a variety of transition zones along its margins.

Acadian Louisiana. Acadia developed in southern Louisiana with the arrival of French settlers from maritime Canada (Acadia) in the 18th century. These Acadians, or Cajuns, formed a cohesive community along the waterways of southern Louisiana and in adjacent areas. Their isolation continued until the discovery of oil in the early 20th century brought oil workers, roads, a new Cajun self-awareness, and money, though little of that came to many of the original inhabitants. Recently, too, tourism has increased.

Acadian Louisiana is a good illustration of the role of culture in creating a distinctive landscape. Inheritance laws required the equal division of estates among the male children. The original squarish land lots were surveyed to face a navigable waterway that provided the primary method of transportation in the region. Louisiana's continuing use of the Napoleonic legal system required that each male child receive an equal share of the estate. Thus, increasingly narrow splinters resulted, in order that each child would have river frontage and, later, access to the through road that paralleled the waterway. Farmhouses were built facing the road and river to create meandering street villages, or *strassendorfs*, with services scattered almost randomly along their length.

The classic Acadian house was a one-and-a-half-story, four-room house with an incised front porch. A central hall may or may not appear to separate the house into two rooms on each side in what would be the Georgian manner elsewhere in the region. Fireplaces were located between the two rooms on each side of the hall. Most had separate kitchens behind the house, and these structures were a smaller mirror image of the main house. Drainpipe systems and cisterns once collected rainwater for household use in low-lying areas that did not have pure groundwater. Houses with partial Acadian features are found, as well as greatly enlarged "plantation" houses, especially in western Louisiana.

Other significant elements of the Acadian cultural landscape include Roman Catholicism, characteristic place-names, a variety of unique dietary preferences, and some retention of the French language. Almost 88 percent of the entire population of St. Martin parish and more than 80 percent of all church adherents in Acadia belonged to the Roman Catholic Church as late as the 1980s. French terminology, especially the names of saints, dominates the region's place-names. The term "bayou" is commonly used and is sometimes said to be French in origin, although, in fact, it is from the Choctaw word "bayuk." The most striking dietary preferences include dark-roast and chickory coffee, rice, and seafood. Crawfish have almost become a fetish in recent years. The Cajun French language is rarely heard on the street and is less commonly used in homes today than even 30 years ago, except among the oldest citizens. Most residents do have a distinct regional accent.

Southern Florida. Southern Florida was only sparsely settled prior to the 20th century and that settlement was rarely of southern origin. Population growth began with the construction of railroads in the 1890s and dramatically increased after World War II. This unfettered development created a unique mélange of early tourist kitsch and 20th-century fads beneath a garish, land-promoter facade.

Most of Florida was originally subdivided by the township-and-range land division system. The straight lines characteristic of such areas are less visible here than in the Middle West because holdings tended to be large and settlement light until the late 20th century. The familiar dominates this landscape. Older towns have rigidly numbered street grids with endless modern, curved-street subdivisions on their fringes. The 1920s are early history here, and the architectural styles and structures of that period, especially art deco and Spanish stucco rococo, dominate the older sections of many towns. The 1950s brought the legitimization and widespread use of stucco-faced concrete block construction that spawned a distinctive, if garish by national standards, architecture.

South Florida's late-developing towns in many ways epitomize strip-development America. Strong central business districts are rare. Chaotic strips of white concrete suburban shopping centers dominate the commercial landscape. Endless walls of high-rise condominiums now separate the beaches from the public along the Florida coastlines.

The arrival of hundreds of thousands of Cuban and other Caribbean immigrants since the late 1950s has transformed many elements of the landscape. Language and other cultural differences have tended to accentuate the Cuban presence, much as they did that of the Italian, Polish, and Czech immigrants in the Northeast. The presence of almost one million people of Cuban descent concentrated in three of four counties in south Florida has had a significant impact on life there, especially when more than a million "other" Hispanics are included in the mix. Like most late immigrant groups, however, the Cubans have built few culturally distinctive edifices. Their presence is primarily felt as a difference in attitude and pace of life, a somewhat more Hispanic flavor to everything from signs to clothing to food. The presence of almost two million permanent residents from the Caribbean and South America in south Florida has made Miami the commercial gateway to Latin America, increasing the numbers of visitors from Hispanic America and the impact of the resident Hispanics within the region.

Possibly even more visible to the visitor has been the transformation of central Florida into the single most important vacation destination in the world. The construction of the Disney complex, which was followed by a stream of imitators, has created a surreal landscape devoted to pleasure, bringing visitors from around the world. A trip to Disney World is no longer simply a day in the Magic Kingdom for Americans. Visitors are likely to be greeted with a greater variety of languages each day here than anywhere else in the nation.

Simultaneously this infusion of capital and infrastructure, as well as the nearby Cape Kennedy complex, has made central Florida a major high technology manufacturing and corporate center as well. Central Florida is evolving into a landscape version of the three faces of Eve; the last remaining elements of the traditional culture vie with the ersatz world of vacation mecca, which in turn vies with the needs of one of the fastest-growing centers of high technology industry in the country. The combination of strange forces seems to fit together far easier than might be expected.

Transition Zones. Nationalization and regional expansion and contraction prevail along several edges of the traditional South today. The expansion of the industrial Northeast into northern Virginia is possibly the most dramatic of these. The rapidly expanding Washington, D.C., commuter zone was followed by governmental offices that were followed by the rise of high technology firms that in turn spawned more suburbanization that has continued the process on a seemingly endless cycle. There is little southern here that has not been consciously preserved, reconstituted, or simply created from whole cloth.

The region's growth cities may be the ultimate southern transition zones. Traditional accents, foodways, and lifestyles are buried under an avalanche of national trends and styles. Simultaneously, the residents of these places sponsor the reclamation of many physical artifacts, historic structures and districts, crafts, folk events, and other "southern" cultural ways of life by creating markets for festivals, attending celebrations of a past that never was, and simply donating money for their maintenance. Urban foraging, the act of these city folk wandering into the surrounding rural countryside to discover the real world, has become big business in America generally and in the South specifically. Boiled peanut stands, revered barbecue pits, farmers' markets, and a host of traditional activities have found new proponents. Crafts and folkways that had almost disappeared have been brought back to meet the demand for them. Some become so enamored that they take the ultimate step of moving out from the cities to these small communities to purchase "historic" housing and a better way of life.

The departure of millions of southerners to find economic opportunity also created cultural islands far beyond the perceived borders of the region. Chicago, Detroit, and New York City contain the most well known of these exclaves, but virtually every industrial city outside the region has a neighborhood or two where one can be served grits for breakfast, listen to country music on the drive to work, and attend a good old-fashioned "come on down and affirm your faith" church service down the street. Dogtrots and tidewater houses may not have been built in these foreign places, but the stamp of the South is as clear as if they had been.

New Directions. Change is carrying the traditional South into a new landscape. Saddlebag houses lie abandoned in overgrown fields. Camp-meeting grounds are deserted. Boarded-up and rusting cotton gins stand beside the railroad tracks, forgotten by almost all who pass. Landscapes are never static, but the nationalization of the southern landscape has been exceptionally rapid. The new era began with the exposure of thousands of young American soldiers to Europe and the migration of southerners to the labor-short northern factories during World War I. World War II sent another generation of young men away but also introduced many northern soldiers to winters without snow shovels. The postwar period saw the end to traditional tenant farming and the virtual depopulation of vast sections of the agrarian South. These shifts in the region's population set the stage for the massive changes in culture and landscape that were to follow.

Television and the national print media have long been considered two of the most potent forces underlying the homogenization of contemporary American culture. They brought national fads, accents, and trends into every living room in the nation. The impact of national retailers and franchisers has been less recognized, but the insensitivity of these players to regional tastes and reliance upon homogenized menus, central purchasing, and standardized inventories have been equally destructive of regional personality. There is little room in this new landscape for men in overalls standing around a country gas station drinking R.C. Colas and eating Moon Pies.

The southern landscape has not been altered uniformly. Change has been most rapid in the cities and least rapid in rural areas. Traditional cuisine, regional vernacular housing, and southern values are increasingly difficult to find in places like Atlanta and Dallas. Department stores, restaurants, specialty retailers, malls, and fast-food chains that strive for national identities dominate these urban landscapes. Pulte, Centex, and other national contractors who build much the same house in one city as another increasingly dominate suburban housing developments. *Southern Living* magazine has promoted "southern" house plans, southern foods, southern gardens, and southern lifestyles to these new suburbanites, but few would have been recognized as southern by hardly anyone's grandmother.

Thousands of small towns are enduring slow deaths as they no longer seem to have a role in modern society. Stores close, buildings crumble, and weeds find their way through the cracks in the streets with no hope in sight. Some, those close enough to the new urban dynamos, are finding new leases on life as residential crossroads, not viable freestanding communities.

The avalanche of incomers has been less pervasive but possibly more important to the region's small towns. Most southern towns went decades without a single "outsider" moving in after the middle of the 19th century. The rising tide of retiring baby boomers from the North, returnees who fled the South in search of better jobs returning home to take care of their parents or just getting away from the pace of urban life, and incomers, people with no ties to the region, are slowly settling into thousands of communities. Towns in favored areas—the coast, the mountains, near lakes and other attractive environments—were the first to receive the incomers, but soon the less favored began to see new arrivals as well. Initially most of these outside of Texas were Native Americans searching for a new life, but increasingly after 1970 nonnative immigrants, initially from Mexico but also from Southeast Asia and China, began arriving in larger and larger numbers throughout the entire South to take low-paying industrial and farm jobs that would otherwise go unfilled. The entire United States has experienced this flood since 1965, but the impact on this region, which had seen few outsiders for more than a century, has been astonishing.

The cultural elements of each new era have always had to compete with those of earlier times. The problem is that the increasing rate of change has left more and more of today's population with a pervasive sense of ennui that is expressed in many ways, from recreating a past that never was to antisocial behavior. The South's contemporary experiences are much the same as those taking place elsewhere in the nation and to a degree the entire developed world. Non-U.S. sales for Kentucky Fried Chicken now exceed the company's sales in the United States. Levi jeans are seen on the streets of every city in the world. The changes taking place are not southern; they are part of a reorganization of the world cultural order. Understanding one's place in that new order has become increasingly difficult. Maintaining one's sense of identity has become nearly impossible. Increasing numbers of Americans have reached back to their regional pasts to create some semblance of order and sense of belonging. The southern regional culture and landscape, because of its strong roots and its strong sense of identity, has become symbolic of what was, and what might be, to many.

RICHARD PILLSBURY
Folly Beach, South Carolina

Thomas R. Ford, ed., *The Southern Appalachian Region: A Survey* (1962); Henry Glassie, *Pattern of the Material Folk Culture of the Eastern United States* (1968); Sam B. Hilliard, *Hog Meat and Hoecake: Food Supply in the Old South, 1840–1860* (1972); John Brincker-hoff Jackson, *American Space: The Centennial Years, 1865–1876* (1972); Terry G. Jordan, *Annals of the Association of American Geographers* (no. 4, 1967), *German Seed in Texas Soil: Immigrant Farmers in 19th-Century Texas* (1994), *Texas Graveyards* (1982); D. W.

Meinig, *The Shaping of America: A Geographical Perspective on 500 Years of History*, vol. 1 (1986); Richard Nostrand and Lawrence Estaville, eds., *Homelands: A Geography of Culture and Place across America* (2002); Howard W. Odum, *Southern Regions of the United States* (1936); Richard Pillsbury, *No Foreign Food: The American Diet in Time and Place* (1998); Richard Pillsbury and John Florin, *Atlas of American Agriculture* (1996); John Rooney and Richard Pillsbury, *Atlas of American Sport* (1990); James R. Shortridge, *Journal for the Scientific Study of Religion* (June 1977); John R. Stilgoe, *Common Landscape of America, 1580–1845* (1984); Rupert B. Vance, *Human Geography of the South: A Study of Regional Resources and Human Adequacy* (1932); Wilbur Zelinsky, *The Cultural Geography of the United States* (1973), *Social Forces* (December 1951).

Agricultural Regions

Agriculture dominated the economic and social life of the South from its beginnings until well into the 20th century. The demands of this activity were responsible for both the very best and the very worst elements of the region's cultural evolution and shaped most aspects of its social life. Today, the rural South may be divided into three quite distinct agricultural regions, with only vestiges of the powerful cotton and tobacco belts that once defined much of its life still remaining (Map 4).

LOWLAND SOUTH. The agrarian Lowland South is characterized by islands of specialized farming amid a sea of inactivity. At least 60 percent of every Lowland state is classified as woodland and less than 17 percent of each is in crop. A mere 7 percent of Alabama is classed as cultivated. Scattered woodlands dominate the visual landscape in most areas. Throughout the region forested patches are visible on the horizon.

Cotton production dominated much of the settled Piedmont from the beginning of the 19th century through World War II (Map 5 and Figure 1). Fortunes were made in its cultivation until the Civil War brought an end to the cheap plentiful labor. Plantation cotton farming was largely replaced by the tenant farm system through the mid-20th century. The boll weevil is often credited with bringing an end to King Cotton, but chemicals were available to control this pest. The capital to purchase and apply them, however, often was not. The most important factors adversely affecting cotton production seem to have been declining prices and competition from highly automated western producers. The dual phenomenon of mechanization and financial and social opportunities to the north that drew tenant farmers out of the region also played a role.

The decline of tobacco came somewhat later (Figure 2). It too was affected by external forces beyond the control of producers as tobacco consumption in the United States declined and the share of imported tobacco in American cigarettes increased. The likely end to the tobacco allotment system, which has set the geography of production since the 1930s, will bring even more change to traditional tobacco farming.

These traditional crops have been replaced by a host of "modern" alternatives. Soybeans, winter wheat, and corn are the most ubiquitous field crops today, though not important nationally. These crops are easily grown, cultivated, and harvested with comparatively low equipment overhead and little labor demand. Comparatively low per-acre returns are countered with increased acreages by renting idle farmland from aging or nonresident owners.

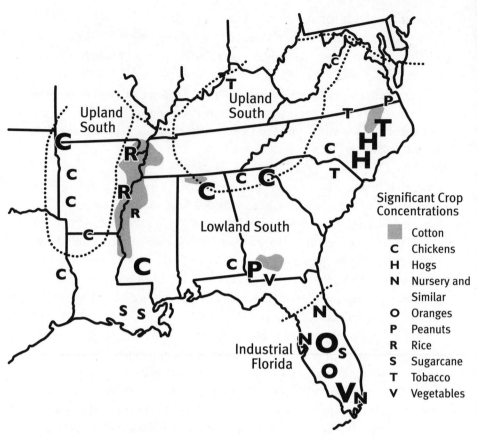

MAP 4. *Agriculture in the South, 2002*

Cotton has made a resurgence in recent years, especially in the Mississippi Delta and lower Piedmont as increased prices and market demand, coupled with rising water costs for western producers, have made it profitable once again. New gins are being built and cotton harvests are now seen in areas where they had not been known for decades. Peanuts were introduced to the United States from Africa where they were a staple food for many of the slaves who were brought to America. Relatively unimportant until after World War II, production has quadrupled since the 1930s. The American diet's increasing consumption of "junk" food has provided an expanding market for peanuts, which are now primarily used in snacks, candy, and peanut butter. Production is very highly concentrated, primarily because of governmental policies. Peanut production is concentrated in 10 smallish counties in southern Georgia and Alabama, on the eastern North Carolina/Virginia border, and in central Oklahoma and Texas, accounting for 23 percent of total production.

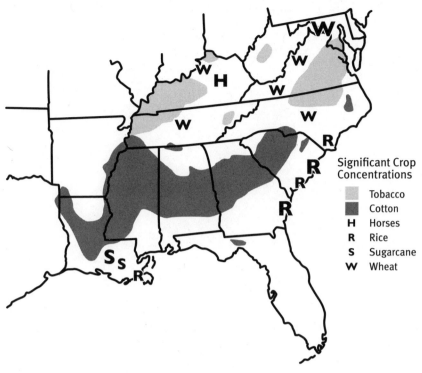

MAP 5. *Agriculture in the South, 1860: Commercial Production*

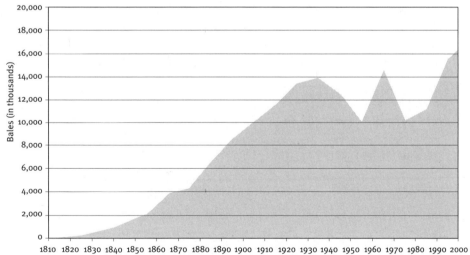

FIGURE 1. *U.S. Cotton Production, 1810–2000*

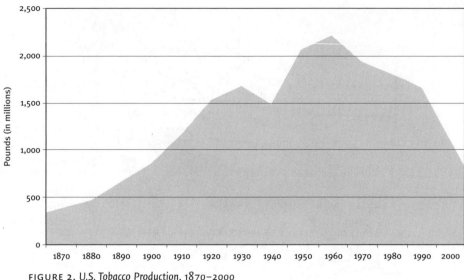

FIGURE 2. U.S. Tobacco Production, 1870–2000

Commercial animal production has been increasing throughout the region over the past 30 years. Broiler chickens supplied the first "factory" animal industry in the Lowland South, primarily in northern Alabama and Georgia. Broiler production actually began in the Upland South and expanded into the lowlands as producers sought better accessibility to markets, labor for processing, and cheap land, especially in southern Mississippi, northern Alabama, and eastern North Carolina. Millions of hogs and turkeys are raised annually using much the same technology as well, especially in eastern and central North Carolina. Catfish and other aquaculture production increased rapidly in the late 20th century, primarily in Arkansas, Mississippi, and adjacent states. Cattle production, especially on the now underutilized Piedmont, increased after 1980 as western beef finishers expanded eastward in their search for heifers for their feedlot operations. Cattle were a good fit for the hobby/part-time farming model popular with many rural southerners looking for farm activities with few capital and labor demands.

UPLAND SOUTH. Upland South agriculture epitomizes the notion of poor farming in the American mind, yet agriculture continues to be an important part of the region's self-image. This was a land of sharp contrasts—horse-drawn plows, ancient agricultural gardening techniques, and hay ricks stood cheek by jowl with high-tech chicken farms and rich thoroughbred horse farms as late as the 1970s. Most picturesque, traditional farming practices have disappeared as

Flue-cure tobacco barn, near Greenville, N.C., 1995 (Richard Pillsbury, photographer)

community elders have died, though for many who are still on the land farming is a labor of love rather than of money. The region has long been characterized by its high rates of rural nonfarm population and part-time and hobby farming.

Isolation from major markets has defined the region's agricultural evolution from the beginning. Poor roads, long distances, steep slopes, and small fields meant that most areas were not well adapted to 20th-century agricultural innovations. Animal fodder, primarily corn, is the dominant field crop in all but a few select specialty areas. Tobacco was the first nationally important specialty crop in the region, followed in the 19th century by westward-moving thoroughbred horse breeders, the latter almost entirely focused upon the Kentucky Bluegrass and Nashville Basin. Broilers were a post–World War II innovation, focused initially in Arkansas, under the leadership of the infant Tyson Farms; later in the Shenandoah Valley, as Perdue and other producers moved toward cheaper production areas; and then in north Georgia and Alabama where food conglomerates, such as Pillsbury, tapped the potential of mass production.

Three important commercial fruit-growing areas that existed at the beginning of the 20th century — the Shenandoah Valley, southwestern Missouri and adjacent Arkansas, and select points along the Illinois Central line — have virtually disappeared today. Winchester, Va., was one of the nation's earliest centers of commercial apple production, focusing upon processed applesauce, juice,

Hay ricks in Appalachian Cove, Fannin County, Ga., 1979 (Richard Pillsbury, photographer)

and cider. Still viable today, it lost relative position in the late 20th century as farmers were slow to adopt the newer varieties and automated techniques found in western production areas. These areas too were hard hit by labor shortages, scarcity of capital for innovation, and competition after World War II.

FLORIDA INDUSTRIAL. Commercial agriculture became viable in south and central Florida with the arrival of rail access to markets in the late 19th century. Off-season vegetables and citrus crops were the focal points of early production, though beef cattle have always been present. Citrus production increasingly focused upon juice after frozen concentrate technology was developed there in 1942. Two-thirds of the annual orange crop becomes frozen concentrate. The nationalization of the nursery/floriculture business has brought large-scale operations to the area in recent years. All of these activities are increasingly threatened by a combination of declining water supplies for irrigation, polluted runoff from fields and groves, and foreign competition, especially from Brazil. Coupled with the ever-expanding urban population, the future of these industries, especially winter vegetables in the far South, is in jeopardy.

Cattle production today focuses primarily on producing calves for western feedlots. There is only a single commercial meatpacking house in the state, and almost 100,000 calves are shipped out of state to feedlots annually. Sugar production around Lake Okeechobee continues primarily because of governmental subsidies and would rapidly decline without them.

Rural life in much of south Florida has been reshaped over the past 30 years by a combination of urban expansion and the arrival of tens of thousands of immigrants from the Caribbean and Middle America. Arriving for the harvests, many Latinos have managed to become permanent, though not always legal, residents. Originating in many different areas, the Latino flavor of agrarian south Florida is a far richer stew of Latino influences than typical of Miami and other urban areas in the state.

OVERVIEW. The changing character of southern agriculture has restructured the rural southern landscape over the past 70 years. The South was always an area of comparatively low population densities, and the reduced viability of most traditional agricultural activities, especially with the limited capital available to most operators of small farms, has meant that millions of southerners, black and white, have abandoned the land and left the region. Crops with low capital and labor requirements replaced traditional activities, or the land was left idle or put into fast-growing pine tree farms. Most of those remaining found jobs "in town," while maintaining their residences on the home place.

The impact of these changes on day-to-day life cannot be overemphasized. Hundreds of small towns and rural communities virtually died after World War II as stores closed, schools closed, and social services disappeared. Three generations of the best and brightest young people of the region fled to the cities, taking with them the drive and risk-taking personalities that are necessary to promulgate change in a stagnant society. The departure of the young and the death of the old brought additional population decline that in turn brought more social decay and service breakdowns. Several south Georgia counties, for example, have residual populations of fewer than a thousand residents today. Most small rural communities outside of the commuting range of the growing cities did not have a single "stranger" move to them in the last half of the 20th century. This pattern has altered somewhat in some areas as expatriates have returned home to care for aged parents and retiring baby boomers have discovered Victorian mansions at bargain prices. For most communities, however, the gentle slide down the economic ladder continues.

JOHN FLORIN
University of North Carolina at Chapel Hill

Sam Hilliard, *Atlas of Antebellum Southern Agriculture* (1984); Richard Pillsbury and John Florin, *The American Cornucopia: Atlas of American Agriculture* (1996).

Appalachia

Appalachia is a single place in the minds of those who do not live there. Indeed there is some correlation between image and reality—a rugged landscape, poverty, physical isolation, mental isolation. There are, however, also significant regional differences within Appalachia. Misunderstanding derives from the very rugged beauty of the land, which has meant that generations of families have lived nestled in coves and small valleys with few visitors, much less new unrelated residents. The very closeness of the rugged landscape gave residents a sense of security until they were literally driven to move, and then only reluctantly. Residents did not see any reason to welcome outsiders who usually were only there because they wanted something. Outsiders, unwelcome as visitors, retained their mythic images of a forbidding place, further enhanced by such books as Harry M. Caudill's *Night Comes to the Cumberland*, Sharyn McCrumb's *Sick of Shadows* and *Ghost Riders*, and the movie *Deliverance*. Myths abound in this place and outsiders know little about it, beyond the statistics and often fanciful accounts of life there.

The regional similarities stemmed from origins and the patterns of settlement of Appalachia. Pennsylvanians settled much of the Shenandoah Valley of Virginia and the Piedmont of the Carolinas during the middle decades of the 18th century. They soon began to push westward into the southern highlands. Their settlement expanded into the uplands, following lowland pathways where possible and cutting across mountainous barriers when necessary. During the period from roughly 1760 to 1820 they occupied the valleys and flatter areas of Appalachia, pushing into smaller and smaller upland valleys and coves, ignoring much of the most rugged mountains. They carried their Piedmont culture, mostly from southeastern Pennsylvania and modified by contact with coastal southerners from the Chesapeake and Carolina Lowcountry, with them.

Time, and changing patterns of national activity, brought differentiation through the last half of the 19th century to what had been a fairly homogeneous pattern of upland culture. Many of those living in more isolated areas became increasingly separated from the rapidly transforming American economy. Poverty became a way of life throughout the highlands, and old ways brought a sense of comfort and security. It was possible in this isolated environment to both retain ancient cultural ways and simultaneously develop variant forms that would be considered aberrations elsewhere. In these isolated coves and valleys, ballad and folktale collectors of the early 20th century found that their richest collections of folk material would trace to Celtic origins. In these isolated places, serpent handling and other religious cult traits also developed. These images of cultural isolation and poverty fueled the national image of an isolated, backward, poverty-stricken Appalachia.

Some areas, however, participated in an entirely different economic experience, though, for many, scarcely more pleasant. Coal was first discovered in southern Appalachia in the late 18th century. Speculators traveled through the future coalfields in the late 19th century purchasing mineral rights, but there was little market for the minerals. The Chesapeake and Ohio Railway linked Richmond with Newport News in 1881 and the western end of that line with the major midwestern railroads in 1888. Coal production skyrocketed from under a million tons per year in 1890 in Kentucky to over 50 million in the 1920s and peaked at 173 million tons per year in 1990. Tens of thousands of hill people turned in their mules and cornfields for weekly paychecks and a tenuous and dangerous future. Their culture became separated forever from their agrarian cousins up in the hollows and coves.

Coal-related manufacturing began growing more rapidly in favored locations after 1890. Chattanooga began calling itself the Pittsburgh of the South about this time; the much larger and more important Birmingham, Ala., nearby tended to compare itself to Birmingham, England. Virtually all of these industries are either gone or ailing today. Birmingham, once the second-largest steel-producing center in the nation, no longer has any significant production. The Kanawha River valley and the adjacent section of the Ohio River are physically a part of the South but culturally and economically have always seemed closer to the midwestern industrial complex. Coal was first used here to help produce salt, but the West Virginia cities of Charleston, Huntington, and Parkersburg became major chemical centers for a host of products during the mid-20th century. The largest synthetic rubber plant in the nation, for example, was located in Charleston during World War II, and major production of coal-based industrial chemicals, synthetic fabrics, and plastics continues to line the two rivers. Whether tied to the larger region or not, these areas tend to operate outside of the arena of southern Appalachian culture.

The industrialized zones notwithstanding, the pervasive image of poverty dominated the national image of the region. Two of the largest federal government efforts at regional economic development — the Tennessee Valley Authority (TVA) of the 1930s and the Appalachian Regional Commission (ARC) of the 1960s — were created to deal with this problem. The TVA began as a program to control the flow of the Tennessee River and its tributaries but soon evolved into an economic development agency in fact, if not in title. The TVA is one of the country's largest electricity generators, a legacy of the decision to utilize its many dams for the production of hydroelectric power. Many argue that most changes would have arrived in the Tennessee Valley with or without the TVA.

John F. Kennedy visited West Virginia many times during the 1960 Democratic primary and presidential campaign and again after his election. His efforts brought renewed national attention to this largely overlooked region. The issue of Appalachian poverty prompted the creation of the ARC, and the impact of the ARC on the region was huge. Adopting the new 1960s model to build and then hope that growth would follow, the ARC channeled money into the region's infrastructure — education, health, and highways — in the belief that private sector industrial growth would follow. The Appalachian Regional Highways network is its most visible regional impact, but some critics have suggested that these highways more often provided escape routes for isolated residents than pathways for incoming investment.

Change came to the region in many other, and probably predictable, forms. The plentiful hydroelectric power of the TVA encouraged the federal government to locate the Oak Ridge research facility in Oak Ridge, Tenn., which at first focused on the atomic bomb but is now one of the country's major centers of government-sponsored research. For a time this plentiful energy supply encouraged a growing industrialization of the valley, although that has waned somewhat.

The late 20th century brought a new economic boom to the region in the form of urban people seeking second and retirement homes. The largest center of this growth has been in and around the Great Smoky Mountains of Tennessee/North Carolina, but this is actually only one of many. Families from Washington, D.C., Richmond, and Pennsylvania have been purchasing derelict farms along the entire length of the eastern edge of the region as summer homes for decades. The impending retirement boom of the nation's most famous population bubble, the baby boom, has widened this trend into a full-scale avalanche with planned communities with all amenities, individual homes, and pure real estate speculation for the past two decades. So many Floridians now own homes in southern Appalachia to escape the sweltering summers of Florida that one Florida politician placed highway ads throughout the mountains of southwestern North Carolina to capture the attention of the thousands of his constituents summering in the region. Like the Lowcountry, southern Appalachia has comparatively well-educated, wealthy incomers now sharing space with the traditional, inward-turned, poor, native population. As cheap land disappears and the natives discover that their lives are being changed, with or without their acquiescence, a degree of stress has begun to appear.

JOHN FLORIN
University of North Carolina at Chapel Hill

RICHARD PILLSBURY
Folly Beach, South Carolina

Harry M. Caudill, *Night Comes to the Cumberland* (2001); Thomas R. Ford, ed., *The Southern Appalachian Region: A Survey* (1962); Terry Jordan, *The Making of the Upland South: The Making of an American Folk Region and Landscape* (2003); Karl B. Raitz and Richard Ulack, *Appalachia: A Regional Geography: Land, People, and Development* (1984).

Central Florida, Disneyfication of

Since 1970, the population of central Florida has exploded, and, as a result, its ever-expanding built environment has expanded over former agricultural scrublands. With the creation of Walt Disney World (opened to the public on 1 October 1971) some 24 miles west of the formal city limits of Orlando, this city has since stretched itself into a regional metropolis, the center of which cannot easily be discerned. Indeed, Orlando is not really a city anymore, or at least anything recognizable as such. Rather it is a veritable archipelago of more or less metropolitanized places, or urbanized bits, only loosely connected by a web of interstates, expressways, and highways. In this sense, the metropolis of Orlando *is* central Florida, stretched along the transportation infrastructure in all directions.

Disney began this growth process. The company has shaped the very social and material substance of the region. Central Florida has been remade, if unevenly, in the image of what the Disney Company represents: a footloose, tourist-based, fantasy-driven, imagineered, built facade overlaying an overwhelmingly low-end, dead-end, service-sector social economy peopled by many who are barely making ends meet. In fact, a major reason that the built environment has expanded in so many directions so rapidly has been the search for affordable housing on the part of those who fulfill the fantasies of visitors to the ever-more-numerous themed attractions of the region, from Disney World to Universal Studios to Sea World.

Yet, there is far more to the story than this summary. The Disneyfication of central Florida should be considered a harbinger of future urbanism in the United States as a whole. Orlando has not only been hollowed out and stretched

TABLE 1. *Orlando Population Growth, 1970–2000*

	Orlando Metropolitan Statistical Area	City of Orlando	Suburbs
1970	522,575	98,965	423,610
1980	804,925	128,291	676,634
1990	1,224,852	164,693	1,060,159
2000	1,644,561	185,951	1,458,610

Source: U.S. Census.

beyond recognition, but its traditional role as the focal point of business and public interaction has been supplanted by the several privatized, Disneyesque "downtowns" of the theme parks. In this, the story of Orlando is not that much different from other cities that have attempted to attract tourists and professionals, and their money, by sanitizing their former industrial pasts, both social and built. Indeed, the construction of festival marketplaces on old wharves, the transformation of warehouses into high-end boutiques, and the renewal of blighted inner cities with sports stadiums, aquariums, and the like is now a common and familiar occurrence.

But the story of the development of Orlando as the Disneyfication of central Florida demands telling, if only as prophecy. Unlike other cities attempting to initiate postindustrial revivals, Orlando never had an industrial past. The city jumped from a small, sleepy, agricultural, crossroads town to a postindustrial metropolitan giant without the traditional transition through the industrial stage. Because of this, Orlando should be considered the quintessential, more finished, more clearly apparent example of the ultimate end product of the still evolving, more dimly perceived, and unevenly understood postindustrial trends in other U.S. cities.

And that underscores the Disneyesque quality of what is taking place in central Florida. After all, the Disney Company is nothing if not the master of facade and fantasy. The Orlando metropolitan region has undergone a boom in the last three decades as a direct result of its image as a safe, clean, happy city of ever-contented residents. Like the many theme parks that lay the ground for this image, the metropolitan region as a whole increasingly is imagined as Disney imagineers would have it. The editing out of relatively unsavory social and built realities via high entry fees, highly regulated social relations, and fan-

Magic Kingdom, Disney World, Orlando, Fla., 1999 (Richard Pillsbury, photographer)

tastic built facades hides more reality than it reveals. Just as in the theme-park imagineering process, so it is with Orlando.

Critics see central Florida as the nation's urban future. The main reason Orlando is now considered to include as many as four counties in central Florida (Orange, Osceola, Lake, and Seminole — and, in reality, most of eastern Polk County) is that its tourist- and low-end service-sector–dominated economy does not provide its ever-increasing workforce enough income to live more centrally. The race for housing is to the more rural, less central parts of these counties. As a result, terms like "inner-city poverty" and "suburban wealth" have no relevance to postindustrial Orlando. The various urban bits of central Florida should be considered either relatively randomly rich or poor or, in fact, quite the opposite of what would be expected according to traditional models of urbanism. Low-end service workers cluster in the most rural parts of Osceola, Polk, and Lake counties, and higher-end professional service workers cluster in the more urbanized areas of Orange, Seminole, and Brevard counties. Among these counties are areas of vast wealth, like Disney's Celebration City in Osceola County, and vast poverty, like the so-called western Black Zone of Orlando city and the "independent" black town of Eatonville, in the middle of the wealth of Orange and Seminole counties.

This randomly placed social and spatial polarization of Orlando has been successfully hidden beneath the happy facade of Disneyfication. Just as the glitter of postindustrial festival marketplaces and wharves and stadiums in other cities generally hide urban problems that have been displaced but not solved, so the many unhappy realities of life in central Florida simply are imagineered away. The region as a whole has been, in this regard, successfully themed.

Perhaps the best example of such large-scale imagineering of the greater metropolitan life is Disney's own new town of Celebration, an even more specific harbinger of urban things to come. On territory once a part of Disney property—and therefore somewhat "in" but not "of" Orlando city—an entire town is being constructed from scratch lands, according to the most recent and best "new urban" practices of urban designers and architects in the United States. This new urban place is physically designed to recover something called "community," commonly understood by new urbanists to have been destroyed in the overly chaotic, strip-malled, automobile-addicted, Las Vegas–obsessed modern city. The belief is that reclustering the built environment will elicit a renewed city social life. The idea is that the residents of the town will rediscover the joy of neighborly socializing through forced proximity and, most interestingly, by attending workshops organized by the Celebration Foundation on such topics as "how to be a good neighbor."

Celebration represents a grandiose plan to social-engineer. The town covers about 1,983 hectares in traditionally rural, cowboy Osceola County, surrounded by another 1,902 hectares of protected conservation greenbelt. Despite grand claims, it appears to be little more than a randomly located urban bit of Orlando. Its 20,000 to 30,000 or so residents are, and will undoubtedly in the future be, virtually all upscale, professional suburbanites, physically and socially isolated from just about everything and everyone outside the town. In this sense, it is as much isolated from its surroundings as the much poorer black town of Eatonville. These are both urbanized but nevertheless disconnected communities within a metropolitan region of other disconnected communities. That such a creation will help solve the problems of American cities, as Celebration's designers contend that it should, remains to be seen.

In addition to adding to the archipelago of disconnected urban bits that constitutes Orlando, Celebration represents a significant deepening of such social and spatial disconnectedness as a result of both its very magnitude and its designers' thematic intent. It represents the most profound example of the ongoing Disneyfication of central Florida—an entire town designed along the lines of a theme park. From its high entry fees (housing costs are some 30 to 40 percent above the average for the metropolitan area), to the physical isolation of its customers/residents, to its fantastic built facades and the overall imagineered nature of its social relations, Celebration is the first large-scale attempt to Disneyfy real, lived life. Jobs and stores are there—and a downtown, along with bedrooms. As if living in a medieval castle, residents may never have to leave the gates. Celebration embodies an attempt to edit out the bad parts of real, lived life by imagineering in only the good, the neighborly, the happy.

KEVIN ARCHER
University of South Florida

Kevin Archer, Economic Geography (1997), in *Growth, Technology, Planning, and Geographic Education in Central Florida: Images and Encounters*, ed. R. Oldakowski, L. Molina, and B. Purdum (1997); Douglas Frantz and Catherine Collins, *Celebration U.S.A.: Living in Disney's Brave New Town* (1999); Andrew Ross, *The Celebration Chronicles: Life, Liberty, and the Pursuit of Property Value in Disney's New Town* (1999).

Crime and Violence

Throughout its history, the South has been labeled a violent region with persistently high rates of homicide. The concept of Southern Violence Syndrome (SVS) is corroborated in research by scholars from many disciplines, including sociologists and criminologists. The reasons cited are varied, with explanations including transference of cultural and behavioral traits to the new world, the existence of a code of honor, and a fascination with guns. Although it is unclear at what point in history an SVS actually developed, the earliest records showed a regional difference in homicide even in the 1800s.

Since the 1930s, the FBI's statistics have confirmed a strong southern regional concentration of violent crime. Although the SVS remains somewhat dominant, current data show that the South has rivals from other areas (Map 6). The region of high incidence comprises the southern half of the country, which includes the West, northward into the Midwest and Middle Atlantic areas. There are specific trends in homicide based on national statistics over the past several decades that partially clarify these patterns. Traditionally, blacks, who are mainly concentrated in the South, are significantly more likely than whites to be homicide victims as well as homicide offenders. Also, although most homicides in all age groups are committed by males, the black female homicide victimization rate is greater than that of white males, giving rise to the term "femicide."

To escape poverty and violence, there was a migration of blacks from the South to northern cities such as Chicago, New York, Detroit, and Washington, D.C., which reached its peak from the 1940s to the 1970s. Ironically, recent census data reveal that black people are returning to the South in small numbers,

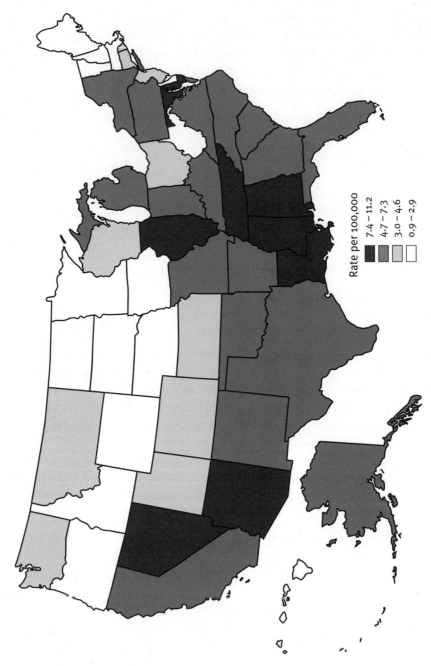

Rate per 100,000

7.4 – 11.2
4.7 – 7.3
3.0 – 4.6
0.9 – 2.9

MAP 6. Homicide Rates, 2001 (Source: Supplementary Homicide Reports, Uniform Crime Reports, FBI)

not only in search of better economic opportunities but also to escape the violence of those inner cities in which they had settled decades earlier.

The South of today is not the same as that of yesteryear. A chronological perspective helps to understand how its pattern of violence has changed and how it fits into the rest of the country. Historically, the rural southerner's attachment to land promoted a suspicion of outsiders. This attitude was at its height during Reconstruction when white southerners, dependent on agriculture for their livelihood, watched as northerners sometimes exploited what was left of their property. Their feeling of rootedness and desire to survive resulted in a deep protective spirit of their space. The highly dispersed rural population also contributed to this defensive spirit by creating an individualized law of the land, with guns as necessities, in contrast to the organized police evident in the densely populated North.

When subsistence agriculture decreased as the primary source of income, increased urbanization in the South spawned another subculture of violence resembling that in other areas of the country (i.e., inner-city violence). An interesting question arises: Is violence hereditary or environmental? Ecological studies on urban crime suggest that people are victims of the environment in which they live. In other words, the place rather than its residents fosters violence. Social conditions, which include poverty through unemployment and low education levels, set up the environment. As residents leave to improve their status, their abandonment of the place attracts criminals to it. Thus, the violence associated with these social stressors is geographically contained.

Another problem facing the New South was that people continued to have large families but no longer had farms to sustain them economically. Research suggests that children living in socially isolated situations created by poverty are more prone to violent lifestyles, and this learned behavior becomes generational. Factors suggested for the high rates of violence today include the emotional and physical status of children, increased availability of drugs, and the breakdown of traditional controls (i.e., parents and community). Therefore, the status of children is a good barometer of the overall social health of a place.

Southern states consistently rank at or near the bottom for certain social indicators (Table 2).

According to law enforcement, the escalation of violence in urban areas today is due largely to the presence of illegal substances. Many drugs (e.g., cocaine, methamphetamines, and designer drugs such as ecstasy) are known to reduce inhibitions and contribute to aggressive and violent behavior. These drugs are also highly addictive, and the need to support a habit becomes des-

TABLE 2. *Child Well-Being State Rankings*

1	Minnesota	18	Rhode Island	35	Oklahoma
2	New Hampshire	19	Kansas	36	Delaware
3	Utah	20	Indiana	37	**Texas**
4	New Jersey	21	California	38	Kentucky
5	Iowa	22	Hawaii	39	**North Carolina**
6	Connecticut	23	Idaho	40	Alaska
7	North Dakota	24	Wyoming	41	**Georgia**
8	Vermont	25	Oregon	42	**South Carolina**
9	Massachusetts	26	Colorado	43	**Tennessee**
10	Wisconsin	27	New York	44	**West Virginia**
11	Nebraska	28	Ohio	45	Arizona
12	Maine	29	Michigan	46	New Mexico
13	Pennsylvania	30	Illinois	47	**Arkansas**
14	**Virginia**	31	Missouri	48	**Alabama**
15	South Dakota	32	Nevada	49	**Louisiana**
16	Maryland	33	Montana	50	**Mississippi**
17	Washington	34	**Florida**		

Source: Kids Count 2003 Data Book, *a project of the Annie E. Casey Foundation.*

perately expensive in a world of poverty. Therefore, ancillary crimes such as prostitution, burglary, and robbery increase. In households where the pot on the stove is as likely to contain crack cocaine as grits, fatalistic attitudes are destined to be the outcome.

In terms of temporal patterns, the South experienced a shift, with the marijuana patch and meth lab replacing the moonshine still. Domestically grown marijuana, with both indoor and outdoor cultivation sites, is a lucrative business. Meth labs, kitchens for methamphetamine drugs, are springing up at a disturbing rate in trailers in remote areas as well as in urban apartments. Conflicts surrounding territorial disputes in trafficking are reminiscent of past disputes between moonshiners and revenuers.

Traffickers of marijuana, cocaine, and heroin are attracted to the South as a distribution venue because of its convenient proximity to major source areas for illegal drug imports—Mexico, South America, and the Caribbean. The coastline along the Gulf of Mexico is appealing to smugglers because its natural configuration provides secluded entries for small boats. The shared border with

Mexico also presents opportunities for traffickers, particularly near cities such as El Paso, Texas, and Ciudad Juarez, Mexico. La Entrada al Pacifico, a new international trade corridor through Mexico, when completed will connect the Pacific port of Topolobampo to Presidio, Texas, giving smugglers a new southwest/northeast route through southern states. However, the illicit drug trade, like bootlegging, is not restricted to this region.

Although drug "mule trains" are common across the border, there are other ways traffickers get their merchandise to market. Interstates serve as drug passageways, as trucks, buses, and automobiles are used to distribute drugs to various locations. Interstate 95 links Miami to New York City, providing a major north-south trafficking route supplying the eastern seaboard, and Interstates 10, 12, and 40 out of Louisiana, where drugs come into port on ships, send the contraband east and west. Interstate 40 continues through Arkansas and Oklahoma as a main pathway for marijuana and cocaine where a high number of seizures are reported by Drug Enforcement Administration officials. Miami, Atlanta, New Orleans, and Orlando are not the only southern cities used as points of entry. Ports once known to pirates and rumrunners, such as Charleston, S.C., are being discovered as alternative destinations for illegal drugs aboard container ships.

Spillover of drug violence from the inner cities into the general population is a growing concern. Smaller cities and particularly suburbs are having the greatest increases in crime. The mobility of gangs and entrepreneurial drug dealers presents a new threat in the South. The micromanagement of drug operations allows for expansion into these areas, making the product accessible to all socioeconomic classes, with youth particularly vulnerable. Recent trends indicate that juveniles are more likely to kill acquaintances than strangers or family members and that the age of their victims is usually between 14 and 25. The availability of guns added to this scenario sets the stage for homicide by juveniles (Map 7). The weapon of choice in the majority of killings by teens is a firearm.

The rates of homicides by guns vary from place to place, and the South, despite its history of gun ownership, is not the only area in the country with this crisis. Accounting for this variability in part is a flow of guns from southern states, where gun regulations are weak, that are used in crimes in other regions.

Although the region has grown in prosperity in recent decades, southerners face the social problems that come with poor urban environments where life is cheap. The diffusion of drugs and gangs, together with an inviting physical and social climate, aids in determining the geographic pathways of violence in the

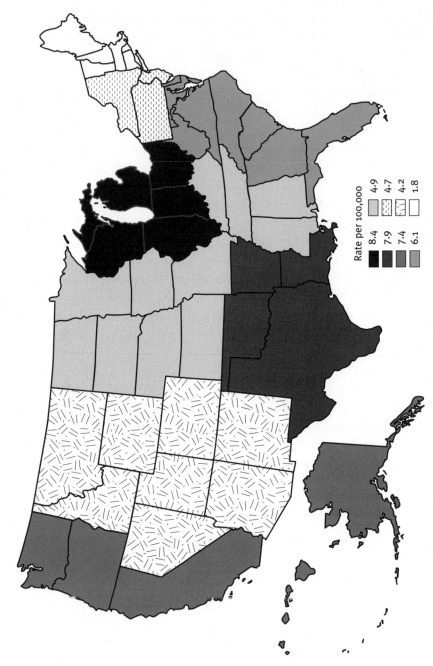

Rate per 100,000

8.4 4.9
7.9 4.7
7.4 4.2
6.1 1.8

MAP 7. *Teen Gun Homicide by Region, 2000 (Source: Homicide Trends in the U.S., Bureau of Justice Statistics, 2001)*

South. It is no longer a cohesive, well-defined violent culture region, but part of an emerging national pattern.

LINDA S. TURNBULL
Roswell, Georgia

Lawrence M. Friedman, *Crime and Punishment in American History* (1993); James Garbarino, *Raising Children in a Socially Toxic Environment* (1995); Keith Harries, in *Atlas of Crime: Mapping the Criminal Landscape*, ed. Linda S. Turnbull, Elaine Hallisey Hendricks, and Borden D. Dent (2000), *Geoforum* (vol. 16, no. 1, 1985); Fred Hawley, *North American Culture* (vol. 3, no. 1, 1987); Wilbur R. Miller, *Revenuers and Moonshiners: Enforcing Federal Liquor Law in the Mountain South, 1865–1900* (1991); Jeffrey D. Morenoff and Robert J. Sampson, *Social Forces* (September 1997); Richard E. Nisbett and Dov Cohen, *Culture of Honor: The Psychology of Violence in the South* (1996); Karen F. Parker and Matthew V. Pruitt, *Social Forces* (June 2000); Linda S. Turnbull, in *Atlas of Crime: Mapping the Criminal Landscape*, ed. Linda S. Turnbull, Elaine Hallisey Hendrix, and Borden D. Dent (2000).

Ethnic Geography

Many of the social systems and distinctive elements of culture that vary within the South and that collectively help distinguish the region can be explained on the basis of ethnicity. Ethnic geography explores the spatial aspects of ethnicity. Place is an important component of ethnicity, and ethnic groups exhibit territorial patterns of organization by clustering in defined areas. Ethnic groups in the South are distributed in spatial units that range from a few relatively large regional concentrations, including Mexican Americans along the borderlands of Texas, Cubans in south Florida, and Cajuns in southern Louisiana, to numerous small rural and urban enclaves scattered throughout the region.

The impact of ethnicity on the culture and landscape of the South, vis-à-vis other large regions of the country, depends to some extent upon the operational definition of ethnic group. Traditionally, ethnic groups have been defined strictly on the basis of common ancestry, national origins, and associated cultural traits. By this standard the South is comparatively lacking in ethnic diversity, considering that the region has attracted proportionately few foreign immigrants, especially foreign-born Caucasians, since the mid-19th century.

Many groups in the South, however, can best be characterized by traits that are essentially ethnic in nature. One of the most significant identifying elements of an ethnic group is an internalized sense of distinctiveness and an external perception of that distinctiveness. Ethnic identity is not ascriptive; it is a matter of individual and group choice. The recognition of minority status tends to

Gullah festival, St. Helena, S.C., 2002 (Richard Pillsbury, photographer)

foster among members of an ethnic group an intense feeling of belonging to a community.

Examples of ethnic indicators might include race, religious affiliation, ancestral or mother language, common settlement and employment patterns, political philosophy, shared literature, folklore, and music, cuisine preferences, and migratory status. By these indicators, blacks, American Indian tribes, mixed-blood groups, various religious sects and groups, and perhaps even selected occupational enclaves in the South may be considered — and are most likely to consider themselves — ethnic groups.

The South has been called the most "native" region of the country because most southerners trace their ancestry in the United States back to settlers who arrived before 1850, and in many cases before 1800. The South's share of the nearly 50 million immigrants who settled in the United States from the beginning of the 19th century up to the 1980s is disproportionately small. The region's inability to attract foreign immigrants was due to limited economic opportunities, a social climate many of these immigrants found unacceptable, and a xenophobia on the part of southerners. The South in 1980 had fewer than 5 million first- and second-generation Americans. Moreover, well over half of these were of Mexican or Cuban descent and resided on the geographical fringes of the region.

The relative lack of foreign immigration is coupled with the fact that the Anglo population of the South is derived overwhelmingly from one source area — northwest Europe, especially the British Isles. The black population, too, though diverse in its African ethnic origins, was rather quickly homogenized into an African American mold.

The consequences of this pattern of settlement were profound, particularly in terms of the relatively uniform cultural milieu that evolved. The narrowed range of religions, for example, resulted in the South's becoming the most Protestant region of the country. This lack of ethnic diversity greatly influenced the shaping of the southern identity and southern attitudes toward both the region itself and the rest of the world. The relative cultural and social homogeneity of the South has even led some scholars to suggest that white and black southerners should be considered ethnic groups in their own right.

The lack of diversity has served to heighten ethnic groups' awareness of their minority status. This has encouraged such groups to settle in well-defined, often small-scale concentrations, thereby increasing their external visibility. Residential segregation likewise tends to increase social interaction and reinforces institutional differences between the group and the larger society, thus perpetuating distinctive ethnic identities. Although ethnic exclusiveness is a source of mutual support and cultural security, it may also lead to conflict through clannish suspicion and distrust of outsiders.

Ethnic groups are the keepers of distinctive cultural traditions. From the Germans of the Ozarks and the hill country of Texas to the Hungarians in Tangipahoa Parish, La., to the mixed-blood Lumbees of North Carolina, ethnic groups foster the continuity of culture and of social systems. These traditions are reinforced through friendships, family ties, business contacts, church affiliations, and social activities. Periodic celebrations and festivals, both secular and religious, also strengthen these ties.

The nonmaterial elements of culture, including language, religion, music, symbols, beliefs and values, along with cuisine preferences, are generally retained longer than most material elements of culture. Yet land-survey systems, settlement patterns, agricultural practices, and architectural preferences, among other material elements, may persist indefinitely among certain groups; they provide graphic imprints of an ethnic group's tenure in an area. Although ethnic groups persist in the South, they also change through the process of acculturation. The Scots-Irish, for example, have been completely assimilated, existing only in the memories of their descendants.

As migration continues to add new ethnic groups to the South, ethnicity continues to enrich the life and landscape of the region. Since the 1980s a dramatic change has occurred in the South's ethnic geography. In 1990 there were 2 million Hispanic Americans in the 10 southern states; by 2000 that population was 4.3 million. This immigration from Mexico and Central America was now being felt not just in Florida and Texas, the traditional states of Latino immigration, but in such states as North Carolina, Georgia, and Tennessee. Most southern states still have relatively small Hispanic populations, but these recent patterns have helped spur the South's overall population growth in the last decade.

JAMES R. CURTIS
University of Miami

Russel L. Gerlach, *Immigrants in the Ozarks: A Study in Ethnic Geography* (1976); Terry G. Jordan, *German Seed in Texas Soil: Immigrant Farmers in Nineteenth-Century Texas* (1966); William Lynwood Montell, *Saga of Coe Ridge* (1970); Lauren C. Post, *Cajun Sketches: From the Prairies of Southwest Louisiana* (1962); Curtis C. Roseman, in *Geographical Identities of Ethnic America: Race, Space, and Place*, ed. Kate A. Berry and Martha L. Henderson (2000); George B. Tindall, *The Ethnic Southerners* (1976); Wilbur Zelinsky, *The Cultural Geography of the United States* (1973).

Ethnicity, Patterns in

Permanent European and African habitation began in the South in the 17th century. Most of the region had been lightly settled with a variety of Amerindian peoples prior to that time, but through a combination of disease, removal, and genocide, the vast majority of these peoples were gone by the middle of the 19th century. Some diffuse elements of this earlier culture were absorbed into the larger traditional southern culture, most notably in the use of a variety of semi-indigenous crops, some specialized buildings, and the use of existing primary route ways, but in the larger scheme of things only modest aspects of Amerindian culture contributed to traditional southern culture as it came into flower in the early 19th century.

The vast majority of early European settlers throughout the region had English ancestry. But other European ethnic groups did play important roles in some areas, most notably the lower Mississippi and its tributaries. New Orleans and its port activities attracted a wide variety of peoples from many areas. The rural areas were settled primarily by French settlers who moved to the mainland from various Caribbean islands and thus brought with them not only their European roots but an often lengthy Caribbean experience as well. Similarly a number of early coastal plantation owners in the Carolinas and Georgia moved there after one or more generations of living in the Barbados and in other

Caribbean housing influences, near Lafayette, La., 2001 (Richard Pillsbury, photographer)

sugar and rice plantation environments. Savannah, Wilmington, and especially Charleston also received settlers from a variety of origin points. Thousands of Germans emigrating to 18th-century Philadelphia, for example, quickly discovered that Penn's cheap land was largely either very far from the coast or too expensive for them to acquire. Many of these moved southward to the Carolinas and Georgia where land was readily available at reasonable cost. The Ebenezer colony of Salzburgers near Savannah was widely known in Germanic Europe and promoted settlement in both the Carolinas and Georgia. Charleston also had a large Huguenot population, many of whom were actually Sephardic Jews escaping persecution in Iberia. It is estimated that a quarter of all American Jews lived in South Carolina at the time of the Revolution. Certainly the majority of people with European origins were from England, but significant variants to that Western European culture were also widely scattered throughout the southern cultural hearth region and shaped traditional southern culture.

Africans were the other important source of traditional southern culture. Although they were brought as slaves from a variety of source areas, their very presence in everyday southern life meant that their impact was both widespread and pervasive. Africans were not randomly distributed throughout the South, especially during the important incubator period of the early 19th century. The geography of African-origin Americans in this period was highly concentrated in areas suited for plantation agriculture, but it should not be presumed that their own varied cultural pasts created a single "African" identity in America.

African slaves were concentrated in three distinct areas in 1820: the rice coast, the Chesapeake and adjacent tobacco region, and the lower Mississippi region. Not only were these distributions distinct, but the origins of those who went to them tended to be distinct as well. Most of the slaves on the rice coast were brought from the Caribbean and had originated in the Senagambian rice production area of West Africa. Many of the slaves of southern Louisiana too had spent considerable time in the Caribbean prior to arriving in mainland America. Most of these people also had Senagambian African origins. In contrast, the vast majority of those going to the Chesapeake tobacco areas originated in other areas of Africa. The southward movement of Virginians, both European and African, meant that much of the Piedmont, especially along the Atlantic coastal section, continued this distinct cultural tradition between coastal and inland inhabitants not only among the European origin population, but the African as well. Finally, the presence of all of these African peoples in the Lowland South is partially, if not mostly, responsible for the dichotomy of Upland/Lowland South cultures.

The single most important source in the creation of the Upland South culture was the stream of "Pennsylvanian" settlers moving along the Great Wagon Road southward through the Valley of Virginia. Not traditionally identified as an "ethnic" group, these settlers were a part of the full-fledged American regional culture that had evolved in southeastern Pennsylvania between Philadelphia and the Allegheny Front. No longer English, German, Welsh, or whatever European origin their ancestors had claimed, these peoples were a part of the newly evolving synthetic regional Pennsylvanian culture, which had blended and modified their various European heritages by the mid-18th century. The literature typically has used the European historical national roots of these people, i.e., as from Ireland, Scotland, England, and the Rhineland, to describe their cultural contributions to the Upland South. A careful analysis of their cultural choices, however, suggests that by the time of this migration they should be identified not by their European roots, but as "Pennsylvanians." These Pennsylvanians mixed with westward moving "southerners," especially where their southward-moving migration stream crossed the Potomac, James, and Little Tennessee rivers. The end result was a distinct Upland South that had strong ties with the Lowland South but that also had a significant admixture of elements from the north. African-origin culture elements are far less evident in this region, partially because of the lack of direct contact in most areas, but also because of the presence of this strong cultural imperative from the North.

The great migrations of the Industrial Revolution largely ignored the South and its post-Reconstruction economy. Those few industries that did venture into the region found plenty of resident labor available. Mountaineers driven from farm production by market forces became the coal miners of southern West Virginia, Tennessee, and Kentucky; lowland small farm operators, or more likely their wives and daughters, became textile mill workers in the Lowland South. There were some intrusions, especially the irrepressible Irish, but their numbers tended to be small and typically had little impact upon the overall cultural evolution of the region. The region was a zone of out-migration — not a destination for outsiders — from the beginning of the Civil War until near the end of the 20th century.

World War II and the civil rights movement brought a new economic prosperity to the South, and the shift in immigration law in 1965 made the region ripe for invasion by international migrants for the first time in a century and a half. The largest single group of these "new" southerners are Middle American, primarily Mexican, immigrants; but substantial numbers of Cubans and Asians have also settled in the region, with increasing visual impact on the traditional southern landscape. As notable as these groups are in rural areas, the region's largest cities have the largest concentrations of foreign immigrants. Miami, suburban Washington, D.C., and Atlanta have had especially large flows of recent immigration. Atlanta alone has had more than one-half million international emigrants arrive in the city over the past 20 years. Not only have Mexican, Vietnamese, Korean, and Indian emigrants settled there, but large numbers of emigrants from less-publicized areas such as Eritrea, Nigeria, the Arabian Gulf, Ukraine, Poland, and a hundred other nations can be found in surprising numbers, often living in a sort of ghettoized suburban environment.

Of even greater numbers in reshaping southern culture in the past 30 years are the hundreds of thousands of other Americans, Yankees in local parlance. This "ethnic" group is even more highly concentrated than international migrants, primarily in the larger cities.

It is impossible to project the future impact of these recent ethnic migrations upon the already rapidly changing southern culture. Typically, new immigrants coming into a large, stable society make few inroads in the larger culture, and those only over long periods of time. This tendency, coupled with the rapid nationalization of southern life generally, suggests that although there will be a broad transformation of the region's culture over the coming decades, the impact of the "new" ethnic groups may be relatively minor, especially considering their numbers.

RICHARD PILLSBURY
Folly Beach, South Carolina

JOHN FLORIN
University of North Carolina at Chapel Hill

James Allen and Eugene Turner, *We the People: An Atlas of America's Ethnic Diversity* (1988); Roger Daniels, *Coming to America: A History of Immigration and Ethnicity in American Life* (2002); Samuel Hilliard, *Atlas of Antebellum Southern Agriculture* (1984).

Expatriates and Exiles

Basil Ransome, a character in Henry James's *The Bostonians* (1886), left his native South after the Civil War and headed for New York City "with fifty dollars in his pocket and a gnawing hunger in his heart." He exemplified what Thomas Wolfe described as the southerner consumed by an "eternal wandering, moving, questing, loneliness, homesickness." The uprooted southerner, Wolfe's Ismael, has been a culturally important figure since the Civil War. Despite the notable southern attachment to localism, mobility has also been a characteristic of 20th-century southerners, but perhaps because of the power of memory and of place, emigrant southerners have continued to ponder the region and its meaning.

"Exile" is used here in the Webster definition of "voluntary absence from one's country or home." Many of the thousands of Confederates who left the region after the Civil War did so for political reasons, as did many blacks at that same time and since, who left to escape the South's racial system. These were political émigrés, of a sort, but they were part of the broader group of individuals who left the region for economic, intellectual, or social reasons, as well as political ones, and yet took their southern identity and customs with them. White working-class emigrants and black emigrants established communities in northern cities, but the focus here is on business leaders, professionals, writers, scholars, teachers, painters, sculptors, and other intellectual and gifted southerners who left the region, causing a "brain drain" of talent out of the South.

In the aftermath of the Civil War, prominent former Confederates headed in all directions, to all parts of the United States and to other areas of the world. Unhappy with postwar conditions and fearful of the Reconstruction future, they left the South seeking better opportunities for financial, social, and artistic success. Confederate cabinet member Judah P. Benjamin went to England and had a successful legal career there. Diplomat John Slidell moved to Paris and was in England when he died. Former Confederate vice president John C. Breckinridge and Confederate general Jubal Early moved to Canada. Three Confederate generals (C. W. Field, William C. Loring, and Henry W. Sibley) went to Egypt to help train that country's army, and a few Lost Cause refugees wound up in Japan and Australia.

Between 4,000 and 6,000 Confederates emigrated to Central America, with Mexico attracting the largest number. Several thousand southerners set up colonies in Mexico, mostly at Carlota and Cordova, between Mexico City and Vera Cruz. Matthew Fontaine Maury, Confederate general and an oceanographer, served as commissioner of immigration to Mexican emperor Maximilian's government and helped to launch a group exodus from the South. At least 17 Confederate generals were part of this migration, including Edmund Kirby-Smith, Thomas C. Hindman, Sterling Price, and John B. Magruder. Other Confederates sought refuge in Honduras and on Caribbean islands such as Jamaica and Cuba.

Between 2,500 and 4,000 southerners reached South America, most of them before 1870 and most settling in Brazilian agricultural colonies. The Brazilian government, like that of Mexico, encouraged the immigration, offering cheap land, advertising in southern periodicals, and providing agents to promote and facilitate the migration. The Reverend Ballard S. Dunn of New Orleans proved to be an especially effective lobbyist for migration, with his book *Brazil, the Home for Southerners* (1866). Four areas of Brazil attracted southerners: Santeram, on the Amazon River; Rio Doce; Iguape, or "Lizzieland," as Ballard Dunn named it in honor of a daughter; and a cluster of three colonies (Campo, Retiro, and Villa America) in the São Paulo region.

Most of the immigrants to Latin America had returned to the United States by the 1870s, but about 20 percent of southern emigrants to Brazil settled there permanently, a greater percentage than in other areas of Latin America. Many descendants of Confederate immigrants to Brazil have lost any sense of their southern ancestry, but some still retain southern identity. Americana, Brazil, has 400 or so surviving descendants and 440 tombstones marked with English inscriptions that mark the graves of ex-Confederates. The Fraternity of American Descendants meets quarterly in the cemetery and holds a potluck dinner. The menu in 1984 included such down-home fare as fried chicken, biscuits, cornbread, pecan pie, watermelon, and soda pop. As well as speaking Portuguese, many of these Confederate descendants can still speak the southern English dialect of their ancestors. Their association sells Confederate flag decals to raise money.

A larger number of southern Confederates went north and west within the United States, but until recently scholars have been less interested in studying their lives than those of the more exotic migrants to foreign lands. "Texas fever" hit the South in the 1870s, and thousands of freedmen and whites went there seeking anonymity and a fresh start. Many became cowboys and participated in the postwar cattle industry. California also proved a popular spot for southern emigrants, but northern cities such as New York City, Philadelphia, and Boston attracted even more southerners. Most of these migrants were young—mostly under 35 years of age—and well educated. Many had lived in the North at times before the war or had been frequent visitors there. The key years for emigration were 1865–68, with a sharp drop after 1871. According to the leading scholar of this movement, Daniel E. Sutherland, 57 percent of a group of 298 subjects who have left detailed records remained in the North after going there.

Southern landowners who had fallen on hard times went north, as did professionals and businesspeople who hoped to find a better market than the postwar South for goods and services. Fear of the future motivated many of them. Northern schools, especially medical colleges, attracted those wanting to further their education. War widows were frequent visitors, sometimes for extended periods. Painters, sculptors, and architects sought training and patrons. Some young southerners, like other restless rural Americans, went north to seek excitement in the region's bustling cities. Sutherland noted, however, that these emigrants "remained southern in mind and heart."

New York City held the greatest attraction of all northern cities for these southerners. It was traditionally a gathering spot for southern financiers and vacationers and a hotbed of prosouthern sentiment during the war. As a result of earlier contacts, friends, relatives, and business acquaintances in the city provided assistance to postwar exiles such as Thomas F. Ryan and John H. Inman, who became financial magnates, and Charles B. Rouss, a former Confederate private who by the 1880s had become a leading wholesale and retail merchant. Roger A. Pryor in law, John A. Wyeth in medicine, William R. O'Donovan in art, and George C. Eggleston in literature were all former Confederates who made their reputations in the North.

Southerners in the North were a self-conscious group. They associated with each other, organized societies, went to church together, and assisted each other in time of need. Proud of their heritage, they donated money to the construction of universities, churches, and public buildings in the South. Many expatriates were sensitive to northern slights and scornful of Yankees. Though some were eager to exploit northerners, they nonetheless played a role in sectional reconciliation. Northerners generally accepted southerners in their midst, and personal contact mitigated political prejudices. Northern businessmen also used southerners with old names and admirable war records as liaisons to win back the southern market for their products.

The New York Southern Society, founded in 1886 by southerners who had succeeded in the North, preserved relics of the Old South, worked toward sectional reconciliation, and helped normalize business relations between the regions. The society welcomed New Yorkers of southern birth or heritage. Southern businessmen were allowed to enjoy the benefits of the club while in town. The society was more a New South organization than an unreconstructed Old South group. It canonized Washington and Jefferson more than Lee and Davis. It typically commemorated Washington's birthday, for example, in a gaudy manner, appropriate to the era. Banjo players provided music, and members dined on dishes such as Old Dominion fried hominy and toasted sectional harmony with large amounts of magnolia punch.

Black southerners are another, larger group that has frequently been in exile from their land of birth. Black migration out of the South in the early 20th century had important meaning for the emergence of a mature and distinct black artistic and intellectual tradition. Writers such as Richard Wright (Mississippi), Zora Neale Hurston (Florida), and James Weldon Johnson (Florida); scholars such as Arna Bontemps (Louisiana) and Carter Woodson (Virginia); performers such as Ma Rainey (Georgia), Bessie Smith (Tennessee), Leontyne Price (Mississippi), Roland Hayes (Georgia), Fletcher Henderson (Georgia), and, later, Dizzy Gillespie (South Carolina), Lester Young (Louisiana), and Thelonious Monk (North Carolina) all were southern born yet made their cultural contributions outside the region. Each took advantage of opportunities in the North that were denied under the South's repressive racial system. Also, the South's paucity of cultural and intellectual resources did not provide support for many kinds of cultural achievements for either race.

The Harlem Renaissance of the 1920s was an outpouring of energy in black literature, music, dance, and entertainment. Coming after the great wave of black migration to the North during and after World War I, many of the leaders of this renaissance were southern born and used southern settings and themes. Sterling Brown wrote a collection of poems titled *Southern Road* (1932). Arna Bontemps's *Black Thunder* (1936) was based on Gabriel Prosser's 1821 slave revolt in South Carolina. Zora Neale Hurston's play *Color Struck* (1925) was set in a segregated railroad coach in the South. Jean Toomer's *Cane* (1923), a series of poems, short stories, and vignettes, captured the life of black people in Georgia lumber camps of the 1890s.

It was natural that black intellectuals, many of whom were born in the South, would turn to the region for material. Exile gave them both perspective and the freedom to work realistically with this material. Earlier black writers, though, had employed genteel literary traditions, frequently writing stories of well-off northern blacks. In the aftermath of the wave of black migration during and after World War I, intellectuals "discovered" the culture of southern black folk. Ohio-born Langston Hughes recalled that his view of black culture was shaped by seeing migrants from the South coming into and through Ohio. Southern blacks in exile, then, gained an opportunity for cultural achievement, using as their raw material their own personal and group experiences from the South.

The maturation of 20th-century southern intellectual life in general has depended on the exile experience. Critic Louis D. Rubin Jr. argues that the writers of the Southern Literary Renaissance were alienated from their communities, partly because of time spent out of the South. All of the contributors to *I'll Take My Stand* (1930), the preeminent statement of southern Agrarianism, had spent time out of the South; Robert Penn Warren's essay for that volume was written while he was in England. These writers' perspective on the region came from leaving it. Future novelists and poets grew up in the traditional South of the 1900s and 1910s, went off to college, and did not return home after graduation. Education and living away from their communities distanced them from their origins. Some left the country. William Faulkner took a walking tour through France and Italy in the summer of 1925. Katherine Anne Porter worked for the revolutionary government in Mexico in that decade. Thomas Wolfe traveled extensively in Europe, especially in Germany. These southern writers were not, however, a part of the lost-generation exile experience, which centered in France and rejected tradition and the general idea of regionalism.

But even more important than European exile, almost all the South's major writers in this period went north at some point. Thomas Wolfe, growing up in Asheville, N.C., dreamed of "the golden vision of the city," as he wrote in *The Web and the Rock* (1939). The city was a place of escape and fulfillment. Southern literature is filled with descriptions of youthful southerners loose without moorings in the big city: Peyton Loftis in William Styron's *Lie Down in Darkness*; Eugene McLain wandering through San Francisco in Eudora Welty's *The Golden Apples*; and Quentin Compson in William Faulkner's *The Sound and the Fury*, who wanders and eventually commits suicide in far-off Cambridge, Mass. All are southerners far from home, estranged from their region, and yet also alienated from the city. Most of these southern writers, however, did not remain in northern cities. Only Wolfe, the great American poet of exile, remained away. But those who returned south did not return to their hometowns. They went to university towns or metropolitan areas. Those few who did return to their home communities, like Faulkner and Welty, were only physically there; they were spiritual exiles, living in what Ruben calls "the faraway country," the South of their imaginations.

Allen Tate stayed in the South in the 1930s, convinced that southerners who leave the South "sacrifice some great part of their deepest heritage." Nevertheless, many of his Agrarian colleagues, those seemingly most convinced of the need to preserve the South as a bastion against modernism, did eventually leave the region and move north. Writing in 1950, Richard M. Weaver admitted that there was "a fairly general exodus of Southern Agrarians to the North," to the big cities and the renowned universities. "The truth about the Agrarians is that they were becoming homeless," he said. "The South no longer had a place for them." A long process of alienation was completed with the move north. Intellectuals who moved north could at least pursue their work in freedom. As Weaver noted, they were "regional expatriates," but in their new home "their ideas are negotiable" and "their convictions did not clash with local immaturities." The Agrarians were engaged in a worldwide battle between humanism and materialism. Instead of a flight of Agrarians, it was a "strategic withdrawal." Weaver betrayed a certain bitterness because the South had been lost. He applied to the region Stephen Dedalus's phrase about Ireland, "an old sow that eats her farrow."

Willie Morris, who was Thomas Wolfe's successor as poet of the southern exile experience, testified to the existence of an "exile" mentality in more recent southerners living outside the South. He wrote in his 1967 memoir *North toward Home* of "New York's burgeoning and implacable Southern expatriate community," and he suggested that Mississippi and a few other southern states were the only states in the nation that "had produced a genuine set of exiles, almost in the European sense: alienated from home yet forever drawn back to it." Morris recalled the importance of the exile experience to a growing understanding of a common background and interest with black southerners. Morris himself returned to Mississippi in 1980 and remarried there, writing mostly about the South but also of his time in the North in *New York Days*.

Sociologist John Shelton Reed has argued for the importance of exile in nurturing cultural nationalism among southerners. By standing at a distance from a culture, one achieves perspective on it. The experience of the provincial youth in the city reminds those away from their homeland that they are from a culture viewed as inferior. Cultural nationalists engage in "the politicization of homesickness," nurturing their memory of the homeland and forgetting the divisions and disagreements back home. Being aware of people with different ways makes one, at times, appreciate the ways left behind. Southerners have been frequently reminded of being southern. The accent has marked one as identifiably southern, and nonsoutherners reacted accordingly by treating those with an accent as different. Many southern whites have been assumed to be racially bigoted. Those nonsoutherners who themselves are prejudiced may treat all white southerners as kindred spirits, and northern liberals may force white southerners to assume the personal burden for all the sins of the region. Southern black intellectuals living in the North have complained of being treated as "rubes" by northern blacks and of hypocritical whites who spoke of equality but distanced themselves from personal relations with blacks. Looking back on his own education in Cambridge, Mass., in the 1960s, Reed has written that northerners "would apparently believe anything at all about the South, provided only that it was weird." The result was that southerners "almost had to think about the South." Many southerners apparently have discovered or intensified their regional identity while living away from the region.

Educated, exiled southerners, when meeting other exiles, frequently discuss where they are from and whether they have common friends or even family. They may complain about the coldness of the North, and of northerners, and exaggerate the legendary southern hospitality. The ritual of food has always been important as a token of retaining and renewing the southern identity in exile. Morris has recalled gathering with two southern black couples, the Ralph Ellisons and the Albert Murrays, for a traditional southern New Year's Day dinner in 1967 in Murray's Harlem apartment, drinking bourbon and feasting on collard greens, black-eyed peas, ham hocks, and cornbread. Morris, like other southerners, discovered the importance of food as a shared ritual of a common regional identity with blacks. He observed that only in Harlem could a "southern white boy greet the New Year with the good-luck food he had had as a child."

The South's economic backwardness has had a discernible effect on the intellectual life of the region by promoting the exile of its intellectuals and artists. A study of the 1932–33 edition of *Who's Who in America* showed that of the 6,015 persons listed there as born in the South, 2,229 were living in other parts of the country. The depletion was largest among editors, authors, educators, lawyers, judges, businessmen, religious workers, medical doctors, politicians, diplomats, army and navy officers, and actors and actresses. The superior opportunities for employment outside the region were singled out as the main reason for the loss of talented personnel. Another study from 1949 found similar findings but concluded that the South was retaining more of its talented offspring. The categories of loss have remained the same over the years, although with improved graduate and professional education in the region the number of those remaining has increased.

CHARLES REAGAN WILSON
University of Mississippi

Wilson Gee, *Social Forces* (March 1937); Eugene C. Harter, *The Lost Colony of the Confederacy* (1985); Alan Huffman, *Mississippi in Africa: The Saga of the Slaves of Prospect Hill Plantation and Their Legacy in Liberia Today* (2004); Lewis M. Killian, *White Southerners* (1970); Willie Morris, *New York Days* (1993), *North toward Home* (1967); John Shelton Reed, *One South: An Ethnic Approach to Regional Culture* (1982); Daniel E. Sutherland, *Journal of Southern History* (August 1981); Richard M. Weaver, *Sewanee Review* (Autumn 1950).

Foodways, Geography of

The mechanisms of the natural environment and the historical processes of culture link food to place. Together, ecology and culture account for the diversity of foodways in the South. Early settlers carried with them knowledge, practice, and predisposition concerning food. Those traditions were usually derived from Europe, but they were also filtered through other parts of the New World such as Acadian Canada. Native Americans provided new culinary inspiration and strategies. African Americans, in slavery and freedom, blended African food preferences, techniques, and even vocabulary with those of the predominantly European agricultural and urban populations.

For settlers, the South's new natural habitats, whether coastal or interior, mountain, piedmont, or delta, established certain ground rules of availability and feasibility that tempered food traditions. Virtually everywhere, for instance, seemed appropriate for raising hogs and corn, two common features of agriculture and diet throughout the South. On the other hand, certain foods are closely tied to particular parts of the South because of ecological factors unique to those areas. Conch salad and conch chowder are known only in south Florida. In comparatively recent times, agribusiness, contemporary food-marketing techniques, and the general blurring of regional boundaries—which is sometimes counterbalanced by the rise of regional self-consciousness—have all had their effects on the southern geography of food.

Corn and pork, two staples of the southern diet, illustrate the ways in which food varies with locality. Ground into meal, corn is the source of a variety of breads. Spoonbread, a puddinglike cornbread, is common in Tidewater Virginia and not unknown in Kentucky, at least in the Bluegrass. In south-central

Iron pot Carolina hash, West Springs, S.C., 2003 (Richard Pillsbury, photographer)

Kentucky and parts of Tennessee, cornmeal is mixed into a batter and fried on a griddle, where it becomes corncakes, hoecakes, or just plain cornbread, depending on whom you ask. Mixed with onion and other seasonings and fried, cornmeal is the main component of hush puppies, a ubiquitous accompaniment for fried fish, especially catfish, a creature whose culinary acceptance appears to be spreading steadily northward from its original Deep South base. Bourbon is, of course, a corn-based distillation. Only Kentucky produces whiskey by that name, although other well-known brands of corn-based sour-mash whiskeys are produced in Tennessee. Bourbon is most popular in the Upper South, although it is also the most commonly consumed hard liquor in virtually the entire South.

The preparation of pork, particularly hams and barbecue, is clearly related to place. If, in the process of curing, hams are hung from six months to two or more years, the resulting country ham is likely to come from either the vicinity of Smithfield, Va., or central Kentucky. Barbecue, which refers both to cooking techniques and to ways of serving the result, is so closely tied to place that for many it seems to serve as an emblem of home. Wherever it is found, barbecue is generally meat cooked slowly over embers and basted with a sauce. In North Carolina it must be cooked so long that it falls apart, and it is supposed to be served in shreds in a sandwich on a hamburger bun. Many North Carolinians add coleslaw to the sandwich as a topping for the meat, illustrating that food traditions may also involve "grammars" or rules concerning appropriate food combinations. In south-central Kentucky, barbecue may be slices of pork shoulder, bones in, dipped in a peppery sauce and served on slices of white bread. In parts of Texas, sausage links are barbecued. And, of course, there are parts of the South in which barbecue is not pork. Texans eat barbecued beef brisket; in western Kentucky, mutton is the preferred meat. The International Barbecue Festival, in Owensboro, Ky., features mutton and chicken.

The potent combination of ecology and culture has yielded a number of very distinctive regional cuisines in the South. The best known of these, and perhaps the most distinctive of all, is that of the southwest Louisiana Cajuns. Journalist Calvin Trillin, a chronicler of regional American food traditions, has written a number of essays on Cajun foodways covering the local crawfish festivals, the liberal use of various sorts of peppers, and the now celebrated and generally familiar repertory of Cajun food traditions.

In south Florida, Cuban immigrants have created another strongly distinctive set of food traditions, a more contemporary example of the same sorts of historical circumstances and cultural processes that underlie Cajun food traditions. Cuban sandwiches — long, narrow loaves of bread stuffed with roast pork, pickles, and other ingredients — are commonly available in south Florida, as is thick, rich Cuban coffee and the black bean soup that merits those same adjectives. And one should also note the Tex-Mex cooking of south Texas, another Spanish-speaking cuisine with a distinct southern accent. In these parts of the South, food is clearly emblematic of the region's plural cultures.

Even when recipes remain the same from place to place, vocabulary may vary. In the Deep South, the term "battercakes" refers to what in the Upper South is generally called pancakes. Reportedly, flitters are pancakes in southern Kentucky. Vocabulary may reflect settlement patterns. The distribution of the terms "smearcase" and "kochcase" in Texas provides a link to the history of German settlements in Texas. Elsewhere in Texas the term "cottage cheese" suffices.

Some southern foods have spread far beyond their original localities. If the "grits belt" was once thought to have covered roughly the same southern territory as the Bible Belt, President Jimmy Carter from Plains, Ga., helped nationalize that southern breakfast food, at least temporarily. A number of fast-food chains have recently begun serving biscuits for breakfast, first in the South where the practice is well known and now throughout much of the country. Population shifts have also helped bring southern food traditions to much of the nation. The large out-migration of African Americans to the North and

Midwest brought soul food, a combination of distinctly African American and regional southern culinary practices and preferences, to most of the cities of the Snowbelt. The geography of southern cooking, then, extends far beyond the South.

BURT FEINTUCH
University of New Hampshire

Linda Keller Brown and Kay Mussell, eds., *Ethnic and Regional Foodways in the United States* (1984); Charles Camp, *American Quarterly* (no. 3, 1982), *Journal of American Culture* (Fall 1979); Floyd M. Henderson, in *This Remarkable Continent: An Atlas of United States and Canadian Society and Cultures*, ed. John F. Rooney Jr. et al. (1982); Sam B. Hilliard, *Hog Meat and Hoecake: Food Supply in the Old South, 1840–1860* (1972); Calvin Trillin, *American Fried: Adventures of a Happy Eater* (1974); Eugene Walter, *American Cooking: Southern Style* (1971).

Hispanic/Latino Origins Populations

Hispanic/Latino populations are exploding across the states of the South. Headlines in local publications from South Carolina to Georgia to Tennessee report "Hispanic Culture Woven into Carolina Tapestry," "Political Parties Seek Share of Hispanic Voters," "Construction Industry Owes Hispanic Employees for Boom." Stories reveal the opening of new Hispanic groceries, the rise of predominantly Hispanic churches, the formation of new Latin soccer leagues, the founding of Spanish-language newspapers, and the creation of new radio stations that broadcast in both English and Spanish. The expansion of Hispanics to the region is part of a larger Latino diaspora that is spreading across the United States.

Historically, Hispanic Americans, also now known as Latino Americans, largely concentrated in Mexican borderland states like Texas, California, Arizona, and New Mexico. Nevertheless, in 1990, Hispanic populations could be found in most U.S. counties, albeit in small concentrations outside of the borderland. Ten southern states in 1990 counted 2 million Hispanic Americans. By 2000, that population more than doubled to 4.3 million. Excluding the peripheral southern states of Florida and Virginia, the number of Hispanics in the South more than tripled from 402,000 to 1.3 million between 1990 and 2000.

Among southern states in 2000, Florida counted the greatest number of Hispanics (1,003,643) and Mississippi the fewest (39,569). Mexican-ancestry Latinos were the largest Hispanic population in seven of ten southern states, including Georgia (275,288), North Carolina (246,545), Tennessee (77,372), Arkansas (61,204), South Carolina (52,871), Alabama (44,522), and Mississippi

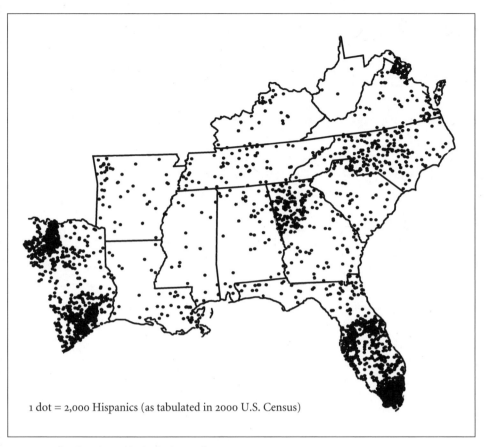

1 dot = 2,000 Hispanics (as tabulated in 2000 U.S. Census)

MAP 8. *Hispanic Population in the South, 2000*

(21,616). In three remaining southern states, Florida, Virginia, and Louisiana, the dominant Hispanic subgroup was "Other Hispanic." This confirms that Central Americans, like Salvadorans, Guatemalans, and Nicaraguans, as well as South Americans like Ecuadorians and Colombians, are more numerous in some southern states. Even Florida, which historically has been chiefly associated with Cuban Americans, is now predominantly Other Hispanic despite the strong concentration of Cubans in metropolitan Miami.

Beyond absolute numbers of Hispanics in southern states, and the variation of dominant subgroups, most southern states have small total percentages of Latinos. In 2000, Georgia (5.3 percent) and North Carolina and Virginia (4.7 percent each) were states with relatively high proportions of Hispanics, yet each was far behind Florida (16.8 percent), which continues to be the most Hispanic southern state. Southern states, nevertheless, have experienced considerable

TABLE 3. *Hispanic/Latino Population of the South, by State, 1990–2000*

State	1990		2000		Largest Subgroup, 2000	
	Number	Percent	Number	Percent	Subgroup	Number
Alabama	24,629	0.6	75,830	1.7	Mexican	44,522
Arkansas	19,876	0.8	86,866	3.2	Mexican	61,204
Florida	1,574,143	12.2	2,682,715	16.8	Other Hispanic	1,003,643
Georgia	108,922	1.7	435,227	5.3	Mexican	275,288
Louisiana	93,044	2.2	107,738	2.4	Other Hispanic	59,353
Mississippi	15,931	0.6	39,569	1.4	Mexican	21,616
North Carolina	76,726	1.2	378,963	4.7	Mexican	246,545
South Carolina	30,551	0.9	95,076	2.4	Mexican	52,871
Tennessee	32,741	0.7	123,838	2.2	Mexican	77,372
Texas	4,339,905	25.5	6,669,666	32.0	Mexican	5,071,963
Virginia	160,288	2.6	329,540	4.7	Other Hispanic	206,089
Total	6,476,756		11,025,028			

Source: Betsy Guzman, The Hispanic Population, 2000 *(Washington, D.C.: U.S. Census Bureau, 2001).*

change: Arkansas was 0.8 percent Latino in 1990 and grew to 3.2 percent in 2000; South Carolina grew from 0.9 percent to 2.4 percent and Tennessee from 0.7 percent to 2.2 percent in the same period.

Whereas most southern states have low percentages of Hispanics, there are higher concentrations of Latinos in specific counties. North Carolina has 26 counties with greater than 5 percent of the population Hispanic. These counties represent concentrations of Latinos greater than the state percentage (4.7 percent). Chiefly, these counties are proximate and peripheral to the major urban areas of the state like Winston-Salem, Charlotte, Raleigh, and Fayetteville. Duplin and Sampson counties east of Fayetteville, for example, have 15 and 11 percent Hispanic populations, respectively. These counties contain some of the state's leading pork- and poultry-processing industries, which employ significant numbers of Latino workers. Similarly, Arkansas has 11 counties where Hispanics exceed the percentage for the state (3.2 percent). Principally, these counties are in the west along the Oklahoma border. Two of these counties, Benton and Washington in the northwest corner of Arkansas, have the largest numbers of Latinos—14,000 and 13,000, respectively. Towns like Rogers in Ben-

Hash house and mercato, Greenwood, S.C., 2003 (Richard Pillsbury, photographer)

ton County and Springdale in Washington County contain plants operated by Tyson, the nation's leading poultry-processing company.

Pork- and poultry-processing industries continue to draw Hispanics to southern states, but additional factors make parts of the South attractive. In Mississippi, for example, Harrison County on the Gulf of Mexico has the greatest number of Hispanics in the state, some 5,000, representing almost 13 percent of all Latinos in Mississippi. Two towns in this county, Biloxi and Gulfport, are major resort centers where 11 casinos and nearly 7,000 hotel rooms create a demand for service-sector and domestic workers. In Georgia, the greater Atlanta area centered on Fulton, Dekalb, Cobb, and Gwinnett counties has the highest concentration of Hispanics in the state. Here each county has between 10 and 15 percent Latino population, more than double the state percentage (5.3 percent). Service-sector employment is a mainstay of any metropolitan area, and Hispanics increasingly fill this niche in large cities. Yet in Atlanta some recent immigrants include Mexican professionals, technicians, and managerial personnel hired by corporations and newly started Mexican companies. Atlanta is now home to the first Hispanic-owned bank in the Southeast outside of Florida.

The presence of Hispanics in some southern towns and cities has created friction among groups. Other communities have adjusted to the new residents. In Greenwood, S.C., tensions run high because Hispanic immigrants compete with African Americans for meat-processing factory jobs. In Birmingham, Ala., improvements have been made to the process of hiring day laborers who are mostly Hispanic to protect workers from crooked contractors. In Hickory, N.C., a community relations council has been formed to ease Hispanic adjustment, and a Latino festival has been launched to promote community well-being.

It would be a mistake to assume that this explosion in Hispanic population in the region is simply a response to labor demand and that it represents a temporary condition. Latinos are moving to the South, not simply migrating for short-term employment. This movement, therefore, is significantly different than the cycles of seasonal migration that have historically characterized Mexican American workers from states like Texas, who moved across the West and Midwest to work and harvest different crops. Hispanics are coming to the South to stay, to put down roots, and to invest in communities, for the present as well as for future generations. And, importantly, the new migrants are not only foreign-born Latin Americans. Increasing numbers of relocation migrants who immigrated first to gateways like Los Angeles, New York, and Miami are now coming to the South. Some from this population are even native-born Hispanic Americans who are choosing to migrate to a region of opportunity. This portends a greater ethnic and cultural plurality in the future of the South.

DANIEL D. ARREOLA
Arizona State University

Daniel D. Arreola, in *Ethnicity in Contemporary America: A Geographical Appraisal*, ed. Jesse O. McKee (2000); Cynthia A. Brewer and Trudy A. Suchan, *Mapping Census 2000: The Geography of U.S. Diversity*, Census 2000 Special Reports (2001); Altha J. Cravey, *Southeastern Geographer* (November 1997); Kevin E. McHugh, Ines M. Miyares, and Emily H. Skop, *Geographical Review* (October 1997); Curtis C. Roseman, in *Geographical Identities of Ethnic America: Race, Space, and Place*, ed. Kate A. Berry and Martha L. Henderson (2002); Cruz C. Torres, *Emerging Latino Communities: A New Challenge for the Rural South*, Southern Rural Development Center, Mississippi State University (August 2000).

Indians and the Landscape

The southern American Indians at the time of the Europeans' arrival represented a population of about one million. These Indians spoke distinct languages of the Algonkian, Iroquoian, Siouan, Yuchean, Muskogean, Tunican, and Caddoan stocks. A short list of the better-documented tribes speaking those languages includes the Powhatan, Shawnee, Tuscarora, Cherokee, Catawba, Yuchi, Choctaw, Seminole, Natchez, Tunica, Chitimacha, and the Natchitoches. After decimation by European diseases and forced movement

Cherokee log corncrib, near Young Harris, Ga., 1970 (Richard Pillsbury, photographer)

west by secretly arranged treaties and violent expulsions, the Indian population in most of the South vanished. Although today their numbers in the region have grown to almost 195,000, this is a mere shadow of their historical presence, and that number is but a small percentage of the modern southern population. More salient than their numbers has been the continuing cultural impact upon the Europeans who settled in the South. Indian trails became traces and eventually highways, their wild and domesticated foods became staples in the southerner's diet, their place-names enhanced the southern landscape, and their ancient earthen monuments are now preserved as parks. Rarely, if ever, has one race intruded into the kingdom of another without drawing from the native culture, and European settlers in the South were no exception.

Even if most non-Indian southerners do not personally encounter their Indian compatriots in daily activities, they do constantly hear Indian words. A number of characteristically southern words are, in reality, of Indian origin. A few of the more familiar examples would include the words bayou, hammock, hominy, opossum, and persimmon. The very names of half the southern states are of Indian derivation: Alabama, Arkansas, Kentucky, Mississippi, Tennessee, and Texas. The same is true of the names of countless cities and towns (e.g., Chattanooga and Tupelo), mountains (e.g., Appalachian), valleys (e.g., Shenandoah), rivers (e.g., Monongahela, Atchafalaya), lakes (e.g., Okeechobee), swamps (e.g., Okeefenokee), islands (e.g., Assateague), and bays (e.g., Chesapeake). Indian place-names are of value for their characteristic euphony, and they lie at the root of much historic research. In innumerable instances the native place-names are the most valuable descriptors of locations and landmarks as they existed before European settlers altered geographical characteristics. For example, few people think of the city name Chattanooga as meaning "a rock rising to a point," yet this Indian name clearly applies to Lookout Mountain nearby.

The attraction to nature is another intangible Indian contribution to southern culture. The traditional southern affection for the pleasures, adventures, and freedom of the outdoors or backwoods was learned from Native Americans. This was not a trait brought from Europe by the majority of the peasants who settled in the South in the 17th and 18th centuries. In fact, few of them could have experienced such freedom under the authoritative oligarchies that prevailed in their native countries. Southerners' love of the outdoors might well be seen as a legacy of the Indian prowess that the colonists learned from and developed. It is ironic that this legacy is so prominent in the South, a region that exerted much energy to rid itself of its Indian habitants.

In the realm of tangible items, the innumerable wild and domesticated food plants known to the Indians aided the European explorers and settlers and then became staples in the diets of populations worldwide. Chief among the food plants was the Native American cultigen maize, or corn, which has proved to be the favorite food for both man and animal in the South and the most notable staple in the southern diet. Other regions of the nation consumed wheat bread, but the mainstay of the southern diet was cornbread. Corn, ground into meal, is not only used to make bread; it is concocted into a myriad of recipes and served as pone, muffins, biscuits, corn dodgers, hoecake, hush puppies, mush, sourings, griddle cakes, and waffles. Corn is also converted to hominy and grits. Nor can one forget the contribution of corn to the manufacture of three particularly southern beverages, sour-mash whiskey, bourbon, and moonshine.

The traditional beliefs, languages, crafts, and lifeways of the South's Native Americans have broadly influenced and immeasurably enriched the culture of the South.

ROBERT W. NEUMAN
Louisiana State University

Alexander P. Chamberlain, *Proceedings of the American Antiquarian Society* (1905); Felix S. Cohen, *American Scholar* (Spring 1952); Sam B. Hilliard, *Hog Meat and Hoecake: Food Supply in the Old South, 1840–1860* (1972); George R. Steward, *Names on the Land* (1945).

Industrial Regions

Throughout its history, southern manufacturing has undergone several significant changes in its structure and composition. In 1972, for example, one in five members of the southern workforce found employment in manufacturing. By 2000 the proportion of those employed in the region's factories had fallen to 11 percent. Over the same period, however, manufacturing as a whole grew in size and witnessed the simultaneous decline of its traditional industries and the rise of more advanced capital- and knowledge-intensive forms of manufacturing. These structural changes have been accompanied by a commensurate spatial reorganization that has taken place in and around the region's metropolitan areas and along the interstate highways that connect them.

TRADITIONAL REGIONS. Southern industrialization had its beginnings in the last several decades of the 19th century, with the rapid growth of the cotton textile industry along the Piedmont corridor, a rolling plateau that extends from middle Virginia into Alabama. By the 1920s the South surpassed the once-dominant New England region in textiles output.

Mill developers typically chose rural sites for their plants, establishing entire villages in which the employees lived and worked. The proliferation of these villages produced a dispersed pattern of population and a consequent lack of large cities. This dispersed pattern emerged in the late 19th century, and it remains as a distinctive feature of the Piedmont region. Also on the Piedmont, in northern North Carolina and into Virginia, the furniture industry developed, attracted by local hardwood forest resources. It too followed a dispersed pattern of development. The cigarette-manufacturing industry concentrated in a few of the region's cities, notably Winston-Salem, Durham, and Richmond.

Although much of the Deep South remained agrarian during this period, an unusual occurrence of self-fluxing coal and iron ore in close proximity to each other formed the basis for the development of an iron and steel industry in and around Birmingham. In 1901 the discovery of the massive Spindletop oil field near Beaumont, Tex., triggered the explosive growth of the petroleum industry along the Gulf Coast in Louisiana and Texas. The extraction of crude oil soon led to the nation's largest refining industry and the subsequent development of petrochemicals facilities, for which petroleum served as the raw material for a host of chemical products.

By World War II, these districts dominated southern manufacturing. There were, to be sure, a host of resource-oriented producers scattered throughout the region, notably paper mills and processors of agricultural products. These

Coal tipple, south of Fairmont, W.Va., 1971 (Richard Pillsbury, photographer)

plants were even more dispersed than textile mills but, like them, supported a strongly dispersed, rural population.

POST–WORLD WAR II GROWTH. The period after World War II brought dramatic changes to the economy of the South. The war effort served as a strong boost to the textile industry and revived it after the slump of the late 1920s and the Depression of the 1930s. The construction of the interstate highway system greatly increased access to northern industrial markets, and the first-hand experience of millions of military personnel created a broad awareness of the region's assets. Rapid industrial development was paralleled by the growth of urban-based service economies. As the industrial base of the Piedmont was diversified by machinery, electronics, and other more capital-intensive industries, textile producers and related apparel producers found it difficult to compete with the wages being offered by the newer industries and the growing urban service economies. This led to an episode of rural industrialization as mill owners sought out new supplies of low-cost workers. The dispersed pattern that had characterized the Piedmont for many decades thus moved onto the Coastal Plain or into the Appalachian mountain valleys. From the 1940s until the early 1970s, textile and apparel employment grew steadily even as these industries were redistributed within the South.

During this period, the petroleum refining and petrochemical industries along the Gulf Coast continued to expand, and the capital generated by them fueled the strong growth of urban economies in places such as Dallas and Houston. However, the Birmingham steel industry began to decline in the face of high operating costs, competition from foreign producers, and mergers with larger U.S. steel companies.

INDUSTRIAL RESTRUCTURING. The OPEC oil embargo of the early 1970s and consequent escalation in domestic oil prices triggered an awareness of a rapidly developing global economy. This globalization and the related technological developments drove a major restructuring of the South's industrial economy. The formation of transnational corporations led to the transfer of industrial production from the South to various low-cost sites in Asia and Latin America. This hit the labor-intensive textile and apparel industries, the backbone of many rural economies, especially hard, ending the era of rural industrialization. Employment in these industries and other traditional southern industries, such as furniture and cigarettes, began to decline rapidly. For example, since 1972 the South has lost an average of 12,000 textile jobs every year, partly through labor-saving technologies and mergers and acquisitions, but mostly through relocations to lower-cost regions in other countries. The pace of job loss in the region's traditional industries quickened during the 1990s, causing the South to lose over three-quarters of its jobs in the textile industry since the 1970s, a pattern repeated in several of its other traditional manufacturing sectors, often with devastating effects on the communities that hosted them.

Although globalization has undercut many dispersed rural areas, it has worked to the benefit of larger urban areas that tend to be the recipients of foreign direct investment. As illustrated in Map 9, industries such as wood products and food processing are widely dispersed throughout the region, and the Gulf Coast, eastern seaboard, and parts of northern Alabama and North Carolina have maintained their petrochemical, paper, and furniture production, respectively. Partly fueled by foreign direct investment, however, substantial production complexes have developed around Atlanta, Houston, Dallas–Ft. Worth, and central Florida. A few quasi-rural areas have benefited from new investment flows, such as the ribbon of industrial machine producers found along I-35 stretching from central Oklahoma through Dallas–Ft. Worth and Austin, Tex. Similarly, foreign direct investment helped develop "auto alley" bounded by I-65 and I-75 in Alabama, Kentucky, and Tennessee, as well as the I-85 corridor of upstate South Carolina. The emergence of motor vehicle assembly and parts suppliers in the South is particularly notable for its implementation of flexible manufacturing processes, which use advanced robotics, programmable machines, and "just-in-time" inventory and supply chain management. These characteristics not only changed the nature of work and the skills demanded by employers, but produced a distinctive industrial pattern to accommodate just-in-time production. New auto assembly plants required new regional agglomerations of suppliers to facilitate "on demand" shipment of inputs. At the same time, many parts suppliers located at distances sufficiently far from assembly plants to avoid direct competition for labor, producing a geography of production that was regionally agglomerated, yet locally dispersed. In these instances, however, none of these plants is very far from a metropolitan area and all are connected to them by an interstate highway (Map 9). As a 1986 report by the Manpower Development Corporation put it, "The sunshine of recent growth in the South is shining brightly on metropolitan areas but casting a dark shadow over rural areas."

In addition to globalization, the southern economy has responded strongly to the emergence of new technologies. Research Triangle Park in North Carolina, for example, is generally regarded as the "hottest" research-oriented industrial park in the country. Companies there specialize in telecommunications, computers, pharmaceuticals, software, and other high-tech research and development industries. Florida also has a substantial concentration of photonics/optoelectronics companies, especially in Orlando and Tampa. Spurred by an abundance of federal procurement contracts and highly skilled and entrepreneurial labor, northern Virginia has developed one of the largest agglomerations of customized computer programming, systems integration/architecture, and telecommunications firms in the nation. Other advanced manufacturing clusters can be found in Austin, Tex., Atlanta, Ga., Asheville, N.C., and Dallas–Ft. Worth, Tex., to name a few.

The traditional sectors of textile mills, textile products, and apparel collectively declined by nearly 47 percent between 1972 and 2000, at a loss of over 592,000 jobs. In the meantime, a host of newer, high-tech industries (machinery, instruments, electric and electronic equipment, motor vehicles, and chemicals) added almost 690,000 employees. This growth, and that in a few other sectors, created an overall increase of 17 percent in the region's manufacturing sector. In the rest of the United States, manufacturing jobs actually decreased by over one million, a 7.4 percent loss. As a result, the South's share of the U.S. total rose from just over 25 percent to nearly 30 percent between 1972 and 2000.

There are two major features of this industrial restructuring. First, the South has shed many of its declining traditional industries, which have been characterized as low-skill, low-wage employment with an average payroll per employee in 1997 of $20,557, only two-thirds of the regional average of $30,230. In

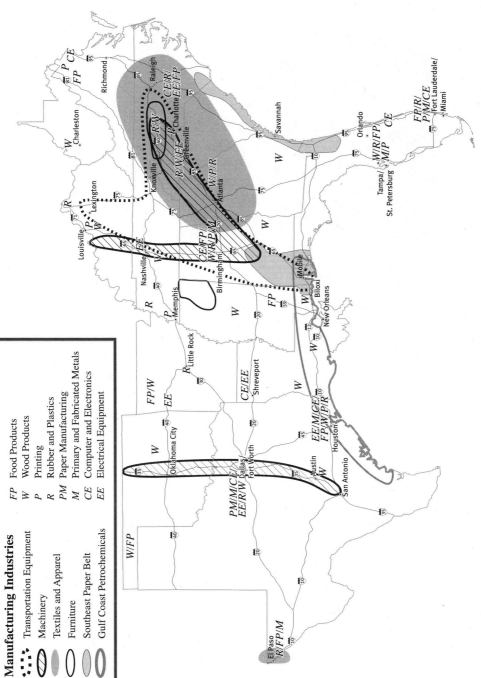

MAP 9. *Industrial Regions of the South* (Adapted from a map by the UNC–Charlotte Cartography Lab; source: *derived from the U.S. Census of Manufactures, 1997*)

Manufacturing Industries

Transportation Equipment

Machinery

Textiles and Apparel

Furniture

Southeast Paper Belt

Gulf Coast Petrochemicals

FP   Food Products
W   Wood Products
P   Printing
R   Rubber and Plastics
PM   Paper Manufacturing
M   Primary and Fabricated Metals
CE   Computer and Electronics
EE   Electrical Equipment

Gristmill, an instant source of power, Sharpsburg, Ga., 1971 (Richard Pillsbury, photographer)

contrast, the newer industries as a group averaged $37,199, more than 20 percent higher than the regional figure. Second, the restructuring of industry has changed the geographic distribution of employment in favor of metro areas. The 1997 Census of Manufactures shows that there were 398 southern counties (out of 1,396) with 500 or more employees in the newer industries group, and over 80 percent of them were in one of the region's Metropolitan Statistical Areas. On the other hand, 70 percent of the 292 counties with 500 or more employees in the traditional industries were in nonmetro areas.

The implications of this distribution are profound. On the one hand, the South's metropolitan areas continue to attract thousands of jobs in higher-wage, higher-skill, capital-intensive manufacturing, even as great losses are being experienced in the lower-wage, low-skill industries that are often found in the more rural parts of the South. The future prospects for many communities in the rural South are thus not encouraging. High-tech industries play more to the strength of the U.S. economy than do traditionally labor-intensive industries, and these industries require a well-educated labor force, as well as accessibility to national and global markets, whether by interstate highways or air service.

Added to the obvious attraction of such industries to urban areas is the shift toward more flexible manufacturing systems that depend heavily on computer-

Vehicle carrier, Charleston, S.C., 2004 (Richard Pillsbury, photographer)

integrated processes. Production runs are smaller, and the uncertainties of volume associated with this production are shifted to subcontractors and suppliers who achieve efficiencies through economies of scope rather than scale.
This favors smaller, more flexible establishments, including those that are affili-
ated with corporate headquarters and research and development functions that
operate over a range of product types. Such operations and the related skilled
jobs in research, innovation, marketing, and finance gravitate toward amenity-
rich urban centers with diverse labor pools and high levels of (inter)national
connectivity. In contrast, the rapid changes associated with developing technologies and markets put any plant that specializes in the manufacture of a
single product at considerable risk. Unfortunately, branch plants producing a
limited number of product lines are the very type of industrial operation that
is found throughout the rural South. Many rural communities have only low-
cost labor with few employment alternatives to offer, but so too do a host of
other countries where labor costs are lower still.

The industrial landscape of the South is now a composite of broad, largely
rural, clusters of traditional manufacturing that are declining remnants of the
past and burgeoning metropolitan areas that comprise nodes and corridors of
modern, information-intensive industries, many of which are active partici-
pants in the global economy. The good news is that the shift toward advanced

manufacturing has brought better wages and working conditions to the South. The bad news is that structural changes in the southern industrial economy present significant challenges to specific states and communities that are forced to cope with the changes that disinvestment and dislocation bring. In short, the economic base of many rural areas is eroding, while metropolitan areas are gaining a host of higher-wage industrial jobs that complement the networked web of suppliers, producer services, and other urban activities. The restructuring of the southern industrial economy has thus shifted the spotlight of growth to shine brightly on metropolitan areas, while throwing some rural areas more deeply into the shadows.

HARRISON S. CAMPBELL JR.
University of North Carolina at Charlotte

ALFRED W. STUART
University of North Carolina at Charlotte

Jacquelyn Dowd Hall et al., *Like a Family: The Making of a Southern Cotton Mill World* (1987); M. L. Johnson, *Southeastern Geographer* (no. 2, 1997); E. J. Malecki, *Technology and Economic Development* (1991); Manpower Development Corporation (MDC), *Shadows in the Sunbelt* (1986).

Jewish Origins Populations

American Jewish history is often said to commence with the migration of 23 Jews from Brazil to New Amsterdam in 1654. Yet much of the early history of Jews in the United States is not a history of the Northeast but of the South. The earliest synagogues were found not only in New Amsterdam, Newport, and Philadelphia, but also in Savannah, Charleston, and New Orleans. The first known Jew in North America was Joachim Gaunse, a mining technologist from Prague, who settled for one year (1585) at Roanoke Island, Va., to serve as a metallurgist in the colony founded by Sir Walter Raleigh.

Until after the Civil War, Savannah and Charleston shaped the character of all of American Jewry. Jews originally came to Georgia because James Oglethorpe, while specifically excluding "Papists" from the colony, apparently "forgot" to exclude Jews. The first group of Jewish settlers in the South included 42 (mostly) Sephardic (Spanish/Portuguese) Jews from London who came in 1733 to settle in Georgia. Congregation Mickve Israel, established in 1735, still functions.

Jews originally came to South Carolina because the Charter written by John Locke granted equality to "Jews, heathens, and dissenters." Congregation Kahal Kadosh Beth Elohim in Charleston was founded in 1749 and is the second-oldest congregation in the country. During the first decade of the 1800s, Charleston had a Jewish population of about 500 and was the largest, wealthiest, and most cultured Jewish community in the United States. One of the earliest examples of an American Jewish self-help group was the Hebrew Orphan Society of Charleston, organized in 1801. It was also in Charleston in 1824 that the first attempt occurred to establish a Reform Jewish congregation, an experiment that lasted only until 1833. (In Baltimore, in 1842, the country's first enduring Reform congregation was established.)

Not until the middle of the 1800s did German (Ashkenazic) Jews arrive in the South, mostly in connection with the cotton industry. When the large migration of Eastern European Jews to the United States began, the vast majority of the 2,326,500 Jewish migrants from 1881 to 1924 settled in the Northeast. Thus, the percentage of American Jews living in the South declined rapidly during this period. Only after World War II did Jews originally from Eastern Europe (Ashkenazic Jews) migrate in large numbers from the Northeast and Midwest to major southern cities, as part of the general movement of Americans to the Sun Belt, leading to a significant expansion of the Jewish population in the South.

Thus, the Jewish population of the South Census Division increased from 157,000 in 1900 to 330,000 in 1940 and to 1,283,000 in 2000. The percentage of the South's population that was Jewish decreased from 1.8 percent in 1900 to 0.8 percent in 1940 and then increased to 1.3 percent in 2000. The percentage of American Jews who live in the South Census Division also shows a similar pattern, decreasing from 14 percent in 1900 to 7 percent in 1940 and then increasing to 21 percent in 2000.

These numbers are a bit misleading, as two areas of the South in which most of the recent increases have occurred—Maryland/D.C. (essentially the Baltimore/Washington corridor) and Florida (essentially Miami, Fort Lauderdale, and Palm Beach)—are not really "southern." Maryland/D.C. is essentially a northeastern city, and the growth in Florida is a result of the migration of (mostly elderly) Jews (mostly) from the Northeast. The Jewish population of the Maryland/D.C. area increased from 38,500 in 1940 to 241,500 in 2000. The Jewish population of Florida increased from 21,000 in 1940 to 628,000 in 2000. Thus, of the increase of 953,000 in the South's Jewish population from 1940 to 2000, 64 percent occurred in Florida and 21 percent in Maryland/D.C. Therefore, 85 percent of the reported growth in the South's Jewish population occurred in areas atypical of the South. Most of the remainder of the growth was in Atlanta, Dallas, Houston, and northern Virginia (essentially a D.C. suburb).

The current distribution of Jews in the South at the state level shows that, after Florida and Maryland/D.C., other important states include Texas

(128,000), Georgia (93,500), and Virginia (76,000). At the metropolitan area scale, southeast Florida (504,000) and the Baltimore/D.C. corridor (275,000) are the two largest centers. Atlanta (85,900), Dallas (45,000), and Houston (42,000) are secondary centers.

But the story of southern Jewry since World War II is even more a story of small Jewish communities that are either decreasing in Jewish population or simply ceasing to exist as Jewish communities. The 2000 *American Jewish Year Book* identifies 140 Jewish communities in the South with 100 or more individuals. More than three-fourths of these Jewish communities contain fewer than 5,000 persons. Only 7 percent are large Jewish communities of 25,000 and over. More important, 44 Jewish communities that existed in 1960 have ceased to exist in 2000 in the sense that they either are totally devoid of members or have dropped below the level of a "functioning" community.

Four different reasons may be postulated to explain the decline of small southern Jewish communities. First, anti-Semitism in the South has varied significantly both spatially and temporally. Both anecdotal evidence and evidence from scientific surveys support its existence at a level commensurate with the idea that some Jews have left the South because of anti-Semitism. But note that researchers have differed on the seriousness of southern anti-Semitism. On the one hand, some of the nation's worst anti-Semitic incidents have occurred in the South (the Leo Frank case and several synagogue bombings), and examples abound as well of insensitivity to the Jewish population. Even the title of Eli Evans's classic work on southern Jewry, *The Lonely Days Were Sundays*, implies that many Jews felt like outsiders in the South. On the other hand, many observers of the southern Jewish scene comment that, although (mostly covert) anti-Semitism did exist, in general the South was an amenable locale for Jews. Many religious fundamentalists in the rural South were respectful of Jews, or even philo-Semitic, viewing Jews as the "People of the Book." In fact, the first Jew to hold elective office in the United States was Frances Salvador, who, in 1775 and 1776, was elected as a delegate to the South Carolina Provincial Congress. Georgia elected the country's first Jewish state governor in 1801. Florida elected the first Jewish senator (David Levy Yulee) in 1845. Martin Behrman served as mayor of New Orleans from 1904 to 1920. Thus, anti-Semitism and insensitivity no doubt played a significant role in the out-migration of Jews from some areas of the South but was probably not the major reason for the out-migration of Jews in many areas.

Second, in small southern towns it was common for a large percentage of the peddlers and merchants to be Jewish. Many of today's largest department and variety stores were started by southern Jews. In some places, Jews were influential in the economy. Raphael Moses and Sam Sommers contributed innovations that led to the growth of the peach and pecan industries. The inventions of Benjamin Ehrlich contributed to the success of Coca-Cola. However, the children of these store owners and businessmen attended colleges (often outside the South) in areas with larger Jewish communities and often decided to not return to the status of being a tiny minority in a small town. The Jewish-owned stores on Main Street were gradually replaced by the Kmarts and Wal-Marts.

Third, many Jews, within a few generations of arriving in a small town, intermarried and assimilated into the Christian population. A National Jewish Population Survey conducted in 1990 showed a very high rate of intermarriage and assimilation in the South.

Fourth, in some cases, those Jewish communities that were lost existed in areas where the general population also declined. That is, the loss in Jews is commensurate with a general downturn in an area.

During the same period (1960–2000) that some small Jewish communities were disappearing, 17 Jewish communities that had not existed in 1960 came into existence. Of the 17, 8 are retirement communities located in Florida, most notably South Palm Beach (Boca Raton/Delray Beach), which increased from less than 100 Jews in 1960 to 93,000 Jews in 2000. Five new small Jewish communities have been established in university towns, reflecting the disproportionately high number of Jews among both the faculties and student bodies of some universities. Two new small Jewish communities have developed in resort areas.

Thus, both the geographic distribution of the southern Jewish population and its places of origin (Spain/Portugal, Germany, Eastern Europe) have changed significantly since colonial times. Although never a large percentage of the southern population, the political and economic contributions of the Jewish population to southern society have been considerable. Jews in the South developed a southern Jewish consciousness, and the full range of political opinions and passions held by other southerners developed among them.

IRA M. SHESKIN
University of Miami

American Jewish Committee, *American Jewish Year Book* (annual); Leonard Dinnerstein and M. Pallson, eds., *Jews in the South* (1973); Eli N. Evans, *The Lonely Days Were Sundays* (1993), *The Provincials: A Personal History of Jews in the South* (1997); Melissa Faye Greene, *The Temple Bombing* (1996); D. D. Moore, *To the Golden Cities: Pursuing the American Dream in Miami and L.A.* (1994); Ira M. Sheskin, *How Jewish*

Communities Differ: Variations in the Findings of Local Jewish Demographic Studies (2001), in *Land and Community: Geography in Jewish Studies*, ed. H. Brodsky (1997); Stella Suberman, *The Jew Store* (1998).

Land Division

Different survey systems were used in the American South, including the metes and bounds system, the state rectangular systems, the French long lot system, and the U.S. township and range system. Each of these helped shape the distinctive physical and cultural landscape of the South.

The metes and bounds survey system was introduced from Europe. It used natural boundary markers such as trees, streams, rocks, and other features. Very few of the areas where it was employed were surveyed before settlement. It created a series of very irregular and unsystematic landholding patterns. Surveyors made every effort to lay out these lots in rectangular shapes, but these patterns generally failed to survive through time. The sizes of the holdings varied greatly but were usually between 200 and 1,000 acres. The metes and bounds survey system was indiscriminate at best. The system created countless lawsuits and challenges concerning property boundaries as well as actual land ownership. This unsystematic survey was employed in the southern Atlantic Seaboard colonies as far south as Georgia, where massive land frauds occurred.

The metes and bounds survey system extended westward in Georgia to the Oconee River. It was also used in some river valleys of the lower Gulf South, notably in the alluvial Mississippi Valley as well as in east Texas. Other vestiges of this survey system can be found scattered throughout the region. The states of Tennessee and Kentucky also employed the metes and bounds survey system.

One of the most spectacular and successful state-controlled rectangular survey systems employed in the American South was implemented in the early 19th century. Between 1805 and 1832 a state-controlled land-lottery system was established in Georgia, and a series of six lotteries were held. By this method the western two-thirds of Georgia was made available to the public at little or no expense to settlers. Each of the lotteries consisted of land districts containing rectangular lots that were surveyed before settlement and then offered to the citizens by public lottery. Several town sites were selected and surveyed at strategic locations, and town lots were offered at public auctions. The individual land-lot sizes varied in different lotteries, but an effort was made to maintain rectangular land districts and land lots. The land-lot sizes in Georgia included lots of 40, 160, 202½, 250, and 490 acres. The land district lines in Georgia were primarily surveyed north-south and east-west. A similar state rectangular survey system was later used in portions of central and west Texas as well.

An unusual and not-so-well-known survey system found essentially in the Gulf South and concentrated in the state of Louisiana is the French long lot system. There is evidence, however, of the use of long lot surveys in Tennessee, North Carolina, and Texas. The major concentrations of long lots in Louisiana are found in the Mississippi alluvial valley and related bayous, the Atchafalaya basin, and the Red River Valley. The long lot survey lines were laid out perpendicular to stream channels and roads; in southern Louisiana most were surveyed perpendicular to water courses. Usually the depth of the lot was three or four times greater than the width. Most of the lots were roughly rectangular in shape; a few were true rectangles. By surveying at right angles to stream courses, landowners were given access to a variety of environmental zones. They had access to the water courses, the well-drained lands along the levee, pasturelands, and woodland swamp areas.

The fourth major survey system used in the South was the U.S. township and range survey, which was initiated in the latter 18th century in northeastern Ohio. The basic unit of measurement was a township or an area of 36 square miles. The survey began with a zero baseline and a zero north-south coordinate; principal meridian units six miles in distance were then measured north and south of the baseline and east and west of the principal meridian. These units were then designated township one north (T1N) and township one south (T1S) from the zero baseline. Ranges were designated range one east (R1E) and range one west (R1W) of the principal meridian. Each of these townships was then subdivided into 36 sections of 640 acres each. These sections were numbered 1 through 36. Section number 1 was always located in the northeast corner of the township, with section 36 in the southeast corner.

Because the range lines were in fact meridians that converge as they extend northward, adjustments were made to prevent reduction in township widths. Four baselines and seven principal meridians were used in the South. This survey system was superimposed on earlier surveys in the states of Florida, Alabama, Mississippi, Louisiana, and Arkansas. However, in many instances, prior survey lines were honored and maintained. This was especially true in the long lot regions of Louisiana. Essentially, the major advantages of the township and range survey system were that land records were more correct and more easily accessible to the public.

GERALD L. HOLDER
Sam Houston State University

Vernon Carstensen, ed., *The Public Lands: Studies in the History of the Public Domain* (1963); Everett Dick, *The Dixie Frontier: A Social History of the Southern Frontier from the First Transmontane Beginnings to the Civil War* (1948); Edward M. Douglas, *Boundaries, Areas, Geographic Centers, and Altitudes of the United States and the Several States*, Geological Survey Bulletin 817 (1930); Sam B. Hilliard, *Geographical Review* (October 1982), *Studies in the Social Sciences*, vol. 12 (1973); Gerald L. Holder, *Pioneer America* (September 1982); Hildegard Binder Johnston, *Order upon the Land* (1976); Roy M. Robbins, *Our Landed Heritage: The Public Domain, 1776–1970*, 2nd ed. (1976); Norman J. G. Thrower, *Original Survey and Land Subdivision* (1966); Payson J. Treat, *The National Land System, 1785–1820* (1910).

Land Use

In its most general form, land use in the South may be viewed from the perspective of an Upland South and a Lowland South. The Upland South includes much of the Appalachian Highland and the Ozark-Ouachita Highland. These hilly-to-mountainous areas with steep slopes and poor soils have rarely supported an intensive and profitable agriculture. The predominant land-use pattern has been that of small, independently owned and operated farms on which woodlands and pastures served as low-quality grazing space for small livestock herds. Such limited farming enterprises, even with their provisional crops, have provided a meager living. Often the owners of such farms have had to seek supplemental work in forestry, mining, or manufacturing.

The Lower South includes the Atlantic and Gulf Coastal Plain and the outer Piedmont. It possesses the best of the southern agricultural resources — especially on the inner Coastal Plain from southern Virginia to southeastern Alabama and Mississippi, the Tennessee Valley of northern Alabama, the Mississippi Delta, the black prairies of Texas, and the Gulf Coastal prairies of Louisiana and Texas. These regions have provided the resources for the traditional cotton and tobacco crops and, to a lesser extent, for the sugar and rice crops. Currently they support such diverse crops as corn, soybeans, peanuts, cotton, tobacco, and rice, and they provide excellent pastures.

Land-use patterns emerge from the interactions of a given culture system with a physical habitat. Changes in the physical-cultural milieu within which these interactions occur induce change in the organization and structuring of land use. Such has certainly been the case in the American South, where, for the past half century, changes in land-use patterns have reflected the economic, social, and technological changes that have engulfed the region. Two broad and encompassing events provide a perspective for understanding recent developments in southern land use.

The first is an agricultural revolution originating in the early decades of the 20th century. Developments such as the boll weevil infestation; agricultural depressions; erosion problems; competition for labor; rising expectations; genetic, chemical, and mechanical advances in agricultural technology; federal agricultural programs; and market forces, all in their own persistent manner, have changed land-use patterns. The imprint of this revolution on the landscape was widely evident by the post–World War II years.

Substantial areas within the South have experienced declining use of agricultural land, particularly cleared land on farms. The entire Piedmont and adjacent segments of the Coastal Plain, the Appalachian Highland of eastern Kentucky, and the interior highlands of Arkansas and northern Louisiana all experienced this loss. The cropland losses can be attributed to modest physical resources, federal programs, and the loss of competitive ability with respect to particular crops. Where agriculture has retained vitality, the cropland has often been converted to the production of alternate crops, such as soybeans, corn, peanuts, and winter wheat. Agriculture has become decidedly more diversified. Other cropland has given way to forest or pasture—with terraces the only visible evidence of former cropland use. Indeed, forestry has become the single most common component of southern land-use patterns.

Sixty-two percent of all land area in the South is forested. Nearly 75 percent of this land is privately owned as woodland on farms or simply forested tracts. Nineteen percent of the forestland is owned by the forest industry, and the remainder is owned by national and state agencies. Though large forested tracts are owned by private corporations and the federal government, most forestland remains under the control and ownership of small holders; the average parcel is 66 acres. The quality of forestland is highly variable because of differences in management practices. Paradoxically, however, even though vast areas are forested and have experienced woodland expansion, other areas such as the lower Mississippi Valley and southwest Georgia have witnessed forest clearing for expansion of agriculture. Adaptation of modern irrigation technology has made some southern lands more valuable for agriculture.

A second major influence on land-use change has been urbanization. The peripheries of most southern cities have experienced a shift from nonurban to urban land use. The "growth zone" surrounding the city shows a curious juxtaposition of old and new patterns of land use. The edges of southern cities now extend far into the countryside—blurring the once-distinct rural-urban boundary and rendering the terms virtually obsolete. Some southerners have chosen to retain a rural environment for residence, and this has increased not only the rural nonfarm population but also the growth of retailing and services in response to that market. Many nonmetropolitan residents commute to metropolitan work sites. This pattern is an outgrowth of new settlement patterns and modern transportation, and it has become extensive throughout the South, reflecting and reinforcing the continued change in nonmetropolitan land use.

The use of land for nonagricultural and nonforestry purposes increasingly extends beyond the metropolitan areas. The economic revolution has focused upon small cities and towns throughout the South — in fact, the nonmetropolitan location of much of southern manufacturing growth has been one of the notable features of the regional experience. Numerous towns and small cities have gained new employment opportunities as a result of major American firms locating branch plants nearby. These local employment opportunities have reversed a long-standing population loss in towns and cities where surrounding peripheries, 20 to 30 miles in extent, realize residential expansion and the growth of retailing and services.

Any attempt to envision the patterns of southern land use in the future must take into account the following forces: (1) the rate of population increase of the South will exceed the national average for the foreseeable future; (2) contemporary patterns of settlement, including urbanization and the spread of urban and quasi-urban land uses into the nonmetropolitan periphery, will continue; (3) the demand for recreational space will increase; (4) the economic growth of the past two decades will continue as part of national decentralization and southern regional development; (5) the demand for prime agricultural land will increase; and (6) the forest industry of the United States, indeed of the world, will increasingly look to the American South. The result of these forces can only be increased competition for use of the best southern land.

JAMES S. FISHER
University of Georgia

J. Fraser Hart, *Annals of the Association of American Geographers* (December 1978 and December 1980), with Ennis L. Chestang, *Geographical Review* (October 1978); Robert G. Healy and James L. Short, *The Market for Rural Land: Trends, Issues, Policies* (1981); Merle C. Prunty and Charles S. Aiken, *Annals of the Association of American Geographers* (September 1968 and June 1972).

Language Regions

Within a national language, regional dialects reflect social experience in the context of land forms. The comparatively recent settlement of the Western Hemisphere by Europeans provides a powerful illustration of the taking of new-found lands. The North American example demonstrates settlement processes, routes of interior migration, political structure, reactions to climate and physical geography, the emergence of cultural centers, the development of urban social structures through sociolinguistic complexity, and the reorganization of urban societies under the pressure of large numbers of recent immigrants.

Of the four major language regions of American speech — Northern, Southern, Midland, and Western — none offers more striking examples of these processes than do the Sub-Potomac varieties. The Northern region extends from Maine to Minnesota, terminating at the 98th meridian, 40 miles west of Fargo, beyond which annual rainfall fails to support traditional midwestern farming. Dominated by the historic speech of Pennsylvania, the Midland region forms a vast transition area, across the midwestern states (North Midland) and the entire Highlands regions to the south (South Midland). Below the South Midland area, the great Southern region extends across the Piedmont, Delta, and Plains to the 98th meridian, 50 miles west of Fort Worth, where the linguistic West begins in the southern states.

Language regions in the American South offer examples of all seven of the aforementioned factors of social mobility: (1) primary settlement areas with large and influential elements in the early population (Richmond, Charleston, and New Orleans), powerfully influencing the form of local speech patterns; (2) migration routes (from Pennsylvania to Georgia via the Great Valley of Virginia); (3) old political boundaries (the Mason-Dixon line, the historic Confederacy, and the Three States of Tennessee — East, Middle, and West); (4) response to physical geography (discovery of the Cumberland Gap, opening Kentucky from the south); (5) response to climate (the northern extent of Georgia Piedmont cotton after the 180-day growing season); (6) cultural centers (Charleston, Atlanta, and Nashville) and urban social structures (New Orleans and San Antonio); and (7) large numbers of new immigrants (Miami).

These processes yield six major language regions (dialect areas) in the southern states: (1) the Highlands; (2) the Piedmont; (3) the Piney Woods; (4) the Coastal Strip; (5) the Plains; and (6) the Delta. Five of these form discrete, linguistically defined domains; only the Plains area lacks basic vocabulary. Instead, it finds distinctiveness in four complex patterns, identified below as 2A Piedmont/Eastern Plains/Piney Woods, 2B Piedmont/Eastern Plains, 2C Piedmont/Mississippi Plains, and 5D Lower Delta/Western Plains.

Each of these areas includes several subdivisions: (1) the Highlands include the Eastern division of Blue Ridge Mountains of Virginia, the Carolinas, Tennessee, and Georgia; (2) the Piedmont (the easternmost province of the eastern Highlands and Uplands) extends across Virginia, the Carolinas, Georgia into

Alabama and the western division of the Interior Low Plateaus (Middle Kentucky and Tennessee), and the Ozark Plateaus of Arkansas, as well as Missouri and Oklahoma; (3) the Piney Woods (Southeastern Pine Forest) extends between the Coastal Strip and the Interior Plains and Piedmont from Virginia to West Texas, interrupted only by the Alluvial Plains (Delta) in lower Louisiana; (4) the Coastal Strip (the eastern domain of the Atlantic/Gulf Coastal Plain) extends from the mouth of the Potomac (Virginia) to the mouth of the Rio Grande (Texas); (5) the Plains (the Interior Atlantic/Gulf Coastal Plain) enters all southern states — Virginia, Kentucky, North Carolina, South Carolina, Tennessee, Georgia, Florida, Alabama, Mississippi, Louisiana, Arkansas, and Texas — as well as Oklahoma and Missouri; (6) the Delta includes (a) the Arkansas St. Francis River Basin, (b) the Upper Mississippi River Basin of Tennessee, Arkansas, and Louisiana, including the Tensas Basin, (c) the Mississippi Yazoo Basin of Mississippi and the Lower Mississippi River Basin of Mississippi and Louisiana, (d) the Louisiana Atchafalaya Basin and the Red River Basin of Louisiana and Texas.

These six language regions (dialect areas) distinguish themselves, one from the other, by characteristic words and phrases, morphological forms, and pronunciation. For convenience, the following markers include only lexical items (words and phrases) reported in conventional orthography. Such words and phrases proceed from the basic set of regional forms that mark southern speech, from Virginia to Texas. These include southern expressions, such as *chop* (cotton) [= weed/thin], *roasting ears* [= corn on the cob], *chifforobe* [= wardrobe], *whetrock* [= sharpening stone], *slop bucket, (corn) shucks, jackleg* [of a carpenter, lacking training and tools], *polecat, peckerwood* [= woodpecker/poor white trash], *pallet* [= bed on the floor], *tote* [= carry], *cherry/peach seed, hoot owl, screech owl, dirt dauber* [= mud wasp], *toad-frog, common* [pejorative], *(white) trash, juice harp* [= Jew's harp], *skin* [= bacon rind], *hominy, grits* [= ground hominy], *feist* [= small noisy dog], *goobers* [= peanuts], *clabber* [= curdled milk], *greens* [= leafy vegetables], *Irish potatoes, butter beans* [= lima beans], *light bread* [= white bread], *varmint* [= small predator], and *chitlins*. Finally, widespread Southern expressions including only the Coastal Strip include *pulley bone, goozle* [= trachea], *tommyto* [= cherry tomato], *branch* [= creek], *terrapin* [= tortoise], *counterpane* [= bedspread], *hunker down* [= crouch or sit on one's heels], *galluses* [= suspenders], *tree frog, flying jenny* [= merry-go-round], *yellow* [= yolk], *haunts* [rhymes with *pants* or *paints* = ghosts], *souse* [= headcheese], and *corruption* [= pus].

1. Southern Highland: *French harp* [= harmonica], *tow sack* [= gunnysack], *barn lot, bawl* [= cry of a calf], *nicker* [= whinny], *green beans* [= string beans],

backstick [= backlog], *(paper) poke* [= paper bag], *sook* [rhymes with book = call to cow], *dog irons* [= andirons], *knob* [= bald hill], *gap* [= mountain pass], *redworm* [= earthworm], and *chigger*.

1A. Tennessee/Arkansas Highlands: *red squirrel, mud turtle, crappie* [rhymes with *happy*, usually = white perch], *springhouse* [= dairy], *plumb (across)* [= completely], *buck* [= male sheep], *shivaree* [= wedding celebration], *(baby) buggy, stick beans* [= pole beans], *double shovel* [= two-shared plow], *be fresh* [= calve], *of a night* [= at night], *coo* [= call to sheep], *corn dodger* [= pone], *wood(s) colt* [= bastard], *clabbered milk* [= curdled milk], *play-pretty* [= small child's toy], and *plunder* [= household goods].

1B. Tennessee Highlands: *open stone/seed (peach), sugar tree* [= sugar maple], *Mammy* [= Mother], *portico* [= small porch], *drag (harrow), bull tongue (plow), jackleg preacher, touchous* [= overly sensitive], *redbud* [= small Judas tree], *goober peas* [= peanuts].

1C. East Highlands (Virginia, Carolinas, east Kentucky, east Tennessee, and north Georgia): *miller* [= moth], *snake feeder* [= dragonfly], *dip* [= sweet topping], *wasper(s)* [= wasp(s)], *cornfield (beans), poison vine* [= poison ivy], *mountain hoosier* [= rustic], *cucumber tree* [= magnolia], *laurel,* and *ivy* [= laurel].

1D. West Highlands: middle Tennessee/Kentucky and Arkansas Ozarks: *hay shed, woodchuck* [= woodpecker], *hollow* [= wooded valley], *country hoosier* [= rustic], *freshen* [= calve], *scrooch owl* [= screech howl], *wildcat whiskey* [= moonshine], *crawdad* [= crawfish], *razorback* [= wild hog], *Indian peach* [= small cling peach], *teeter-totter* [= seesaw], and *sweet corn*.

1E. Tennessee/Carolina/Virginia Blue Ridge: *(hay) mow* [rhymes with *cow* = hayloft], *(milk) gap* [= outdoor milking place], *boomer* [= brown squirrel], *glib* [= lively, of elderly], *airish* [= cool, brisk, of weather], *shelly (beans), (Irish) cobblers* [= white potatoes], *wardrobe* [= built in closet], *fishworm, hillside plow, baker* [= covered pot], *crawfish(y) land, whirligig* [= merry-go-round], *meal room* [= pantry], *hornyhead (fish),* and *johnny house* [= privy].

1F. Highlands and Piney Woods (American Midland, historic Pennsylvania, vocabulary): *serenade* [= wedding reception], *boogerman* [= devil], *rock fence, flitters* [= pancakes], *boil (coffee)* [= prepare coffee], *granny (woman)* [= midwife], *middling(s)* [= bacon side], *favors* [= resembles, of a child's appearance], *swingletree* [= singletree], *catawampus* [= cater-cornered], *antigodlin* [= cater-cornered], *dairy* [= cellar], *ridy-horse* [= seesaw], *widow woman,* and *mushmelon* [= muskmelon].

1G. Highlands/Piedmont: *press(ed) meat* [= headcheese], *souse meat* [= headcheese], *plum (peach)* [= cling (peach)], *rich (pine/splinters/wood)*

[= resinous kindling], *side meat* [= bacon], *salad/sallet* [= greens], *ground squirrel* [= chipmunk], *fatback* [= salt pork], *davenette* [= small sofa], and *fire-board* [= mantel].

2. Piedmont: *salad tomatoes* [= small tomatoes], *(quarter/fifteen) of* (the hour), *tumblesault* [= somersault], *tumbleset* [= somersault], *thunderwood* [= poisonous bush], *(Louisiana) pink (worm)*, *stump (whiskey)* [= moonshine], *streak of lean* [= salt pork], *liver hash, nut grass* [= field weed], and *come in* [= calve].

2A. Piedmont/Eastern Plains/Piney Woods: *harp* [= harmonica], *veranda* [= large porch], *spring onions* [= green onions], *crocus sack* [= gunnysack], *lightwood* [usually rhymes with *mitered* = resinous kindling], *Confederate War* [= Civil War], *bateau* [= rowboat], *collards, bream* [= sunfish], *ground peas* [= peanuts], *scooter plow, egg bread* [= cornbread with egg], *flambeau* [= make-shift lamp], *rank* [= rancid], and *hooting owl*.

2B. Piedmont/Eastern Plains: *bath cloth, sorghum syrup, lamp oil* [= kerosene], *stove room* [= kitchen], *poison ivory* [= poison ivy], *boiling meat* [= fat bacon], *countryman* [final syllable weak = rustic], *reared* [= brought up/raised], *battercakes* [= pancakes], *beau* [= boyfriend].

2C. Piedmont/Nashville Basin/Mississippi Plains: *snake doctor* [= dragon-fly], *sowbelly* [= salt pork], *clabber milk* [= curdled milk], *candlefly* [= moth], *coal scuttle*, and *come up* [= giddyup].

2D. Piedmont/Piney Woods: *firedogs* [= andirons], *breakfast bacon, crocus bag* [= gunnysack], *guano* sack [= gunnysack], *guinea wasp, waistcoat* [= vest], *nest onions* [= green onions], *white potatoes* [= Irish potatoes], and *liver pudding*.

3. Piney Woods: *pineywood(s) rooter* [= range hog], *splinters* [= resinous kindling], *smut* [soot], *shiner* [= minnow], *pinders* [= peanuts], *press (peach)* [= cling (peach)], *find a calf* [= calve], *horn owl, skeeter hawk* [= dragonfly], *cow pen, boar hog, (potato) bank, whicker* [= whinny], *sweep (plow), multiplying onions, mantel board* [= mantel], *croker sack* [= gunnysack], *fox squirrel, proud* [= glad], *fair off* [= clear up, of weather], *green frog* [= small frog], *kerosene oil*, and *haslet(s)*.

3A. Eastern Piney Woods: *fat lighterd* [= resinous kindling], *corn dodger* [cornmeal dumpling], *co-ench* [= come, wench, call to cow], *lye hominy, cane syrup, puny* [= sickly], *spider* [= frypan with legs], and *Joe (harrow)*.

3B. Western Piney Woods: *free jack* [= mulatto], *corn dodger* [= cornbread], *farm-t-market (road), chunk* [= throw], *(potato) house* [= potato cellar], *white perch, side harrow, stone fence, plum tomato* [= small tomato], *baker's bread*

[= white bread], *hog(s)head souse* [= headcheese], *gee-whiz (harrow)*, *squinch owl* [= screech owl], *mark* [= castrate], and *shinny* [= moonshine].

3C. Piney Woods/Coastal: *hog(s)headcheese, mosquito hawk* [= dragonfly], *mouth harp* [= harmonica], *soft-shell (turtle)*, *red bug* [= chigger], *live oak, blood pudding, cat squirrel* [= gray squirrel], *lowland(s), spicket* [= spigot], *hopper-grass* [= grasshopper], and *gopher* [= burrowing tortoise].

4. Atlantic/Gulf Coastal: *shell road, collard greens, (red) snapper, croaker (fish)* [= grunt], *mantelpiece, cherry tomato, throw up* [= vomit], *rainfrog* [= small frog], *pail*, and *store-bought bread* [= white bread].

4A. Atlantic Coastal: *(peach) stone, (peach) pit, whiting* [food fish], *scallions* [= green onions], *layer/laying hen, mouth organ* [= harmonica], *cracker* [= rustic], *sea turtle, white bacon* [fat bacon], *spring frog* [small frog].

4B. Florida/East Central Gulf Coast: *alligator turtle, grouper* [food fish], *piazza* [= large porch], *oil* [= kerosene], *rock road, croker bag* [= gunnysack], *fatwood* [= resinous kindling], *muck(y) land, cooter* [= turtle], *cooter* [= tortoise], *(corn) buck* [= moonshine/beer], *red-neck* [= rustic].

4C. Texas/West Central Gulf Coast: *pilón* [= something extra/lagniappe], *jabalina* [= wild hog], *(blue) norther* [= wind from the north], *arroyo* [= large gulch], *caliche (road)* [= dirt road], *gringo* [= white], *Anglo* [= white], *new potatoes, Johnson grass, mesquite, salt bacon* [= fat bacon], *chinaberry (tree)*, and *liverwurst*.

4D. West Central Gulf Coastal/Lower Delta: *gallery* [= large porch], and *cream cheese* [= cottage cheese], *armoire, snap beans* [= string beans], *pirogue* [= Cajun rowboat], *skiff* [= rowboat], *red(fish), mud dauber* [= mud wasp], *gunnysack*, and *blood sausage*.

5. Delta: *bayou* [= backwaters], *bayou* [= creek], *grass sack* [= gunnysack], *middlebuster* [= lister plow], *coal oil* [= kerosene], *salt meat* [= fat bacon], *stout* [= strong], *cush* [= cornmeal mush], *buffalo (fish), frogstool* [= toadstool], *hunkers* [= backs of thighs], *clear stone (peach), white perch, Catahoula (cur), coco (grass), loggerhead (turtle), gumbo* and *buckshot* [= mud].

5A. Lower Delta: *lagniappe, banquette* [= sidewalk], *orphan child, beignet* [= square doughnut], *boudin* [= spiced pork sausage with rice], *cush-cush* [= mush], *jump the broomstick* [= marry], *(gasper) goo/goo (fish), shallots, picket(s), guts* [= chitterlings], *scrape (cotton), pave road* [= paved road], and *gar(fish)*.

5B. Lower Mississippi Delta: *kyoodle* [= worthless dog], *sheepshead (fish), (potato) pump* [= potato cellar], *irons* [= andirons], *lord god* [= pileated woodpecker], *bootleg (whiskey)* [= moonshine], *locker* [= clothes closet], and *Cajun*.

5C. Atchafalaya Delta: *coulee, flood rain, pee/kee* [= calls to chickens], *cho/choo* [= calls to hogs], *croquinole* [= cracklings], *coonass* [= Cajun, pejorative/jocular], *blackjack (land), champignon* [= mushroom], *choupique* [= Atchafalaya mudfish], *sacalait* [= Atchafalaya crappie], *steps* [= small porch], and *charivari* [= shivaree].

5D. Lower Delta/Western Plains: *prairie, (corn) husks, bellow* [= moo, of a cow], *burlap sack, blackland (prairie/soil), lunch* [= snack], *cottonwood (tree), hackberry (tree), passed* [= died], and *mustard greens.*

LEE PEDERSON
Emory University

Craig M. Carver, *American Regional Dialects: A Word Geography* (1987); William A. Kretzschmar Jr. et al., *Handbook of the Linguistic Atlas of the Middle and South Atlantic States* (1993); Hans Kurath, *A Word Geography of the Eastern United States* (1939); Hans Kurath and Raven I. McDavid Jr., *The Pronunciation of English in the Atlantic States* (1961); Raven I. McDavid Jr., "Dialect Areas of the Atlantic Seaboard" (1985), Lee Pederson, "Piney Woods Southern" (1996), and Lee Pederson, "Dialects" (2001), all in *The Linguistic Atlas of the Gulf States*, ed. Lee Pederson et al., 7 vols. (1986–1992).

Log Housing

Until the arrival in the backcountry South of central Europeans after 1723, notched-log construction was not popular in the region. A few log houses may have survived from the Swedish settlement in the Delaware Valley, but the distinctive traits of that area did not become those of the southern log-building tradition. The log buildings of the South were of either British or central European plan and were executed with central European techniques.

Pioneer German and Scots-Irish settlers in the backcountry built houses much like those in the Old World. Even today, a few directly transplanted German log houses dot the Virginia Valley and the Piedmont (for example, at Winston-Salem). By the eve of the American Revolution, however, a small set of distinctively New World models had emerged. These forms became characteristic of the broad expanse of the South, spreading out to cover a million square miles between 1775 and 1835.

The forms that spread so suddenly and so extensively were six variant arrangements of a British pen, or bay, made using German methods. The basic unit was the single-pen house, an oblong, one-room house having its gables to the side, its doors on the eave front and rear, its chimney against the outside of one gable end, a wooden floor, and a foundation of piers. If built to stand alone, such a house would have measured from 16 by 20 feet to 20 by 26 feet.

Two versions of this basic pen spread, in succession, across the South. The earlier one, built of logs joined by half-dovetail notches, usually had a loft supported by joists that had been let through the front and rear walls by means of mortises. At the same tier or the next up, wall logs extended about 12 feet to the front and rear as cantilevers that supported the roof. The extension of the continuous-pitch roof permitted the plan to include a gallery in front and a room in back, both half the depth of the pen. The facade of the oldest of these had only a door, centered on the wall.

The second version, which followed the first by about a generation, had walls formed by V-notched logs. Its loft, if present, was supported by joists that had merely been sharpened and wedged between logs at the front and rear. Any porch or rear room added to the V-notched pen was usually a lean-to addition, rather than space lying under a cantilever-supported roof. The front facade commonly had a single door off center, plus one window between the door, and the end had the chimney.

In time these two forms blended, so that later, and especially more western, versions were likely to have traits of each. The half-dovetail forms of the northern South often lacked galleries, whereas those emanating from the back-country west of Charleston, the entry point of Caribbean immigrants, almost always had broad galleries.

To form larger houses, two pens were joined in one of three set ways. The most favored enlarged house, the dogtrot, was formed by setting two pens together along a common, central, open hallway. The other two plans involved separating the two pens either by a chimney (saddlebag) or a common wall (double pen). Any of these three types of houses may have had a gallery, loft, shed rooms, separate kitchen, dormers, or any of a host of architectural additions.

When the owner was more prosperous, these two-room plans may also have been built in two stories. Such houses, known academically as "I houses," may have had one or both stories built of logs. I houses existed both with and without open dogtrots, central halls, and central chimneys.

Log construction extended also to the outbuildings. Log barns were built of various arrangements of units, known in this case as "cribs." The single-crib barn was an ancient, central European form. Its gable roof extended out over the area in front, sheltering the step to the door. The single-crib barn usually held corn still on the cob; consequently, the structure was set upon piers made

Porch on dogtrot house, Hickory Flat, Miss., 1968 (William Ferris Collection, Southern Folklife Collection, Wilson Library, University of North Carolina at Chapel Hill)

of rocks or blocks of wood. The walls were formed of horizontal logs notched at their ends to join the tiers. Although all kinds of notches were used in barns, the saddle and V notches were the most common. Crib sizes differed widely, ranging from 8 by 10 feet to 20 by 30 feet, the length lying along the ridge.

The single-crib barn was put to many uses and served many functions. Many had dirt floors and shed-roofed areas on one or more sides. In some, a crib and a dirt-floored side room shared the same roof. Single-crib forms also served as smokehouses, well houses, and root houses. Single cribs were also combined to form larger structures. Two cribs set facing each other across a common drive-through space formed a double-crib barn. Four cribs under a common roof and sharing two crossing driveways formed a four-crib barn. Two sets of three facing a common driveway formed a transverse-crib barn. Some double-crib specimens had large, cantilever supported lofts.

The making of log walls required shaping the log, forming the notches, and finishing the walls. Traditionally, the logs were split to form one face, the other being hewed to a line with a broadax; otherwise, both faces would be shaped by the broadax or sawed into the shape required. During the heyday of the log house, notches were formed on logs that had been raised to the top of the finished part of the crib; axmen standing atop the walls cut the bottoms of

Saddlebag house, near Eatonton, Ga., 1986 (Richard Pillsbury, photographer)

notches as needed. Once notched, the logs were rocked into place and the tops of their notches were cut to receive the next logs. The most common notches for houses were half-dovetail and square (for one variety), V and saddle (for the other). Log walls were finished either by chinking between the logs with wood or stone chips and mud or mortar or by "sealing" the inside with sawn lumber. Cribs generally lacked any finish siding, the cracks aiding in the drying of the corn.

Notched-log construction is a technique, not a type or a style. Nearly any kind of building made of logs also appears in other material. Southern log work is Central European in origin; the buildings are mostly British New World in form. That American log construction is basically southern is seen in the near uniformity of frontier log buildings, their specific forms having developed in the backcountry between Lancaster and Augusta.

M. B. NEWTON JR.
Baton Rouge, Louisiana

Terry G. Jordan, *American Log Buildings: An Old World Heritage* (1985), *Texas Log Buildings: A Folk Architecture* (1978); Fred Kniffen, *Pioneer America* (no. 1, 1969); M. B. Newton Jr., *Geoscience and Man*, vol. 5 (1974); Eugene Murphy Wilson, "Folk Houses of Northern Alabama" (Ph.D. dissertation, Louisiana State University, 1935).

Migration, Black

To black southerners, migration has symbolized both the limitations and the opportunities of American life. As slaves, many suffered forced migration and the heartbreak of separation from family and community. As freed men and women they seized upon spatial mobility as one of the most meaningful manifestations of their newly won emancipation. Subsequently, black southerners sought to better their conditions by moving within the rural South, to southern cities, and finally to northern cities in a frustrating quest for equality and opportunity. Simultaneously, white southerners acted to restrict such movement, because, until the mechanization of cotton agriculture, black geographic mobility — like black social and economic mobility — threatened the racial assumptions and labor relations upon which the southern economy and society rested.

The first significant migration of black southerners followed the American Revolution and the subsequent opening of the trans-Appalachian West to settlement by slaveholders. The enormous expansion of cotton cultivation in the early 19th century, combined with the closing of the foreign slave trade (1808), soon transformed a forced migration dominated by planters carrying their own slaves westward to one increasingly characterized by the professional slave trader. Although the Chesapeake remained the major source for the interstate slave trade after 1830, North and South Carolina, Kentucky, Tennessee, Missouri, and eventually Georgia also became "exporters" of slaves. The plantations of Alabama, Mississippi, Louisiana, Florida, Arkansas, and Texas were worked largely by these early black "migrants" and their children. Although it is difficult to determine the volume of the domestic slave trade, one historian has recently estimated that over 1 million black southerners were forcibly relocated between 1790 and 1860.

The forced migrations of the antebellum South were complemented by barriers against voluntary movement. Although each year hundreds of slaves escaped, they represented but a fraction of the southern black population. Even free black southerners were hemmed in, and by the 1830s their movement across state lines was either restricted or prohibited.

During the Civil War, white fears and black hopes generated opposing migration streams. Many slave owners responded to the approach of Union troops by taking their slaves west, either to the western, upcountry areas of the eastern states, or from the Deep South to Texas and Arkansas. Thousands of slaves, on the other hand, fled toward the advancing army.

Ex-slaves continued to move away from plantations after the war ended. For many, like Ernest J. Gaines's fictional Miss Jane Pittman, the act of moving constituted a test of the meaning of emancipation. Others sought to reunite with family separated by antebellum forced migration. Much of the movement grew out of a search for favorable social, political, and economic conditions, especially the chance for "independence," which was closely associated with land-ownership. The flurry of migration generally involved short distances, often merely to the next plantation or a nearby town or city.

Southern cities offered ex-slaves the protection of the Freedmen's Bureau and the Union army, higher wages, black institutions, political activity, and freedmen's schools. But under pressure from whites—and often faced with the prospect of starvation—many of the thousands who moved to the cities soon returned to the plantations. Urban whites considered the black city dweller a threat to social order, and planters sought to stabilize and reassert dominance over their labor force. Vagrancy laws provided a temporary mechanism, and even after the legislative reforms during Reconstruction, the economic structure of the cities limited the urbanization of the black population. Few jobs outside the service sector were available to blacks, and black men especially found that survival was easier in the countryside. Black southerners continued to migrate to cities in modest numbers; by 1910 less than one-fourth lived in communities larger than 2,500. Some people moved back and forth, mainly between farm and small town, following seasonal labor patterns. This kind of mobility also characterized rural nonfarm labor and established what one historian has called a "migration dynamic," which later facilitated movement to northern cities.

Most black southerners who migrated longer distances in the 19th century headed for rural destinations, generally toward the south and west. During the 1870s and 1880s rumors and labor agents drew blacks living in the Carolinas and Georgia to the Mississippi Delta and other areas in the Gulf states with promises of higher wages and better living conditions. Usually, migrants found social and economic relations similar to what they had left behind. The search for "independence" continued, with black southerners trying Kansas in the 1870s and then Arkansas and Oklahoma between 1890 and 1910. Movement became as central to southern black life as it has been to the American experience in general. But because blacks for so long had been unable to move freely, it acquired a special mystique manifested as a major theme in black music and symbolized by the recurrent image of the railroad as a symbol of the freedom to move and start life anew. By the 1890s one black southerner in twelve would cross state lines during the decade in search of the still-unfulfilled promise of emancipation. Local moves remained even more frequent.

The direction and historical impact of black migration shifted dramatically during World War I. Northern industrialists, previously reluctant to hire blacks when they could draw upon the continuing influx of white immigrants, turned their attention southward as immigration ceased and production orders began pouring in. Some sent labor agents into the South, but news about opportunities and conditions in the North traveled more often via an emerging black communications network comprising letters from earlier migrants, northern newspapers (especially the *Chicago Defender*), and railroad workers. Observers and subsequent scholars offered various catalogs of "economic" and "social" factors that "pushed" migrants from the South and "pulled" them toward the North. Floods, boll weevil infestations, and credit contractions contributed to the urge to move to northern cities offering higher wages than those available to black southerners. Jim Crow, lynching, disfranchisement, and discrimination in the legal and educational systems contrasted with seemingly more equitable and flexible race relations in the North. Most migrants left because of a combination of motivations, which they often summarized as "bettering my condition." For the first time, however, thousands of black southerners looked to industrial work, rather than landownership, in their hope to enjoy the prerogatives of American citizenship.

Nearly a half million black southerners headed north between 1916 and 1920, setting off a long-term demographic shift, which would leave only 53 percent of black Americans in the South by 1970, compared with 89 percent in 1910. Nearly all of these migrants went to cities, first in the Northeast and Midwest, and later in the West. Most followed the longitudinal routes of the major railroads, although by World War II California was drawing thousands of migrants from Texas, Oklahoma, Arkansas, and Louisiana. At the same time, black southerners moved to southern cities, which by 1970 contained two-thirds of the region's black population. Even the massive urban unemployment of the Great Depression only moderately slowed the continuing flow northward, and movement accelerated to unprecedented levels during World War II and the following decades.

Many white southerners initially responded to this "Great Migration" by continuing the tradition of constructing barriers in the paths of black migrants. As always, landlords and employers feared the diminution of their labor supply, a threat that in the 19th century had stimulated the enactment of a corpus of legislation designed to limit labor mobility. As a social movement and a series of individual decisions, however, the Great Migration also constituted a direct — although unacknowledged — threat to the fiber of social and economic relations in the South. The system rested upon the assumption that blacks were by nature docile, dependent, and unambitious. The decision to migrate and the evolution of a "movement" suggested dissatisfaction, ambition, and aggressive action. As they had in the past, white southerners tended to blame the movement on "outside forces" (in this case, labor agents), and localities ineffectively sought to stem the tide by tightening "enticement" laws and forcibly preventing blacks from leaving.

The Great Migration transformed both American urban society and African American society, as migrants adapted to urban life while retaining much of their southern and rural culture. It was not unusual for southern communities to reconstitute themselves and their institutions in northern cities. Frequent visiting among relatives in the South and North has contributed to this interchange between regional cultures, and the South is still "down home" to some northern black urbanites.

The 1970s saw a return of blacks to the South, a reverse migration that escalated in the 1990s. According to the 2000 census figures, the non-Hispanic black population of the South grew in the 1990s by 3,575,211 people, more than in the Northeast, Midwest, and West combined. This number doubles the black population that the South attracted in the 1980s (1.7 million). Southern cities, especially Atlanta, attracted most African American migrants in the late 1990s, at the same time that such major urban areas as New York, Chicago, Los Angeles, and San Francisco experienced the largest out-migration of blacks. Demographers have attributed the dramatic reversal of the Great Migration north during the early 20th century to the South's economic development, its improved race relations, the growth of a black middle class in southern cities, and historic, cultural, and family ties to the South.

As a historical process, black migration within and from the South suggests some important continuities suffusing much of southern history: the coercive implications of white dependence on black labor, the refusal of blacks to accept their "place" as defined by whites, and the search for identity and opportunity articulated by black writer Richard Wright, whose personal migration experience began with the hope that "I might learn who I was, what I might be."

JAMES GROSSMAN
University of Chicago

William H. Frey, in *Immigration and Opportunity*, ed. Frank D. Bean and Stephanie Bell-Rose (1999), *Population Today* (May/June 2001); James R. Grossman, *Land of Hope: Chicago, Black Southerners, and the Black Migration* (1989); Florette Henri, *Black Migration: Movement North, 1900–1920* (1975); Allan Kulikoff, in *Slavery and Freedom in the Age of the American Revolution*, ed. Ira Berlin and Ronald Hoffman (1983); Nicholas Lemann, *The Promised Land: The Great Migration and How It Changed America* (1991); Larry Long, *Migration and Residential Mobility in the*

United States (1987); Nell Irvin Painter, *Exodusters: Black Migration to Kansas after Reconstruction* (1976); Arvarh Strickland, *Missouri Historical Review* (July 1975); Carter G. Woodson, *A Century of Negro Migration* (1918).

Migration Patterns

The historical and geographical dimensions of southern culture are partly the product of human migration. Migration streams have brought to the South a mix of peoples, spawning a unique cultural milieu. The variation of culture within the region is the product of an intricate pattern of migration streams within its boundaries. Migration has also brought many aspects of southern culture to other parts of the United States.

By 1700 the most populous of the European settlements along the Atlantic shore of North America were in the Chesapeake region. During the next century additional footholds gained prominence, especially Charleston, and the English and black-slave populations were supplemented by a variety of other ethnic enclaves. In the mid-18th century, 200,000 Germans and 250,000 Scots-Irish migrated to the colonies and spearheaded a movement from the Philadelphia area down the Great Valley of Virginia, then ultimately westward across the mountains. That new immigration wave, plus various changes in agricultural systems, eventually led to additional migration pathways, which carried persons of European origin westward within the South.

Migration forced upon a group or impelled by circumstances also played an important role in the South. After 1750, Cajuns began arriving in Louisiana as refugees from Acadia. Their imprint on the cultural landscape of Louisiana remains today. European settlements encroached on the American Indians, forcing them to relocate, and mass expulsion of Indians to the Indian Territory occurred between 1820 and 1840. At least 50,000 Cherokee, Chickasaw, Choctaw, Creek, and Seminole were driven from their home areas in several southern states. The mass exodus, with its resultant high mortality rate as the Indians journeyed from northern Georgia through Tennessee, western Kentucky, southern Illinois, and southern Missouri, became known as the Trail of Tears.

Numerically, the most significant forced migration affecting the South was one having worldwide impact—the importation of slaves from Africa and the West Indies. This resulted in what has been perhaps the most important juxtaposition within one location of large and nearly equal numbers of people of European and African descent anywhere in the world. By 1750 there were more than 200,000 slaves in the colonies, and from 1750 to 1800 as many as 1 million additional slaves were imported. Changes in agriculture on the Atlantic Coastal Plain led to a variety of internal slave trade routes that shifted the center of the black population from Virginia in the 18th century to northern Georgia in the 19th century.

During the 19th century a number of important new black migration streams developed: migration to the Liberian colony, which involved 15,000 émigrés; the underground railroad routes, which carried about 90,000 blacks into the North before the Civil War; a postwar movement of thousands to Kansas, resulting in a series of all-black towns in that state; and steady post–Civil War migration streams to northern cities.

The truly great mass exodus of blacks from the South, however, occurred in the World War I era. Both the "pushes" by agricultural labor surpluses and heightened social conflicts and the "pulls" of industrial jobs in northern and western cities are well documented. The net migration of blacks out of the South totaled about three million between 1910 and 1960.

A parallel movement of whites from the Upland South sent hundreds of thousands of people to northern cities, especially in the 1940s and 1950s. In both black and white movements the dependence upon friends and relatives as sources of information, advice, and comfort led to "channelized" streams of migration that connected migrants from the South with acquaintances in northern cities and even particular neighborhoods within those cities. These channelized flows initially followed rail lines and created regional connections, such as northern Louisiana to Los Angeles, Mississippi to Chicago, the Carolinas to New York City, eastern Kentucky to Hamilton, Ohio, and southern West Virginia to Cleveland. Today, the nonmetropolitan South can still be divided into a complex mosaic of small subregions that traditionally depended upon different cities in the North and West as migration destinations, such as St. Louis, Mo., Gary and Muncie, Ind., Youngstown, Ohio, and Wilmington, Del.

Two other major migration patterns of the post–World War II era had earlier roots. The first was the rapid population growth in southern regional centers such as Charlotte, Atlanta, Jackson, Memphis, and Houston. Each gradually exerted a powerful draw on surrounding nonmetropolitan populations. The second was the rapid growth of Florida, which continues unabated today. Florida attracted migrants via mechanisms such as land developments and promotion, and it rapidly became the most important destination for elderly interstate migrants in the United States. The elderly, plus significant numbers of other migrants, streamed from the Midwest to the Gulf shores of Florida and from the Northeast (New Yorkers who moved to Miami and Miami Beach) to the east coast of Florida.

Beginning in the late 1960s, two new major population redistribution patterns affected the nation as a whole but especially the South. First, the South became a part of a broad population growth area, the Sunbelt. Decentralization of employment from the traditional northeastern "core," plus the emergence of a great variety of new amenity growth regions, including the Arkansas Ozarks and extensive areas in the southern Appalachians, fueled the broad Sunbelt migration movement. The balance of migration toward the Sunbelt was significant, because for every migrant headed for the Snowbelt, two were moving to the Sunbelt. Also, many fewer persons moved from the rural South to cities outside of the region in the 1960s and 1970s, contributing to this migration pattern. Because for many years people in their 20s had moved out of the South and birthrates had fallen, there were simply fewer people in the group that tended to move away from the rural South by the 1960s. By 1970 the South was attracting overall net in-migration from the Midwest and Northeast but was still losing migrants to the West, a region that had a considerable pull on southern out-migrants in the 1940s, 1950s, and 1960s. By the end of the period 1975–80, the South had a net gain of 800,000 from the Northeast, 700,000 from the Midwest, and 160,000 from the West. Blacks, lagging behind the population as a whole in these migration trends, left the South for all regions through migration in 1965–70; yet by 1975–80 the South was gaining black migrants from each of the three other regions.

A second recent trend was more abrupt than the broadening of the Sunbelt migration. A nonmetropolitan population turnaround occurred, whereby for the first time in memory more people were moving away from metropolitan areas than toward them. This pattern has been seen both within the South and in the nation as a whole. However, compared to the North, a large number of metropolitan areas in the South are still growing rapidly, primarily because of the Sunbelt migration streams.

Migration made another contribution to southern culture in the 1970s. In the 19th and early 20th centuries the South was not a major destination for European or Asian immigrants (as were the West and the North), but in the 1970s such immigration became much more important to the region. Primary examples include an expansion of the traditional Mexican immigration into Texas, significant additional numbers of Cuban refugees settling in south Florida, large numbers of Haitians moving to Miami, and a pattern of settlement of Southeast Asian refugees in Houston and other cities, including some "remigration" from the Snowbelt. Partly as a result of these recent migration streams, the cultural mosaic of the South continues to change.

According to census data, between 1980 and 1984 the South's population grew by 7 percent, increasing from 74,139,633 in 1980 to an estimated 79,340,321 as of 1 July 1984 (these figures include the 13 states traditionally considered southern, plus Maryland and Oklahoma). Florida's population grew by 12.6 percent, the most marked growth in the region. Texas followed, with an increase of 12.4 percent in its population. The growing population and increasing cultural diversity will affect many elements of lifestyles in the South.

CURTIS C. ROSEMAN
University of Illinois

George A. Davis and O. Fred Donaldson, *Blacks in the United States: A Geographic Perspective* (1975); Martin Gilbert, *American History Atlas* (1968); Daniel M. Johnson and Rex R. Campbell, *Black Migration in America: A Social Demographic History* (1981); M. B. Newton Jr., *Geoscience and Man*, vol. 5 (1974).

Plantation Morphology

The southern plantation symbolizes large-scale agricultural operations and landscapes and contrasts with the smaller family farm in the South. Whether the site of sugarcane, cotton, rice, indigo, or tobacco production, the southern plantation has left its mark on the landscape.

For nearly two centuries the characteristics of traditional plantations included large, level fields extending over hundreds, even thousands, of acres. Plantations were located primarily in the flat terrain of the Atlantic and Gulf coasts and Mississippi floodplains or in the rolling fields in the Upland South. A web of ditches, canals, and field roads was etched into the landscape. Centrally located outbuilding complexes consisted of sugarhouses, cotton gins, rice mills, mule barns, tractor and implement sheds, storage tanks and sheds, blacksmith and mechanical repair shops, stores, and churches. Laborers' quarters formed characteristic patterns. And, at a distant site, set amid moss-draped oaks or in the shade of magnolias and pines, stood the plantation mansion—a symbol of power, opulence, and cultural achievement.

The architecture of plantation mansions reflects the ethnic traditions of their builders. Creole plantation mansions on sugar plantations in southern Louisiana show the taste of French Creole planters. Anglo plantation mansions are associated with Anglo-American planters who used architects from the Tidewater region of the Atlantic Coast, from Virginia to Georgia. Furthermore, Anglo plantation mansions with Upland traits largely reflect the tastes of Anglo-American planters from western Virginia, Kentucky, Tennessee, the Carolinas, Georgia, Alabama, Mississippi, and northern Louisiana.

Creole plantation mansions are characterized by (1) interior central chimneys at the center of the roof line (never exterior chimneys on the outside gabled ends of the house); (2) multiple front doors that allow all front rooms to open onto the gallery or front porch; (3) floor plans several rooms wide and one or two rooms deep, without a central hall; (4) all stairs on the exterior; (5) hip roofs; (6) galleries, a wide front porch, and often wide porches on all sides of the house; (7) one-and-a-half- to two-story heights; and (8) half-timbered walls or all wood construction.

The traits of Anglo-American plantation mansions include (1) exterior chimneys; (2) a single front door; (3) floor plans usually one to two rooms deep and no more than two rooms wide; (4) inside stairs; (5) a central hall or passage extending from front door to back; and (6) construction materials of all wood, brick, and plaster but never half-timbered construction.

Anglo houses of Tidewater origin further display a front-facing gable, two full stories, pediments, porticos, large white pillars, end chimneys (outside end or inside end), a single front door and hallway, and, in some cases, side pavilions or wings, common to the Georgian style. Other modest Anglo plantation structures of the Upland South have traits of the southern pen tradition — one to two rooms wide, deep, and tall; single front door; central hall; and exterior brick chimneys.

Settlement patterns based on the arrangement of quarter houses within the plantation complex also have distinctive traits. On modern sugar plantations in Louisiana, the quarters — a villagelike settlement that once housed slaves — contain the dwellings of field laborers, tractor operators, sugar mill workers, field overseers, and mill foremen. The arrangement of dwellings follows traditional 18th- and 19th-century linear settlement patterns marked by parallel rows of quarter houses divided by a road that bisects the long axis of the plantation landholding. Traditional land surveys from the French long lot system created long narrow landholdings, which dictated the arrangement of structures into a linear settlement pattern that is characteristic of early French plantations.

On other present-day Louisiana sugar plantations, on early cotton, rice, indigo, and tobacco plantations of the Tidewater, and on cotton plantations of the Upland South, distinctive block-shaped or gridded quarters are associated with Anglo-American plantation origins.

Elsewhere on southern cotton plantations, the antebellum quarters disappeared in the post–Civil War era, to be replaced later by individual sharecropper and tenant houses widely scattered among cotton fields. Blacks often insisted that quarter houses near the plantation mansion be relocated as a symbol of their new status. Such a dispersed pattern remained until the 1940s, when agglomerated plantation settlements reappeared on cotton enterprises in the lower Mississippi Valley and other parts of the South.

JOHN B. REHDER
University of Tennessee

Lewis C. Gray, *History of Agriculture in the Southern United States to 1860*, 2 vols. (1933); Merle C. Prunty, *Geographical Review* (no. 45, 1955); Robert L. Ransom and E. Richard Sutch, *One Kind of Freedom: The Economic Consequences of Emancipation* (1978); John B. Rehder, *Delta Sugar: Louisiana's Vanishing Plantation Landscape* (1999), *Geoscience and Man*, vol. 19 (1978); Edgar T. Thompson, *Plantation: A Bibliography* (1957).

Population

In 2000, 84,283,000 persons lived in the 11 former states of the Confederacy, as shown in Table 4. This number is a 19.1 percent gain since 1990, when 70,774,000 lived in the region, and a 94.0 percent gain since 1960, when the population was 43,436,000. At the time of the first census in 1790, the South's population of 1,454,000 was 37.0 percent of the national total. That share declined steadily until reaching a low of 23.4 percent in 1930. It has since rebounded, rising to 27.1 percent in 1980 and 30.0 percent in 2000.

For more than a century after initial settlement, the South was less a destination than a point of origin for migrants. Alabama, Arkansas, Georgia, Mississippi, and Tennessee each recorded over a million more out-migrants than in-migrants from 1870 to 1960. Only Florida (2.8 million) and Texas (1.3 million) consistently gained population from migration over this period. By the late 1960s the general pattern of net out-migration had begun to reverse. For the period from 1995 to 2000, all southern states except Louisiana had net gains from domestic migration, and the region as a whole recorded a net population gain of 1,807,000 as a result. Over the same five-year period, 926,000 international immigrants settled in the South, primarily in Florida (378,000) and Texas (299,000).

The 19.1 percent growth rate between 1990 and 2000 is higher than the nation's growth rate of 13.1 percent. Increased migration to the South is primarily responsible for the region's dramatic growth in recent decades, although a higher birthrate also has contributed. The South has long had a birthrate above the national rate; even when out-migration was high in the 1940s and 1950s, large numbers of births enabled the South to grow. Rates have declined since 1960, when the South recorded 25.0 births per 1,000 population and the na-

TABLE 4. *Population of the South, by State, 1790–2000 (in thousands)*

State	1790	1860	1900	1940	1980	2000
Alabama	—	964	1,829	2,833	3,894	4,447
Arkansas	—	435	1,312	1,949	2,286	2,673
Florida	—	140	529	1,897	9,746	15,982
Georgia	83	1,057	2,216	3,124	5,463	8,186
Louisiana	—	708	1,382	2,364	4,206	4,469
Mississippi	—	791	1,551	2,184	2,521	2,845
North Carolina	394	993	1,894	3,572	5,882	8,049
South Carolina	249	704	1,340	1,900	3,122	4,012
Tennessee	36	1,110	2,021	2,916	4,591	5,689
Texas	—	604	3,049	6,415	14,229	20,852
Virginia	692	1,220	1,854	2,678	5,347	7,079
Total	1,454	8,726	18,997	31,832	61,287	84,283

Source: U.S. Census.

tion recorded 23.7 births per 1,000 population. In 2000, the South recorded 15.0 births per 1,000 population, and the nation's rate was 14.7. Of the ten states with the highest birthrates, three are in the South: Texas (second nationally with 17.8 births per 1,000 population); Georgia (fourth, 16.7); and Mississippi (tied for eighth, 15.8). Utah led all states with 21.9.

The South is slightly younger than the nation as a whole. The median age is 35.1 years, almost identical to the country's 35.3 years. This gap would have been even greater were it not for Florida; deleting that state with its median age of 38.7 years results in a median age for the remaining ten states of 34.2 years. The proportion of southerners who are aged 65 and over, 12.4 percent, is almost exactly the same as for the entire country, 12.6 percent. In Florida, more than one in six residents is at least 65 years old, the highest proportion in the country. Excluding Florida, the remaining ten southern states have a combined population 65 and over of 11.2 percent. More women live in the South (31.5 million) than men (29.7 million), resulting in a sex ratio of 96.1 men per 100 women. This ratio is almost identical to that for the entire country, 96.3.

In 2000 the South's death rate was 8.8 deaths per 1,000 population, about the same as the 8.7 recorded for the entire nation. This similarity of the two rates is misleading, however; because the South has a younger population than the nation as a whole, it has relatively more of its population at those ages where the fewest deaths occur. When rates are adjusted for age, mortality in all southern states except Florida is higher than the national rate of 876.68 deaths per 100,000 population (based on 1998–2000 annual averages). Higher age-adjusted mortality in the South is a pattern that has held since adequate death statistics became available in the 1930s. The most recent life expectancy figures, for the 1989–91 period, confirm this higher mortality. Nationally, babies born in that period could expect to live 75.4 years on average, but this figure was surpassed in only one southern state, Florida, at 75.8 years. The four states with the lowest life expectancies were all in the South: Georgia (73.6 years), Louisiana (73.0), Mississippi (73.0), and South Carolina (73.5). (The District of Columbia had the nation's lowest life expectancy—68.0 years.) Infant mortality has been relatively high in the South as well; in 2000 there were 7.5 deaths in the first year of life per 1,000 births, compared to the national rate of 6.9 such deaths per 1,000 births. Among individual states, three of the five with the highest rates were in the South: Alabama (9.4 infant deaths per 1,000 births), Mississippi (9.6), and Tennessee (10.3).

The South has a larger proportion of its population in rural areas (26.6 percent) than the country as a whole (21.0 percent). One state, Mississippi, remains predominantly rural (51.2 percent), and only two states — Florida (10.7 percent) and Texas (17.5 percent) — have proportionately fewer residents in rural areas than the nation as a whole. This relatively low rate of rural residence is a new phenomenon in the South: as recently as 1950, over half of all southerners lived in rural areas.

The South also has proportionately fewer metropolitan residents (76.7 percent) than the United States as a whole (79.8 percent). Arkansas (49.4 percent) and Mississippi (36.0 percent) have fewer than half of their residents living in metropolitan areas; only Texas (84.8 percent) and Florida (92.8 percent) exceed the national rate. A total of 18 of the 50 largest metropolitan areas in the country are in the South: Atlanta; Austin–San Marcos; Charlotte-Gastonia–Rock Hill; Dallas–Fort Worth; Greensboro–Winston-Salem–High Point; Houston-Galveston-Brazoria; Jacksonville; Memphis; Miami–Fort Lauderdale; Nashville; New Orleans; Norfolk–Virginia Beach–Newport News; Orlando; Raleigh–Durham–Chapel Hill; Richmond-Petersburg; San Antonio; Tampa–Saint Petersburg-Clearwater; and West Palm Beach–Boca Raton. Dallas–Fort Worth (5,222,000, ninth largest nationally), Houston (4,670,000, tenth nationally), Atlanta (4,112,000, eleventh nationally), and Miami–Fort Lauderdale (3,876,000, twelfth nationally) are the region's largest metropolitan areas. Also, part of Washington, D.C.–Baltimore, the nation's fourth largest (7,608,000), is located in northern Virginia.

The South's population is concentrated in two states, Texas (20,852,000 inhabitants in 2000) and Florida (15,982,000 in 2000). Combined, they contain almost 44 percent of the region's population. Next largest, according to the 2000 census, are Georgia (8,186,000), North Carolina (8,049,000), and Virginia (7,079,000). Arkansas (2,673,000) and Mississippi (2,845,000) have the fewest residents.

The population of the South is largely of African and European stock. In 2000 one in five southerners was black (20.0 percent). These 16,836,000 persons made up almost half (46.2 percent) of the total African American population in the United States. Mississippi (36.6 percent), Louisiana (32.9 percent), and South Carolina (29.9 percent) have the largest relative black populations, although in absolute numbers, Texas (2,493,000), Florida (2,472,000), and Georgia (2,393,000) have the largest black populations. All 11 southern states have a higher African American proportion than the nation's 12.9 percent, except for Texas (12.0 percent). Hispanics make up the next-largest racial ethnic group, with 11,025,000 persons (13.1 percent). Hispanics are concentrated in Texas (6,670,000, or 32.0 percent of the state's population) and Florida (2,683,000, 16.8 percent). Asians (2.2 percent), American Indians and Native Alaskans (0.9 percent), and Hawaiians and Pacific Islanders (0.1 percent) compose much smaller shares of the South's population.

Many southerners trace their ancestry to northern and western Europe. German ancestry is reported by 9.3 percent, Irish by 8.4 percent, and English by 8.2 percent. (Some persons claimed more than one ancestry group.) Southern and Eastern European immigrant groups are underrepresented in the South; only 2.9 percent of southerners indicate any Italian ancestry, and only 1.3 percent have Polish ancestry. Other ethnic groups, uncommon in much of the South, are locally concentrated. Over 12 percent of all Louisianans claim French ancestry, for example, and 24.3 percent of Texans are of Mexican descent. Also, 67.1 percent of all U.S. residents who claim Cuban ancestry live in Florida.

The South's population has the lowest educational attainment of any region in the country. In 2000, 77.4 percent of southerners aged 25 and over had received a high school diploma or equivalency; the national proportion is 80.4 percent. Only one southern state, Virginia, with 81.5 percent, exceeds the national share. Similarly, the proportion of southerners with at least a bachelor's degree, 22.4 percent, is lower than the national figure of 24.4 percent, and Virginia (29.5 percent) is the only southern state that exceeds the national figure. Of the ten states with the lowest percentage of the population aged 25 years or older with a high school diploma, eight are in the South (percentages are in parentheses): Alabama (75.3), Arkansas (75.3), Louisiana (74.8), Mississippi (72.9), South Carolina (76.3), Tennessee (75.9), and Texas (75.7).

Per capita income in the South in 2000 was $26,773, considerably lower than the $29,469 for the nation as a whole, but a gain of more than 50 percent from the $17,575 recorded in 1990. Four of the ten poorest states in the nation are in the South—Alabama ($23,521), Arkansas ($21,995), Louisiana ($23,090), and Mississippi ($20,900). Only Virginia ($31,120) exceeds the national per capita figure. The South had the same share of its population living in poverty in 2000 as the nation, 12.4 percent. Southern states with the highest poverty rates in 2000 were Arkansas (22.1 percent), Louisiana (16.3 percent), South Carolina (14.4 percent), and Tennessee (14.5 percent). The lowest poverty rates in the South were in Florida (10.0 percent), North Carolina (10.0 percent), and Virginia (7.5 percent). A total of four of the ten poorest counties in the nation are in the South: East Carroll Parish, Louisiana (40.5 percent of the population living in poverty); Holmes County, Mississippi (41.1 percent in poverty); Starr County, Texas (50.9 percent); and Zavala County, Texas (41.8 percent).

The rapid growth in the South since the late 1960s is likely to continue in the near future, particularly in Florida and Texas. From 2000 to 2002, Census Bureau estimates indicate that Texas grew by 928,000 inhabitants (4.5 percent), and Florida grew by over 731,000 (4.6 percent). Other southern states that grew faster than the national average of 2.5 percent from 2000–2002 were Georgia (4.6 percent), North Carolina (3.4 percent), and Virginia (3.0 percent). All southern states grew over the two-year period. Arkansas (1.3 percent), Mississippi (1.0 percent), and Tennessee (1.9 percent) grew the slowest. Taken together, southern states grew by 2,839,000 (3.4 percent) from 2000 to 2002.

JOHN P. MARCUM JR.
Presbyterian Church (U.S.A.)

Historical Statistics of the United States, Colonial Times to 1970, Bicentennial Edition (1975); National Center for Health Statistics, Fastats A to Z <http://www.cdc.gov/nchs/fastats/Default.htm>; National Center for Health Statistics, *U.S. Decennial Life Tables for 1981–89*, vol. 2, State Life Tables (1988) <http://www.cdc.gov/nchs/data/lifetables/life89al.pdf>; *Statistical Abstract of the United States: 2002* (2003); 2000 United States Census of Population and Housing <http://www.census.gov/main/6 www/cen2000.html>.

Religious Regions

Viewed from a national perspective, the South is remarkably homogeneous in its religion. Protestantism predominates, and, in the majority of counties, Baptists and Methodists together account for nearly all the church affiliation. This is true for black and white southerners alike. The region is further distinguished by having high rates of church membership in comparison with other sections of the country. Within the general uniformity of southern religion, however, a degree of diversity exists that is worthy of attention.

The dominance of Baptist groups is perhaps the most striking feature of southern religion. They predominate in most counties, reaching maximum strength along a corridor extending from southern Appalachia through Georgia, Alabama, and Mississippi and into northern Louisiana and Texas and southern Arkansas and Oklahoma. Baptists came to the South during the Great Awakening in the mid-18th century. They were extremely successful evangelists, in part because of a reliance on farmer-preachers who settled among the people they served.

Methodists were the chief rivals of Baptists within the southern missionary field. The two groups grew at similar rates throughout the 19th century, but they employed differing strategies. Methodist expansion emphasized a well-organized system of circuit riders and regular camp meetings. Over the last 60 years the growth of Methodists has lagged behind that of Baptists, possibly because of the latter's strong regional ties through the Southern Baptist Convention. Methodism remains tremendously important, however. Large Methodist minorities exist in most counties, and majorities are found frequently in Kentucky, Maryland, North Carolina, and the Virginias.

Baptists and Methodists together constitute the core of southern conservative Protestantism. Other groups of similar orientation include Disciples of Christ, Presbyterians, and the larger Pentecostal and Holiness denominations. These denominations are widespread throughout the region but have special concentration in the Upper South (where several of them originated) and in the Carolinas.

Concentrations of Catholics form the most significant exceptions to the Baptist-Methodist domination of the South. Some Catholic groups existed in the region before the growth of evangelical Protestantism; others are relatively recent immigrants. Catholics frequently represent not only religious diversity in the South but ethnic diversity as well, and locations where they are concentrated are major cultural "islands" in the region.

Catholicism in the South is most firmly established in southern Louisiana and southern Texas. The Catholic presence in Louisiana dates from the early 18th century, and it became firmly established in the middle of that century when French-speaking Catholics deported from Nova Scotia arrived in large numbers. Catholicism in Texas is even older, beginning with Spanish missions in the late 17th century. Catholics now constitute nearly half of the total church membership in Louisiana and nearly one-third in Texas. The cultural identities of both Cajuns and Mexican Americans are strongly intertwined with their faiths.

Smaller regions of Catholic influence occur along the northern border of the South. The oldest of these has its core in Maryland, a colonial center of Catholicism and of general religious tolerance under Lord Baltimore. Immigration of Marylanders to north-central Kentucky created another Catholic concentration. Farther west, along the Ohio River in Illinois and Indiana and along the Missouri and Mississippi rivers in east-central Missouri, Catholic clusters occurred through the migration of German and Swiss settlers. Relatively recent migration is responsible for Catholicism in southern Florida. First came a general flow of retirees and other northerners in the middle decades of the 20th century. Cubans, Haitians, and other emigrants from the Caribbean region constitute the latest component of Florida Catholicism.

Subtle variations within Protestantism provide a second departure from the norm of southern religious geography. Areas best described as pluralistic, places where Baptist and Methodist strength is somewhat diluted (although rarely replaced), have a cultural or historical background different from the mainstream and are among the most religiously diverse places in the South.

Peninsular Florida and the suburban areas of Atlanta and Washington, D.C., became major areas of pluralism during the 20th century. The amenities of booming economies and the Sunbelt attracted Protestants of various persuasions, Jews, and Catholics alike. Episcopalians, Lutherans, the Reformed churches, and the United Church of Christ, as well as Disciples and Presbyterians, are all found in greater proportion here than throughout most of the region.

Another distinctively pluralistic religious subregion is the Carolina Piedmont, where Friends, Lutherans, Moravians, Presbyterians, and the United Church of Christ are all well represented. North Carolina's lack of restrictions on nonconformists attracted these groups to the area as early as the late 17th century, but the major immigration came during the 18th century. A scarcity of available good land in Pennsylvania prompted many people of varied religious backgrounds to migrate southeastward along the Appalachian front into the Carolinas. The Christian Church, now part of the United Church of Christ, was founded in North Carolina and Virginia.

German, Scandinavian, and Eastern European immigration to the hill country of central Texas during the mid-19th century created a distinctive religious and ethnic complex. Lutherans remain the most numerous group there, but

Northern Transition Zone

N.C.
Anomaly

Southern Domain

South
Louisiana

South
Florida

South
Texas

N.C. Anomaly: Historic Zone of Mixed Denominations
Northern Transition Zone: Predominately Methodist
Southern Domain: Predominately Baptist
South Florida: Predominately Catholic and
　Other "Nonsouthern" Denominations
South Louisiana: Predominately Catholic
South Texas: Predominately Catholic

MAP 10. *Southern Religious Adherence, 1990 (Source: E. Gaustad, Philip Barlow, and R. Dishno, New Historical Atlas of Religion in America, 2001)*

Evangelical and Reformed adherents (now part of the United Church of Christ), Moravians, and Catholics are also important components of the hill country complex.

Appalachia should also be considered as a religious subregion within the South. Its distinctiveness derives not from immigration but from the local emergence of numerous strongly fundamentalist denominations, mainly Pentecostal or Holiness in belief but sectarian in orientation. Religion here reflects the individualism, traditionalism, and localism of Appalachian society generally. In many ways this religion is a relic of the emotional, evangelical faith that characterized the interior South during the 19th-century frontier period.

A final zone of religious diversity lies along the northern border of the South, an area where northern and southern denominations intermix. Catholic concentrations here have already been noted, but one also finds Lutherans, Episcopalians, United Church of Christ congregations, Presbyterians, and other Protestant groups in occasional concentrations.

JAMES R. SHORTRIDGE
University of Kansas

ROGER W. STUMP
State University of New York at Albany

Sydney E. Ahlstrom, *A Religious History of the American People* (1972); Martin B. Brady, Norman M. Green Jr., Dale E. Jones, Mac Lynn, and Lou McNeil, *Churches and Church Membership in the United States, 1990* (1992); Edwin S. Gaustad and Philip L. Barlow, *The New Historical Atlas of Religion in America* (2000); Charles Heatwole, *Southeastern Geographer* (May 1986); Samuel S. Hill, ed., *Encyclopedia of Religion in the South* (1984); Terry G. Jordan, in *Ethnicity on the Great Plains*, ed. Frederick C. Luebke (1980); O. Kendell White Jr. and Daryl White, eds., *Religion in the Contemporary South: Diversity, Community, and Identity* (1995); Peter W. Williams, *America's Religions: Traditions and Cultures* (1990).

Retirement Regions

There were 35 million persons over 65 in the United States in 2001, and it is estimated that there will be about 70 million by 2010. Most of these will remain in their communities. Increasing numbers will not. The impact of those who choose to relocate after retirement has been significant upon the areas where they have tended to concentrate, both in the South and elsewhere. The affluent have long relocated to more salubrious climes after retirement, but the practice has rapidly expanded to all but the least economically well-off since the end of World War II. Whether it is a move back "home" to where the retiree grew up, to a favored vacation area, or just to an area of "better" climate, larger and larger numbers of families with their loosened ties to community and increased financial resources have made this practice not only a dream but a reality.

Families began leaving the farms for city jobs in large numbers soon after the turn of the 20th century, but the combination of increasing farm costs associated with mechanization and specialization, the industrial boom, and the worldliness brought on by World War II turned this flow into a flood. The nationalization of the economic system brought increased mobility — managers were shipped to new locations every few years, and, with the restructuring of the nation's industrial geography, even hourly workers no longer routinely retired at the work location where they had started. Increasingly the middle years

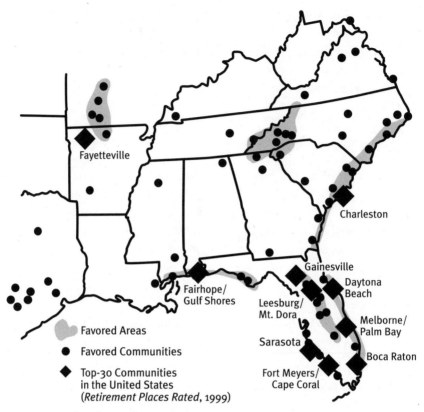

Favored Areas

● Favored Communities

◆ Top-30 Communities
in the United States
(*Retirement Places Rated*, 1999)

Fayetteville

Charleston

Gainesville

Fairhope/
Gulf Shores

Leesburg/
Mt. Dora

Daytona
Beach

Melborne/
Palm Bay

Sarasota

Boca Raton

Fort Meyers/
Cape Coral

MAP 11. *Favored Southern Retirement Areas*

of family raising took place far from traditional family and community for an ever-larger group of Americans. It was thus a logical step for people to look even further afield for their final golden years, preferably in a location that the equally scattered children would wish to visit.

The decision process of the "last" move is complex, and in fact for large numbers the last move becomes several moves as they search for that perfect place that does not exist. Many, especially from the South, dreamed for decades of moving back to their birth communities once they were released from the northern assembly lines. Others believed peace would be found at the golf course, beach, mountain, lake, coastal spot, or in a university community. Still others relive the dream of restoring a historic house in a small community. The South abounds with all of these options. Taken as a whole, these individual decisions have created a number of retirement regions where large numbers of incomers have congregated in search of their desired amenities. Florida is clearly the largest center of in-migration, with distinct colonies developing in several areas of the east and west coasts, as well as in several zones stretching south-ward from Gainesville toward Lake Okeechobee.

The sea islands of Georgia and the Carolinas are almost as well known and have been growing in recent years, and the Mississippi and Alabama Gulf Coasts are now also emerging as important destinations. Inland, the Smokies, espe-cially Cashiers to Asheville, N.C., have been long known as a retirement des-tination, but developers have expanded the target area in all directions with vacation/retirement communities such as Big Canoe in northern Georgia. Lake of the Ozarks, Branson, and other Ozark/Ouachita upland locations are less known nationally but are the destinations of choice for thousands of midwest-erners. Smaller areas, such as Pinehurst, N.C., and the horse country stretching north from Charlottesville, Va., also are notable on any list of retirement des-tinations.

The impact of large numbers of retirees on any area is huge, both economi-cally and culturally. The most obvious, in the eyes of the traditional residents, are rising real estate values, taxes, and the general cost of living. Most retirees are more affluent than those who have lived in their target destination areas for generations, even if the retirees are returning "home." They also have higher expectations of services, see the value of real estate from the perspective of an outsider, and expect more sophisticated goods in the stores, especially in gro-cery stores. Even more far reaching are their other expectations. They bring more aggressive attitudes about "saving" what is there as they acculturate to the region, whether it be the environment or the culture. With time on their hands, outside experience, and an appreciation and sense of the fragility of tra-ditional life, many choose to work to save the place from itself, as they might phrase it. Environmental projects are the most obvious beneficiaries of this out-siders' view, but they also become interested in improving the arts, libraries, and schools and in saving traditional crafts and ways of life through festivals and exhibits. They may not be willing to actually eat chitlins or grits, but they see a festival celebrating these foods as a part of saving traditional life.

Their retail demands bring new national retailers into their larger centers. Not only do pizza, tacos, and salad bars appear where they have never existed before, but bagels, hummus, and sushi make an appearance as well. These changes take place partially because of the overall nationalization of the cul-ture, but the presence of a resident market demand makes the transition more rapid and easier in the areas of highest densities of retirees. The typical fried fish, fries, and coleslaw, which dominated menus in coastal areas, for example, has been rapidly broadened to include grilled fish and exotic vegetables, to say nothing of "Early Bird" specials at restaurants of all kinds. The amount of fat-

Folly Beach, S.C., 2004
(Sandra Weinwurm, photographer)

back in greens and peas has declined, at least in restaurants that cater to the incomers. An inexorable shift in virtually everything has taken place in the process of saving it exactly "as it always was" for posterity.

The visual landscape too is a focus, with not only restoration of traditional housing for newcomers' own enjoyment, but with restoration of public, historic, and other structures as well. It is now estimated that in Charleston, S.C., for example, "nonnatives" own more than half of the great mansions in the South of Broad district. The sounds of restoration hammers and saws seemingly never cease as the average house sale price in this district has climbed above seven figures.

Traditionally, the diffusion of cultural change, in this instance the replacement of classic regional ways of life with national preferences, begins in the largest cities, centers of connectivity with the outside, and passes from there downward through the urban hierarchy. This process is certainly taking place in the South, as Atlanta, Charlotte, and elsewhere increasingly appear to be little different from similar cities elsewhere in the nation. The region's inordinate supply of amenity-laden nonurban areas attractive to retirees, however, has meant that that some semirural areas are increasingly becoming important centers of nationalization as well. Ocala, Hilton Head, Myrtle Beach, and similar places today often are as replete with national traits as regional ones. The impact, however, has tended to take on a different shape as the incomers in these areas typically are more amenable to retaining at least the vestiges of a regional past, if not the realities. In essence, the traditional culture remains more vibrant and more visible under the steady hand of the incomers in these places, but it has been forever changed as it is tuned to this new group of consumers. As one observer described these communities, "They are more like they used to be than they used to be."

RICHARD PILLSBURY
Folly Beach, South Carolina

David Savageau, *Retirement Places Rated*, 5th ed. (1999).

Rice Plantations

Early English settlement of colonies along the southeastern coastline of North America centered on the search for the commodity that could generate the greatest profit. The identification of that crop initiated a period of rapid population and economic expansion and did much to establish the enduring social character of the area. For the Chesapeake Bay that commodity was tobacco. For the lowlands between the Cape Fear River in North Carolina and the Altamaha and Satilla rivers in Georgia, and especially along the South Carolina coast between Georgetown and Charleston, those core products were indigo and, most importantly, rice. Opinions differ about when rice was introduced to the Carolina Lowcountry, but the crop became a permanent part of the coast's economy in the mid-1690s, when Landgrave Smith successfully cultivated Madagascar rice. The crop was an immediate success. In 1700 the governor of South Carolina wrote to the Lords Proprietors with the lament that the colony's output had outstripped the availability of ships for transportation.

The series of circumstances that enabled the transfer of a rice economy to the Lowcountry is intricate. Carolina's contacts with the plantation system of Barbados were substantial. By 1664 Carolina encouraged migration from that intensely used and densely crowded sugar island with the promise of grants of land for every slave brought to the mainland. The ancestors of most of these slaves were from the Upper Guinea coast extending from present-day Senegal southwestward to Liberia, an area where rice had been a dietary stable for several thousand years. There is evidence that Lowcountry slave owners became willing to pay a higher price for captives from Senegambia because of their knowledge of rice culture. Recent scholarship increasingly verifies that these African migrants carried with them knowledge of rice cultivation, milling, and consumption. They shared this knowledge with the planter class. It has been suggested, although not proven, that they used this knowledge as a "bargaining chip" in the establishment of the task system (which granted slaves more free-dom than the more common gang system) that dominated the Carolina rice economy. Evidence suggests a vigorous, extensive informal economy among at least some rice plantation slaves. The plantation system of the Lowcountry, then, was a blend of the harsh and profoundly hierarchically structured plan-tation society introduced from Barbados and an understanding of rice culture brought by slaves from the West African littoral.

Labor demands in the creation of Lowcountry rice fields were extremely harsh. Writing in 1735, a Charlestonian argued that "I am positive that the Com-modity can't be produced by white people. Because the work is too laborious, the heat very intent, and the whites can't work in the wett [sic] at that sea-son as the Negroes do weed rice." In short, though the task seemed impos-sibly difficult, planters saw no problem in demanding that Africans perform the work. By 1750 nearly all rice was grown in drained swamps through a sys-tem of tidal flooding. Most rice plantations were some miles from the coast, along that margin where freshwater stream flow interacted with tidal fluctua-tions. Tidal movement was used to help capture stream flow, and water from the stream was diverted onto the rice fields. Creating these periodically flooded fields was laborious. Heavy, moist swamplands had to be cleared, if necessary leveled, ditched, and enclosed with dikes made from the ditched mud. Trunk locks, or floodgates, were built to control the flow of water onto the fields, and smaller drains were built to enable the water to run off. Once the field and irri-gation system was in place, production could start, though it would demand heavy labor inputs for maintenance as long as production continued.

The rise and fall of the tide was used to irrigate the fields several times during the growing season. Periodic flooding held down weeds, but fields were never-theless hoed each time they were drained. Finally the crop had to be harvested, processed, prepared for market, and transported. Prior to the introduction of the first water-powered rice mill in 1787, slaves milled the rice by hand with a mortar and pestle and winnowed with baskets commonly made of woven grass. Again, the entire system demanded a tremendous outlay of labor and energy.

A distinctive and profitable plantation system developed on the backs of this African labor. Production boomed. During the colonial period most rice was exported to mainland northern Europe, where it was used by both humans and animals. Less than 20 percent was sent to the West Indies. Although the core of production always remained along the mid-coast of South Carolina, mar-ket demands and the high profit potential of the crop pushed production into the lower Cape Fear River Valley in North Carolina and along several Georgia coastal streams after the middle of the 18th century. Plantation ownership be-

Trunk gate in rice field, ACE *Basin, S.C., 2004 (Richard Pillsbury, photographer)*

came increasingly concentrated as production grew, and most major plantation owners eventually controlled a number of units. The 1850s was likely the most prosperous period for Carolina rice. In 1860 there were probably fewer than 200 rice plantations in the Lowcountry. Yet, 29 of the 80 U.S. plantations with more than 300 slaves, and 9 of the 14 with over 500, were concentrated along the rice coast. Joshua Ward of Waccamaw used the labor of 1,092 slaves (one of the few American plantations with over 1,000 slaves) to produce almost four million pounds of rice in his best years. The labor demands of rice production, and the scale of operation, meant that slaves accounted for an increasing share of the region's population. In 1700 there was a rough regional balance between slaves and freemen. By 1860 nearly 90 percent of the population in the most productive areas was slave. The common use of slave overseers meant that many African slaves on the larger plantations rarely laid eyes on Euro-Americans.

The elite of the rice economy lived in a style that recalled Barbados in its heyday much more than the rest of the Southeast. They were wealthy. Most had summer homes in locations separated from the fearsome malaria of the rice lands in nearby places like Charleston or Pawleys Island on the coast, inland on the drier Piedmont, and even at more distant ones like Newport, R.I. The winter season, following a return to the plantation house in early November, was the season of large parties, especially around Christmas. Rice planters dominated South Carolina politics and were most influential in encouraging the state in its withdrawal from the Union in 1861.

By comparison with slaves in most other plantation areas of the South, rice coast slaves had far greater freedom during much of the year. The task system minimized oversight, and most whites were away in healthier locations during half the year anyway. Still, a slave had a hard life. The rice culture was not the only thing slaves brought from Senegambia. With them also came malaria and yellow fever. The *Anopheles* genus of mosquito, the primary vector for malaria, was already common in the coastal swamps. Malaria and enteric diseases killed Lowcountry slaves, unable to join their owners in their annual retreat from the swamplands, at an extraordinary rate. Records suggest that one in three slaves on cotton plantations died before age 16. In the rice counties the rate was two in three, and over one-third failed to reach their first birthday.

The Lowcountry rice economy collapsed in the decades after the Civil War. Reasons for this collapse are complex. Emancipation, and the unwillingness of African Americans to work as hard as they had as slaves, played a role. So did a series of devastating hurricanes that struck the coast in the late 19th century. Scholars have recently argued the importance of the emergence of global capitalism and the arrival of less expensive rice from Southeast and South Asia in northern European markets. Rice farmers in Arkansas, Louisiana, and Texas had the funds and the experience to adopt capital-intensive approaches and could compete in the new marketplace. Lowcountry growers, in contrast, lacked the necessary capital after the Civil War to mechanize, and the proper equipment to work their heavy muck soils would not be created for another half century.

Visible landscape reminders of the rice plantation era are modest. Remainders of the ditched, diked landscape are occasionally visible in the swamps from the ground, though they are still strikingly visible from the air. More important are the continuing social consequences. To the extent that it exists in today's environment, much of the surviving Gullah culture of some isolated areas along the coast has been attributed to the West African coast, especially today's Sierra Leone. More important is a pervasive rural African American poverty. None of the rural replacements for rice has offered opportunities similar to that once offered by rice.

JOHN FLORIN
University of North Carolina at Chapel Hill

Judith A. Carney, *Carolina Rice: The African Origins of Rice Cultivation in the Americas* (2001); Peter A. Coclanis, *The Shadow of a Dream: Economic Life and Death in the South Carolina Low Country* (1989); Charles W. Joyner, *Shared Traditions: Southern History and Folk Culture* (1999).

Roadside

Donald Davidson wrote in *The Attack on Leviathan* (1938) that southern cities reflecting "the finest flavor of the old regime" could not be reached except by passing "over brand-new roads where billboards, tourist camps, filling stations and factories broke out in a modernistic rash among the water oaks and Spanish moss." Davidson saw the roadside in the South as a prime symbol of the evils of modernization, which were destroying the best of the region's agrarian tradition.

The automobile indeed reshaped the southern roadside in the 20th century, promoting Americanization and standardization through billboards, service stations, fast food restaurants, trailer camps, motels, and other aspects of the car culture. But for travelers in motor vehicles, the roadside also reflects and reinforces an awareness of southern history and culture and promotes the consciousness of being in a landscape that is different from that elsewhere. It has thereby promoted regional self-consciousness.

Historic sites, for example, especially Civil War battlefields, have become modern locales for pilgrimage. The war marked the southern roadside for generations. Most of the fighting during the conflict was on southern soil, and the countryside long after the war held tangible memories of the past. As Mary Winn, a traveler in the region, wrote in 1931, "At intervals on the road one passes a group of magnificent live-oaks, in the middle of which rises a tall chimney, all that is left of the 'great house' that was once the center of a feudal property." Virginia pioneered in erecting historical markers by the side of the road, and now the history of every state in the region is revealed in concise statements on signs, markers, and monuments on the roadside. Historian Thomas D. Clark suggested in 1961 that traffic congestion from automobile tourists made it more dangerous to pull off the road "to take a leisurely look at the scene of a Civil War battlefield than it was to have engaged in the battle itself." Historic markers now lead travelers to sites of African American history, especially pertaining to figures from the civil rights movement. State tourism boards in Mississippi and Alabama encourage organized pilgrimages to such roadside places.

Natural attractions have been roadside lures in the South. "See Rock City" and "Ruby Falls" were the most pervasive of signs painted on the sides of southern barns, nailed to a tree as placards, or displayed on standard billboards. But there were also signs for Silver Springs, Natural Bridge, or even Dog Patch. "The southern landscape has been sacrificed in many places to this mad campaign to snatch the tourist dollar," wrote historian Clark. "Scarcely a roadside post, tree, fence, or barn has escaped the signmaker. On some of the main highways there is hardly a quarter of a mile left undefiled."

Engineers in the South, as elsewhere, generally adopted the utilitarian approach to the countryside in road building, with aesthetics having little role. Wildflowers and trees, for example, were discouraged, although Lady Bird Johnson's wildflower campaign in Texas spurred other southern states to plant wildflowers along highways. Southern roadsides were, however, so naturally luxuriant, especially in the warm humid areas, that they could not be kept down, and the simple attraction of the region's plant life has always added a distinctive look to the roadside, one noted by outsiders looking for regional differences. In a 1938 book, native southerner Jonathan Daniels recalled the road north of Greenville, S.C., where "the dogwood, the mountain magnolia, the azalea and the tiny nameless wild flowers bloomed in profusion on the May highway."

Tourist traps also grew up to give a distinctive ambience to the southern roadside. Billboards and handmade signs for miles announced what were sometimes rip-off businesses. "Pet baby alligators" would be a typical come-on. Reptile farms, bears on display, Shetland ponies to ride—all were designed to lure tourists off the road and out of their cars to buy souvenirs, gasoline, or food. South of the Border, located on Interstate 95 near the North Carolina–South Carolina border, has a 220-foot-high Mexican sombrero, an artifact that certainly draws attention. Billboards from Virginia to Georgia announce its importance. Started in 1949, South of the Border has a gas station, campground, and volunteer fire department. Sometimes the artifacts at such places are a kind of folk/pop art. Mammy's Cupboard is at the top of a hill near Natchez, Miss. A 28-foot-tall black woman stands atop the rise, embodying the "mammy" image, down to her apron. Her "cupboard" lies beneath her crinoline skirt, which covers a 20-foot area. It was built in 1940, and its owners serve southern plate lunches inside. The king of the southern roadside businesses is Stuckey's, whose spread nationwide represents an example of the "southernization of America." Gaudy red-and-yellow billboards dot the countryside advertising

Roadside store between Tuscaloosa and Greensboro, Ala., 1936
(Walker Evans, photographer, Library of Congress Prints and Photographs Division
[LC-USF-342-T01-008282-A DLC], Washington, D.C.)

the place to buy pecans, candy, gifts and souvenirs, gasoline, and fast food. William Sylvester Stuckey, from Eastman, Ga., founded his roadside business in 1932, in the middle of the Great Depression, with only a few sacks of peanuts and a $35 loan. He sold pecans to tourists passing through Eastman headed from New York to Florida, supplied candy to the military during World War II, and then expanded his roadside service nationwide after the war.

Souvenirs, artifacts of perceived "southernness," are part of the roadside in the South. They are localized, suggesting place. T-shirts, clothing, and ashtrays are common everywhere but are marked with local references. There are country music references in Tennessee (hairbrushes in the form of guitars, Dolly Parton dolls); Confederate flags and miniature cotton bales are sold in Mississippi; moccasins and other Indian goods are in North Carolina Cherokee country and in Florida Seminole land; hillbilly characters, outhouses, and scatological artifacts can be purchased on Appalachian roadsides; and seashells and seashell art are common along the coasts. Natural products of the region are also popular souvenirs giving a sense of place—a packaged sack of oranges in Florida, grapefruit in south Texas, peaches in Georgia, boiled peanuts in south

Alabama, and fresh honey everywhere. Folk and pop art, whether quilts, velvet paintings of Elvis, or ceramic animals for the yard, are common beside the road. Fireworks stands are pervasive in certain areas and increase before holidays. These sell Chinese fireworks that are repackaged to strike regional themes (as in the Robert E. Lee collection of firecrackers seen in one Kentucky stand).

Religious folk art has flourished on the southern roadside, especially in the Appalachians and Ozarks and in rural areas. Both handmade primitive signs and mass-produced ones are found. These provide among the most distinctive of regional touches to the roadside, because their messages are evangelistic, reflecting the region's predominant religious outlook and style. Statements include "Get Right with God," "Prepare to Meet Thy God," "Where Will You Spend Eternity," "Jesus Is the Answer," or simply "Jesus Saves." Scholar Samuel S. Hill has speculated that these signs are most common in areas undergoing the trauma of modernization; they are most likely associated with Protestant sectarians. One rough drawing on wood in North Carolina had a stark picture of a hand with a nail through it, and blood spurting forth. "He Loved You So Much It Hurt" were the words under the drawing. Such signs are folk art reflecting the intense, passionate southern faith. Appropriately, Flannery O'Connor refers to them in *Wise Blood*. While driving along the road, Hazel Motes sees a gray boulder, emblazoned with white letters that said, "WOE TO THE BLASPHEMER AND THE WHOREMONGER! WILL HELL SWALLOW YOU UP?"

In the contemporary era the roadside along southern interstate highways is becoming more bland, although southerners in cities, in small towns, and on smaller roads maintain in places the colorful manmade landscape. The use of portable signs—the small, metal-framed and illuminated signs on wheels—is especially popular in the South. *New York Times* reporter William E. Schmidt noted in 1984 that they "seem to be crouched everywhere beside highways across the South these days." Since the mid-1970s, over 100,000 of them have appeared throughout the nation, providing a useful message board to the small businesses who use them. They are most typically found along suburban commercial strips. Their garish flashing lights and arrows effectively catch the eye of the motorist; and garages, service stations, barber and beautician shops, bakeries, and night clubs all use them. Marietta, Ga., attempted to restrict their use, but the Supreme Court ruled in 1984 that restrictions were unconstitutional limitations on the First Amendment rights of businesses. Churches have adopted them widely, delivering for the motorist not only evangelistic messages but also general moral precepts and homely proverbs.

Religion has also been central to the most recent outcropping in the South

—crosses commemorating highway deaths. Although individual southerners have long put up crosses to mark their grief at automobile deaths, the region witnessed a dramatic expansion of such landscape markings after 1990. The Midwest has also seen an increase in the creation of new sacred spaces. In the South, roadside crosses are usually simple wooden constructions, sometimes with the names of automobile fatalities that occurred nearby. Often the crosses witness, in good evangelical fashion, to the faithfulness of the deceased or to hopes of heavenly reunions.

CHARLES REAGAN WILSON
University of Mississippi

John Baeder, *Gas, Food, and Lodging: A Postcard Odyssey through the Great American Roadside* (1982); Warren J. Belasco, *Americans on the Road: From Autocamps to Motel, 1910–1945* (1975); Thomas D. Clark, *The Emerging South* (1961); Holly Everett, *Roadside Crosses in Contemporary Memorial Culture* (2002); Tim Hollis, *Dixie before Disney: 100 Years of Roadside Fun* (1999); John Brinckerhoff Jackson, *The Southern Landscape Tradition in Texas* (1980); John A. Jakle, *The Tourist: Travel in 20th-Century North America* (1985); John A. Jakle and Keith A. Sculle, *Fast Food: Roadside Restaurants in the Automobile Age* (1999); Jan Jennings, ed., *Roadside America: The Automobile in Design and Culture* (1990); Chester H. Liebs, *Main Street to Miracle Mile: American Roadside Architecture* (1986); William E. Schmidt, *New York Times* (19 October 1984).

Southwest

The term "Southwest" has long been used popularly and by scholars to refer to a major subregion of the South. The Old Southwest of the early 19th century included lands recently opened to white settlement—Alabama, Mississippi, Tennessee, Kentucky, Arkansas, and Louisiana. By the 1840s the Southwest included Texas. With the acquisition and settlement of land reaching to southern California, the "Southwest" grew to the west, but the relationship of this land to the South was increasingly unclear.

The problems in defining the Southwest are important ones to understanding the complexities of southern culture and its cultural boundaries. Until recently, scholarly attempts to define regions have reflected physical and economic patterns rather than broader cultural ones. Some scholars have seen the American Southwest as a distinct region, altogether separate from the South. Sociologist Howard W. Odum in *Southern Regions of the United States* (1936) wrote that Texas, Oklahoma, New Mexico, and Arizona were the Southwest, one of six major American regions. Using over 200 indices of specific sociocultural characteristics, Odum concluded that "Texas and Oklahoma qualify as 'southern' in less than a third of the indices selected." He insisted that placing the Southwest with the Southeast was inaccurate and "detrimental to genuine regional analysis and planning." Ruth F. Hale identified the same four states as the Southwest in a more recently developed "Map of Vernacular Regions," based on a mail sample of people's identification with region. Cultural geographer D. W. Meinig identified New Mexico and Arizona as the main focus of the Southwest, exploring the cultural contributions of Anglos, Indians, and Hispanics to its distinctiveness. Although not a part of the "South," Meinig's Southwest was formed partly through contributions of southern whites, particularly Texans, who, he wrote, were "a special regional type, differentiated by political and racial attitudes, religion, and social mores."

Political scientist Daniel Elazar in *Cities of the Prairies* (1970) defines the Southwest to include Louisiana, Arkansas, Missouri, Oklahoma, Texas, and New Mexico (with half of Texas and Oklahoma in what he calls the Greater South and half in the Greater West). Elazar's definition is based on "the expression of social, economic and political differences along geographic lines." Cultural geographer Wilbur Zelinsky divides the United States into five regions, with Texas divided between the South and the West. In creating his division, Zelinsky uses such indicators as food habits, religion, language, and self-identification with region.

Most of these definitions of the Southwest come from broader attempts to chart the nation's overall regional boundaries. From the viewpoint of southern history and culture, questions about the nature of a western part of the South center on Texas and Oklahoma. In one effort at defining regions, Raymond D. Gastil has placed most of Texas and Oklahoma in a "western" subregion of the South, based on secondary cultural factors "induced by differences in the origin of the people, the requirements of particular geographical situations, or subsequent creativity." Although Joel Garreau, in *The Nine Nations of North America* (1981), does not use traditional regional terminology, he carves up Texas and Oklahoma, placing the eastern portions of each in "Dixie" and the western parts in the "Breadbasket" (along with southern and far western Texas in Mex-America).

The Southwest is clearly, then, a borderland area of the South, but it offers the opportunity to observe the cultural configuration of a subregion of Dixie, one that has a distinctive history and identity that is, nonetheless, closely related to that of other areas of the South. Texas is the core area of the South's Southwest, the centerpiece for any attempt to understand the line dividing the Southwest into "southern" and "western" spheres. Writer Willie Morris recalls the Texan who insisted that the dividing line was Conroe, Tex., because west of there bar fights occur indoors and to the east they are outdoors. The "bar fight" line has never been formally charted, but environmental, demographic, historical, and cultural factors suggest an answer. For a study of the South, the Southwest is a most significant area for the clash of cultures, where a southern white-black tradition came into contact with a more pluralistic Hispanic-Indian-frontier culture.

Environmental and climatic factors suggest that much of Texas is southern. A fault line, the Balcones Escarpment, is a geological dividing line, marking in solid rock a physical separation between east Texas—the center of southern influences—and west Texas. In the middle of the state the land changes from piney woods in the east to grassy prairies to the west, with increasingly barren-looking plains and desert even farther west. Markedly decreased rainfall in west Texas reinforces the sense of a western physical landscape, nurturing different forms of animal and plant life. These physical differences were matched by differing settlement populations as well—blacks form a major population group in east Texas, gradually diminishing in numbers to the west, where Hispanics increase in numbers and cultural influence. Texas in general has been more ethnically diverse than the rest of the South, with Indians, Hispanics, Germans, Czechs, Danes, Swedes, and, more recently, Vietnamese the significant populations in different areas of the state. The dividing line between southern and western parts of Texas based on these environmental and demographic facts, in any event, seems to be somewhere between the 98th meridian and the 103rd meridian. Walter Prescott Webb's *The Great Plains* (1931) was a landmark exploration of the response of frontier settlers to the challenges of a new environment in the West. Webb argued that the West began near the 98th meridian—or at that point where water becomes scarce.

In addition to environmental and demographic factors, history made Texas partly southern and partly western. The Anglo founder of Texas, Stephen Austin, was born in Virginia, and most early Anglo settlers were southern whites who brought their black slaves with them when they immigrated to Mexican soil. Cotton grew well in east Texas, and historian Frank Vandiver has noted that early Texans saw wealth in southern terms as "land, cotton, and slaves." The Republic of Texas (1836–45) was surely the creation of aggressive southern white Americans, symbolized by leaders such as Sam Houston, born in Virginia, and Davy Crockett, from Tennessee. The evangelical churches that dominated the rest of the antebellum South also dominated in Texas, among both whites and blacks, a situation that remains true in east and central Texas. Texas was a Confederate state, and with defeat in the Civil War Texans claimed the Lost Cause.

Wheaton, A Texas Rancher *(date unknown) (San Antonio [Texas] Conservation Society)*

The erection of Confederate monuments all the way west to El Paso established a southern landscape.

East and north Texas were dominated by sharecropping after the Civil War. George Sessions Perry's *Hold Autumn in Your Hand* (1941) is a major novel of southern social life under crop lien. These areas were among the centers of Populist agrarian discontent in the 1880s and 1890s, befitting their location between other areas of unrest in the Deep South and on the Great Plains. V. O. Key Jr. discussed Texas as a southern state in *Southern Politics* (1949), showing that the state produced the kind of early 20th-century rural demagogues (James Ferguson, W. Lee "Pappy" O'Daniel) found elsewhere in the South, but they did not exploit the race issue to the same degree as elsewhere. Key noted that Texas was less concerned with race than "about money and how to make it."

The post–Civil War period had seen increasing southwestern divergence from southern patterns. The range cattle industry seemed by the end of the 1860s to be an economic substitute for the cotton economy. Cattle culture generated capital but perhaps more importantly a new mythology for the Southwest, one not shared with the rest of the South. The rancher became a southwestern hero and the longhorn a near mythic animal, but the prime new legendary figure was the cowboy, a symbol of western freedom. The cowboy, to be sure, had southern roots. Owen Wister's *The Virginian* created the model, a romantic figure who had much of the honorable cavalier in him. Black and white southerners after the war did go west seeking opportunity and some became cowboys, but they were seeking to escape the South. The cowboy's real life of hard work and loneliness made him more a working-class frontiersman than a cavalier. The cowboy has shown an enduring appeal for 20th-century Texans and other southerners, especially country music entertainers from Jimmie Rodgers to Charlie Daniels, who have nurtured the cowboy legend. Cowboy hats and boots spread eastward to become common southern rural working-class badges of identification with the Southwest.

Discovery of oil at Spindletop near Beaumont on 10 January 1901 further differentiated the Texas economy from the southern, and oil and natural gas would provide a southwestern economic bond among Texas, Oklahoma, and Louisiana. Petroleum lore created another new mythology for the Southwest, as colorful wildcatters such as Dad Joiner became Texas legends. The massive amounts of money generated by petroleum would enable Texas culture and society to escape much of the enervating southern culture of poverty.

Twentieth-century southwestern culture has continued to reflect both southern and western influences. Before the 1920s, for example, Texas Anglo music came out of a southern heritage. Rural Texans played the same instruments and sang the same kinds of songs found elsewhere in the South. Western swing emerged in Texas and Oklahoma in the 1930s, showing the influence of ethnically diverse Texas and becoming a major genre of country music. Its creators, including Bob Wills and His Texas Playboys, dressed in western costume but played music drawing on blues and jazz as well as southern white fiddle music. The first country star, Jimmie Rodgers, lived his last few years in Texas and promoted a western, "singing cowboy" image. Later Texas country music performers such as Ernest Tubb and Gene Autry made "western" music a southwestern contribution to "southern" country music. Lightnin' Hopkins was similarly a major figure in a southwestern blues tradition centered in east and central Texas. Contemporary Tex-Mex music represents a blending of Mexican, German, and southern musical styles.

Southwestern writers have been, until recently, preoccupied with the frontier, which has been a source of the region's enduring mythology. Southwestern literature was traditionally peopled principally by hardy frontiersmen, gruff ranchers, romantic cowboys, and always-just Texas Rangers. The greatest literary achievements until the 1950s were in nonfiction. Folklorist-biographer J. Frank Dobie, historian Walter Prescott Webb, and naturalist Roy Bedichek were dominant forces. Novelist Larry McMurtry has noted that the "Big Three," as he calls them, "revered Nature, studied Nature, and hued to Nature." It was a literature celebrating western triumph rather than exploring the complex, tragic themes of modern southern literature. Since the 1950s, writers such as William Humphrey, William Goyen, Bill Brammer, John Graves, Cormac Mc-Carthy, and Larry King have created a southwestern fiction tradition that draws on themes earlier articulated by Faulkner and other southern writers. Larry McMurtry is perhaps the most accomplished and successful novelist, telling the story of the movement of Texans off the land and into a new urban Southwest.

Southwestern cooking illustrates the meeting of southern, western, and Mexican cultures. Southern dishes such as grits, biscuits, cornbread, turnip greens, fried chicken, country ham with redeye gravy, and pork sausage are all popular in Texas. Texan Elmore Tora was founder of the National Blackeyed Pea Association and marketed the pea in Asia. Chicken-fried steak is particularly popular fare in Texas truck stops and cafés; it applies a southern style of cooking to a piece of beef—battering and frying it like cooking fried chicken. A cream gravy is the essential accompanying sauce. Larry McMurtry insists that "only a rank degenerate would drive 1,500 miles across Texas without eating a chicken-fried steak." Barbecue is the object of cultlike obsession, although southwestern barbecue is beef, not the pork found in the Deep South. Tex-Mex cooking is a particularly revealing product of a cultural borderland, combining ingredients and styles of cooking from Mexican, Indian, and Anglo traditions. Texas produces about 10 percent of the world's jalapeño pepper supply for its cuisine. Texans in 1951 formed the Chili Appreciation Society International in Dallas, launching a crusade for chili that has brought increasingly passionate identification of chili with the state. South, west, and central Texas are the centers of Tex-Mex cooking, but on the cultural borderland its popularity has spilled over into east Texas, Louisiana, and other parts of the South.

The 1970s saw the emergence of an energetic southwestern culture in central Texas. It was a youth culture, the southwestern version of the counterculture. Drinking beer (preferably the regional Lone Star Longnecks), smoking marijuana, listening to "progressive country" music (especially Willie Nelson), eating Tex-Mex food, admiring armadillos—all were rituals of a lifestyle that self-consciously identified with the region. Periodicals such as the *Texas Monthly* (begun in 1973), the *Texas Observer* (a reform journal that began publishing in 1954 and calls itself "a window on the South"), and the *Southwestern Historical Quarterly* explore the cultural dimensions of the Southwest, including its southern ties. In a January 1977 feature entitled "How to Be Southern," for example, *Texas Monthly* noted that through the years "we Texans have been the perfect fair-weather friends of the South." Texans had "the credentials to be Southern when we wanted," but in trying times "we've been able to step neatly aside into our Southwestern identities." With Jimmy Carter's inauguration, the Southwest seemed to reclaim a part of its southern heritage. By the late 1970s, though, the symbols and rituals of Texas culture had come to predominate over either the western or the southern identity.

The last 30 years have seen the Southwest emerge as one of the nation's leading high-tech cultures. Texas Instruments and then Dell Computers were among the most famous companies that represented a new commitment after the mid-1980s to cutting-edge research and development in technology. The state government, universities, private companies, and urban governments collaborated on incentive programs to attract entrepreneurs and their sometimes high-risk technology culture, which boomed in the early 1990s and then crashed afterward. The region's sports and music continue to draw from western and southern influences, feeding into a Southwest that continues to be a cultural borderland.

CHARLES REAGAN WILSON
University of Mississippi

J. Frank Dobie, *A Guide to the Life and Literature of the Southwest* (1943), *Some Part of Myself* (1967); T. R. Fehrenbach, *Lone Star: A History of Texas and the Texans* (1983); Neil Foley, *The White Scourge: Mexicans, Blacks, and Poor Whites in Texas Cotton Culture* (1997); Lawrence Goodwyn, *Texas Observer* (27 December 1974); Ruth F. Hale, "A Map of Vernacular Regions in America" (Ph.D. dissertation, University of Minnesota, 1971); Jon Holmes, *Texas: A Self-Portrait* (1983); Paul Horgan, *Southwest Review* (Summer 1933); Joseph Leach, *The Typical Texan* (1952); Terry G. Jordan, *Annals of the Association of American Geographers* (December 1967 and September 1970); Larry McMurtry, *In a Narrow Grave: Essays on Texas* (1968); D. W. Meinig, *Imperial Texas: An Interpretive Essay in Cultural Geography* (1969); Ben Proctor and Archie P. McDonald, eds., *The Texas Heritage* (1980); Ronnie C. Tyler, Douglas E. Barnett, and Roy R. Barkley, eds., *The New Handbook of Texas* (1996); Frank Vandiver, *The Southwest: South or West* (1975); Walter Prescott Webb, ed., *Handbook of Texas*, 2 vols. (1952).

Sports, Geography of

A trio of national games clearly dominates the South. Football is the premier sport, but baseball and basketball are also played, enjoyed, and in some places avidly followed. The best gauges of a sport's grip on an area are per capita involvement and the number of high-quality performers originating locally. The per capita production of major college and professional football (NFL) players

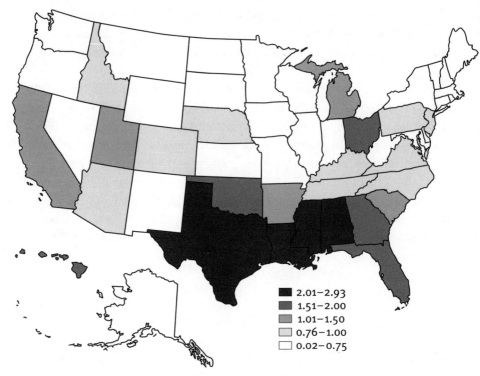

MAP 12. *Blue-Chip Football Players, 2003: Origins of Collegiate Scholarship Players (1.00 = national average)*

has been calculated for the period 1990–2004 in order to identify regional differences. The geographic origins of major league baseball players and collegiate basketball players have been charted for the same period.

The relative importance of baseball, football, and basketball varies across the South, as seen in Map 12. A value of 1.00 indicates that a state's per capita talent output is equal to the national average. Values in excess of 1.00 indicate that a state produces more players than would be expected, and values of less than 1.00 suggest that the state is placing less emphasis on the sport than the nation as a whole. The majority of southern states are near or above the national norm for America's three major sports. Among southern states, Louisiana, Mississippi, and Texas stand out as great producers of football talent; Kentucky and Tennessee are the basketball leaders; Florida is the dominant baseball producer. The majority of the southern states (unlike most northern ones) are above the national football norm.

Football is a national game, but the ability to play it well is concentrated in the South. The South adopted a northern game, absorbed it fully into its culture, and gradually outdid the innovators. Based on the basketball evidence for the period 1970 to the present, the same pattern is being repeated for that sport. Football mania peaks each autumn in towns like Knoxville, Tuscaloosa, Auburn, Oxford, Gainesville, Baton Rouge, Grambling, Athens, Clemson, and Columbia. In February, the annual recruiting saga now overshadows basketball and other ongoing sporting activities. In high schools, the level of community pride associated with football is unparalleled. It is in these small towns where the sport/place bind is strongest, where sport is the glue that bonds people to their places. And football is that sport.

Football mania is still intensifying throughout the South. Young players with football promise are frequently held back, "redshirted in the eighth grade," so that they will be physically capable of meeting the challenges of high school and college ball. Since the early 1970s, black athletes have had full access to the southern university of their choice, and they have selected big-name football schools with increasing regularity. In fact, much of the growth in southern player production can be attributed to the rise of the African American athlete.

As a result of the emphasis on football, most high school sports programs in the South are lacking in breadth. High school boys throughout the region have very limited access to competitive swimming, gymnastics, wrestling, and soccer. Georgia and Florida are the only states above the national norm in soccer participation, although most southern states have made great strides since the 1980s. Track-and-field and cross-country programs are relatively scarce, and Texas is the lone state above the national average. Golf and tennis are still absent from a sizable portion of the high schools.

Women's sports receive little support in the South. Federal legislation requiring equal opportunity for women in sport has thus far failed to bring the South up to national standards, although considerable progress has been made since 1990. Indeed, Kentucky, Tennessee, and Louisiana are among the leaders in women's collegiate basketball, with the University of Tennessee, the University of Texas, and Louisiana Tech leading the way. Texas and Oklahoma, possessing long-standing women's high school basketball traditions, have long been exceptions.

The South is very involved in a variety of other sports. Stock car racing was spawned from the region, and even today the majority of the great drivers are of southern origin. Thoroughbred racing and breeding are concentrated in Kentucky and Virginia. Foxhunting and horse shows are common throughout the Upland South. Tennessee walkers are a distinct southern breed, and the quarter horse continues to grow in popularity throughout the Southwest. Florida is the shuffleboard capital of the world.

Though most southern states are below the national average in number of golfers and golf courses per capita, new course construction is proceeding at a rapid pace. Golf-oriented communities and golf resorts are highly concentrated within the region, creating the ultimate in luxury sports landscapes. Despite its lack of facilities, the South leads the nation in the output of male professional golfers.

Lacrosse, rugby, and crew are largely absent from the southern sports scene, and for obvious reasons most activities requiring ice and snow are poorly developed.

JOHN F. ROONEY
Oklahoma State University

THEODORE GOUDGE
Northwest Missouri State University

John F. Rooney, *American Demographics* (September 1986), *Geographical Review* (October 1969), *Geography of American Sport* (1974); John F. Rooney Jr. and Richard Pillsbury, *Atlas of American Sport* (1992).

Towns and Villages

Early urban communities in the South were not founded by investors or entrepreneurs as they had been in New England and New York, nor were they created by government-subsidized railroads as in much of the Midwest and West. Rather, towns and villages that formed across much of the frontier South as service centers for a primarily agrarian clientele evolved out of transplanted European tradition and law. The plantations of the Tidewater colonies produced cotton, tobacco, and other commodities on a commercial scale, but their proprietors preferred to trade directly with Caribbean or European markets. Consequently, the market town did not develop early in eastern Virginia or the Carolinas as it did in the North, where farmers sold their surplus produce in village markets. Inland from the coast, the first hamlets were established by English, Scots-Irish, and German settlers moving south from Pennsylvania along the Great Valley and Piedmont. At mill sites or where open country roads met, a farmstead or two and a church, school, and store would eventually coalesce into a loosely ordered crossroads hamlet.

The tradition of English law as established in the South was administered through a system of counties. County government was conducted at the county seat, usually the largest and often the only real town in the county. Government attracted professionals who served it and were served by it, and the county seat became the home of politicians, lawyers, bankers, enforcement officers, surveyors and engineers, and merchants — in short, the economic and social elite of the county. Their offices often faced a central town square on which stood the courthouse and jail, a county seat pattern that has diffused widely throughout the South from its origin in Pennsylvania. Few farmers lived in the county seat. If they lived in an urban place at all, it would be the crossroads hamlet. As the South grew, towns built around the central square appeared in adjacent territory and in newly formed counties.

Variations on this urban scheme appeared as early as the 1760s when French Acadian migrants from Nova Scotia moved into Louisiana's Mississippi River Delta marshlands. There they built small villages atop the natural levees of major streams according to a system of community organization and land division that had begun to mature in French Canada.

Before the Civil War, the economy of the South remained largely agricultural, and its urban settlements were small and parochial. The largest towns were coastal cotton-shipping ports: Galveston, New Orleans, Mobile, Charleston, and Savannah. Inland, a string of river or fall line towns grew up at mill sites and navigational breaks: Richmond, Petersburg, Raleigh, Columbia, Augusta, and Macon.

After the Civil War, fundamental changes in regional and national culture and economy began to lay a foundation for dramatic alteration of the urban system. Freed slaves created a new type of settlement in some areas. Freedmen on many cotton plantations settled on dispersed parcels of plantation land in an initial stage of the sharecropping system. On sugar plantations in Louisiana and the livestock estates of the Kentucky Bluegrass, a somewhat different pattern of black resettlement occurred. In Louisiana, sugar plantations had large labor requirements during harvest and refining. Consequently, freedmen working on plantations were housed in small linear hamlets, often located near sugar mills. In Kentucky, large Bluegrass estates required workers to handle livestock and produce hemp and tobacco cash crops. Slave quarters were eliminated, and freedmen were given, or were allowed to rent or buy, housing in small hamlets, which were often subdivided out of a portion of estate property.

The end of the Civil War marked the rebuilding and extension of the southern rail system and the establishment of reliable trade links with the North. Rail lines focused at coastal harbors, river bridging points, and mountain gaps; when a new rail line was built into an existing town there was often a small boom in development as local entrepreneurs built lumberyards, tanneries, furniture plants, textile mills, and cotton gins. Towns on the Piedmont near streams that could provide small-scale hydroelectric power or those near the hardwood stands of the Appalachian uplands tended to benefit most from this transportation revolution. In peninsular Florida, the effect of rail building was substantially different. Inhospitable marshlands became accessible for the first time, allowing rail companies to establish a number of new towns and resorts along the coasts.

The extension of railroads into the South also brought entrepreneurs seeking resources to fuel northern industry. Pennsylvania coal, for example, was used in local iron furnaces until high-strength steel rails and rolling stock made mining in the central Appalachians a profitable alternative. After 1870, northern industrialists sent representatives into the southern mountains to buy mineral rights over broad areas. As coal mines were established in eastern Kentucky, Tennessee, western Virginia, and West Virginia, company towns were built to house the men that the companies hoped to employ. Some towns, constructed by poorly financed companies, were small and pitifully built. Others, such as Lynch and Wheelwright, Ky., were extensive, planned communities housing populations of 1,000 or more within a year of completion. Southern blacks, European immigrants, and local hill farmers were hired to mine coal and were settled in socially stratified towns. Small miners' houses were often crowded together in a valley bottom. More substantial mine managers' homes were usually placed upslope, away from dust, noise, and the miners. About 1870, several small company towns grew amid the ridges and hardscrabble farms of north-central Alabama, where local coal, iron ore, and limestone were used to produce iron. Gradually, the town of Birmingham grew from several such towns.

By the 1880s and 1890s, the textile-milling industry, so strongly entrenched in New England before 1860, was beginning to migrate to the Carolina and Georgia Piedmont. Mill owners, as they had done in England a century before and in New England after about 1790, built small towns at their mill sites to house workers. Many Piedmont farmers, burdened by debt and constrained by poor farming practices that produced little more than eroded fields, sent their wives and children to work in nearby mills. Mill homes clustered around a central company store, where workers purchased food and dry goods or used the post office or barbershops. Pay was often in scrip negotiable only at the company businesses.

Recreational towns began to appear at Virginia's thermal springs in the ridge and valley country west of Roanoke by the turn of the 19th century. Their growth was paralleled by high-altitude resort towns in the southern Blue Ridge Mountains such as Asheville and Highlands, N.C., which attracted wealthy Coastal Plain planters and merchants seeking relief from oppressive summer heat and miasma.

Lexington, Ga., the Oglethorpe county seat, 1970 (Richard Pillsbury, photographer)

The broad pattern of small market towns interspersed with large numbers of crossroads hamlets and clusters of specialized company towns changed little until about 1930, when improved roads and automobiles allowed greater residential flexibility. After World War II, the population of many small towns stagnated or even declined, and a new urban form, the linear roadside housing strip, evolved. Today, people purchase road-front lots from farmers, build homes, and commute to work in nearby towns. Consequently, town populations may not change noticeably, but rural nonfarm densities have increased substantially. This process is especially evident in the Carolina Piedmont.

Since the 1950s there has been a broad reorganization of the small-town landscape of the United States in general and of the South in particular. Massive rural depopulation, especially since 1950, has reduced demand for services in rural areas, and almost-universal access to automobiles and the construction of a network of paved roads has allowed easier access to larger service centers with greater variety and lower prices. The resulting decline in the availability of rural services has further escalated the decay of all services, and much of the rural service network, including schools, churches, and medical and retail services, practically collapsed in the decades after 1950. Tens of thousands of villages and hamlets lie virtually boarded up today across the entire South, with only a few aged storekeepers remaining. Some communities have disappeared entirely, except for a grove of trees and a sign still announcing that Ocee or Garden Grove is (was) here. It is not uncommon for smaller rural counties to have insufficient students to maintain even one high school in this era of state-mandated school consolidation, and many have only a single elementary school.

Life has returned to some of these places since the 1990s as retirees and others fleeing suburbia have discovered the attractive supply of historic homes found in many communities. Low house prices and taxes and a chance to restore a historic structure have attracted thousands of "incomers" from throughout the region and nation in search of refuge from the urban pace of life. Some services have returned, but more likely these are antique and artisan shops than grocery stores and doctors' offices.

KARL B. RAITZ
University of Kentucky

Conrad M. Arensberg, *American Anthropologist* (December 1955); Dwight Billings, *Planters and the Making of a "New South": Class, Politics, and Development in North Carolina, 1865–1900* (1979); John C. Campbell, *The Southern Highlander and His Homeland* (1921); James C. Cobb, *The Selling of the South: The Southern Crusade for Industrial Development, 1936–1990* (1993); Robert D. Mitchell, *Commercialism and Frontier: Perspectives on the Early Shenandoah Valley* (1977); M. B. Newton Jr., *Geoscience and Man*, vol. 5 (1974); Peter Smith and Karl Raitz, *Geographical Review* (April 1974).

Acadian Louisiana

Frenchmen from west-central France crossed the North Atlantic to become Acadians living on the far eastern margins of 17th-century *Nouvelle France*. Caught up in their tragic diaspora, *le grand dérangement*, many Acadians became Cajuns in the 18th century and created a new homeland, *Nouvelle Acadie*, in south Louisiana. In both places, Acadia and south Louisiana, these French-speaking people created homelands by imposing their culture traits over time onto the landscape and by modifying their ways of living to accommodate foreign physical environments and interaction with other peoples. In both places, these Francophones bonded to one another and to their lands, homelands that they not only came to control but to love, to protect, and—ultimately—to lose. And in both places, invasions by Anglos caused the demise of these Gallic-derived homelands.

Early 17th-century French settlers of Acadia, present-day Nova Scotia, faced two important geographical challenges. A harsh climate, which in January and February had temperatures 15 to 20 degrees lower than in western France, forced the Acadians to make a wide range of adaptations in foods, clothing, and housing. Although the Acadians, after some difficulties, succeeded in cultivating their traditional crops of wheat, barley, and oats on the reclaimed saline marshes and brought the apple tree from France, they depended greatly upon a vibrant avenue of transculturation with the Micmac Indians that provided ways to supple-ment an initially precarious subsistence agricultural economy. The Acadians learned to make maple syrup and beer brewed with spruce buds, a noted anti-scurvy concoction preferred over the traditional apple cider.

Most Acadians abandoned their French two-story, wood and masonry houses for the warmer, one- or two-room *poteaux-en-terre* cottage, a marriage of European design, Acadian building materials, and Indian construction and insulation techniques in which walls consisting of posts bound together by small branches and coated with a mixture of mud and clay sealed out the arctic blasts and supported a small attic and a European-styled roof thatched with reed and bark. And their French vernacular began to include Indian words to describe the new ways.

The second geographical problem was simply isolation. Acadia was not in the mainstream of French colonization nor was it on a favorable route of transportation, having been located on the shores of a relatively dead-end bay with unusually great tidal extremes. Thus the 17th-century Acadians forged a unique blend of French and Indian folkways on an isolated edge of the North American frontier but in doing so became increasingly distant from their native French culture that continued on its own path of evolution.

Although 18th-century Acadian neutrality and later recalcitrance were strategies that tried to navigate swirling geopolitical events, the Acadians nevertheless lost their homeland, fought off Anglicization in the American colonies as well as assimilation into a conde-

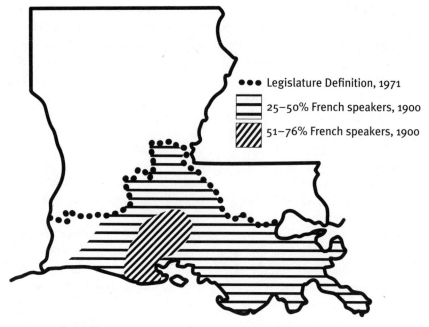

● ● ● Legislature Definition, 1971

25–50% French speakers, 1900

51–76% French speakers, 1900

MAP 13. *Acadian Louisiana*

scending society in France, and thus spent years in their *grand dérangement* searching for a *Nouvelle Acadie*—a land in which they again became pioneers. For many Acadians, the tragic diaspora came to a close in subtropical south Louisiana far from their frozen Canadian homeland.

Between 1765 and 1785 most of the 4,000 Acadians who ended their diaspora in present-day south Louisiana settled on the back slopes of the lower Mississippi River and its distributaries. Spurned by their own French monarch, about 1,600 Acadians, the largest single group, were transported by the Spanish crown to Louisiana in 1785 to try to stabilize Spain's economically unprofitable colony.

Throughout the late 18th century, the Acadians, contrary to current

automobile-society images of the Atchafalaya Swamp as an impenetrable watery barrier infested with reptiles, saw the basin as a highly porous landscape that allowed them to roam widely within it, to settle its western edge along Bayou Teche (displacing such native peoples as the Houma, Opelousa, and Attakapas), and to have a constant contact between the Mississippi and the Teche. Indeed, the lower Mississippi River, its distributaries, and its Atchafalaya Swamp form a natural system of waterways, perhaps finer than any other on the continent, that ensured ease of early Cajun transportation.

Cultural change was pervasive in south Louisiana. The Acadians abandoned wheat, barley, and oats for Indian corn, oriental rice, and West African okra. Flax would not grow in

A classic Acadian house, Bayou Lafourche, La., 1978 (Richard Pillsbury, photographer)

the hot, wet climate, so cotton fields and pre-Whitney gins began to dot the countryside. Broadcasting seed no longer worked in soil that needed furrows. Apples and cider vanished. Figs, peaches, and wine from vines of concord, white, and muscadine grapes were enjoyed. Agricultural practices thus radically changed, as the Cajuns plowed rows for new crops that took advantage of a far-longer growing season, fought off seemingly incessant and infinitely varied hordes of insects, and, perhaps most important, became slaveholders, thereby deserting a proud heritage of egalitarianism.

Sheep flocks shrank significantly at the expense of burgeoning cattle ranches — the huge *vacheries*, an industry learned from the Spanish. Barn size likewise shrank since cattle no longer needed large winter refuges. The numbers of horses increased exponentially as the animal became central to agrarian Cajun life for both work and pleasure. Cornbread replaced whole wheat, sugar cane replaced the maple tree for syrup, and filé gumbo replaced *soupe de la toussaint*. French Creole (non-Cajun French born in Louisiana), Indian, and African cooking methods, particularly the red sauces introduced by West African slaves, crept into Cajun cuisine.

Louisiana's subtropical climate forced Cajuns to change their entire wardrobe to loose-fitting, cotton clothing. The Canadian woolen shawl became the Louisiana cotton *garde-soleil*, a headdress with a wide, rigid brim that provided protection from the sun. Moccasins were worn in the short winter but were forsaken altogether during the remainder of the year.

Not only was the thick-walled, heavily insulated *poteaux-en-terre* cottage unbearable in Louisiana's heat, but the high water table rotted the structure's wooden-post foundation and termites ate away the wood at ground level. The Acadian cottage was quickly abandoned for what has come to be known as the Cajun house, a simple structure raised off the ground by cypress blocks and having large doors, matched windows, and a front gallery for increased cooling by ventilation. Cypress shingles called *merrain* cover a steep, gabled roof for better nocturnal heat radiation from the attic. The Cajuns borrowed this architecture from the French who had preceded them in settling Louisiana and who had brought the prototype from the West Indies. *Pieux*, roughly hewn cypress boards, and *bousillage*, nogging of mud and moss, were the main construction materials for the Cajun house, which, except for its painted front, weathered to a dull grey color.

In the 17th and 18th centuries, geographical relocation into alien physical environments caused the French settlers to make striking cultural adaptations and borrow ways of living from Indians, French Creoles, Spaniards, and African slaves to survive in Acadia and south Louisiana. In the 19th and 20th centuries, although the Cajun homeland would become geographically stable, invasions of Anglo-Saxon Americans by the thousands and new, exciting technologies would profoundly change Cajun life.

Historic events filled 19th-century Louisiana — the Louisiana Purchase, statehood, the Civil War, and Reconstruction — and new technologies swept the state — steamboats, railroads, telegraphs, agricultural mechanization,

electricity, and telephones. And the 19th century was one of critical, tumultuous cultural transformation in which an aggressive Anglo-Saxon nation displaced the French as Louisiana's predominant people.

As early as the 1830s railroads began to track across the south Louisiana countryside, and the Gallic community enthusiastically supported rail transportation. The railway revolution was also a communications revolution. Mail between New Orleans and Franklin on the lower Teche was delivered every third day in 1848. During the next decade, the mail runs of the New Orleans, Opelousas, and Great Western, the state's second longest railroad, made it possible for Franklin's residents to read a New Orleans morning newspaper the same evening. But perhaps of greater significance was that the railroad introduced antebellum Cajun Louisiana to the precursor of today's electronic age — the telegraph.

After the Civil War, schooners again sailed up the Lafourche, Teche, Vermilion, Mermentau, and Calcasieu to engage in lucrative extraregional commerce based on south Louisiana's agricultural and timber production. Again the ubiquitous steamboat skimmed into the most remote locations for commerce and industry. Farmers shipped tons of agricultural commodities to market from "Louisiana's garden" along Bayou Teche; customized steamboats hauled 300 to 400 head of prairie cattle at a time to New Orleans auction lots; and swampers towed huge rafts of cypress logs out of the Atchafalaya Swamp.

In the 19th century, south Louisianans thus felt the pervasive effects of transportation revolutions that rapidly pierced whatever barriers of geographical isolation remained. Cajun communities were no exception; they too were transformed by the steamboat and the railroad. Easy transportation throughout south Louisiana surely encouraged extensive Anglo settlement in *Nouvelle Acadie*, thereby changing its landscape and its culture.

In the early 19th-century Cajun homeland, as in every southern region, there existed a complex mix of white and black, free and slave, rich and poor, educated and ignorant, mansions and shacks. An increasingly important part of this cultural milieu were the thousands of Anglo-Americans who began to stream into Louisiana even before the Louisiana Purchase and who brought their English-speaking slaves deep into the Cajun homeland. During the century's first decades, an intense Franco-American cultural clash developed. But by the 1840s, Anglo economic and political hegemonies controlled Louisiana and had irreversibly begun to change the Cajun social fabric. American encroachment, in which Anglos bought up and consolidated fragmented, uneconomical French long lots, forced some Cajuns, mainly from the old "Acadian Coast" along the lower Mississippi in Ascension and St. James parishes and from the upper reaches of Bayou Lafourche in Assumption Parish, to move westward in what some scholars have termed the "second expulsion" and rapidly Anglicized those who remained.

Anglos won the battle for state political hegemony. At the time of the Louisiana Purchase in 1803, there were roughly seven Frenchmen for every one Anglo-American in Louisiana, and at least a three-to-one ratio at statehood in 1812. By the Civil War, 70 percent of Louisiana's population was Anglo. Fully appreciating the implications of the swelling Anglo ranks, the Gallic leadership secured a majority of delegates at the state's first constitutional convention and contrived its promulgation to ensure long-term French political control. Out of the Constitution of 1812 came the "French Ascendancy" of the 1820s. This Gallic political dominance was short-lived, however. After years of calling for political equity, Anglos captured control of the state government through their majority in the Constitutional Convention of 1845. The gubernatorial election of Cajun Paul Hebert in 1853 was the last gasp of French domination in Louisiana.

South Louisiana towns, like those throughout the United States, were caught up in a wave of late 19th-century innovation. Three years after Alexander Graham Bell invented the telephone in 1876, a "talking telegraph" company was incorporated in New Orleans. Just two years later, Donaldsonville, 80 miles up the Mississippi into the Cajun region, inaugurated a local telephone exchange that linked the town to New Orleans in 1883. Ten years later, construction began on an ambitious telephone system that by 1900 connected most towns and villages in or near the Teche country: Jeanerette, Olivier, New Iberia, Loreauville, St.

Martinville, Lafayette, Breaux Bridge, Arnaudville, Sunset, Grand Coteau, Opelousas, Washington, and others. In 1887, New Orleans installed its first electric lights. Within little more than a decade, New Iberia, Lafayette, Crowley, and Opelousas did likewise. In 1902, a New Iberia physician purchased one of the first automobiles in Louisiana. In 1909, Donaldsonville began to enforce automobile speed ordinances. Of course, if most Cajuns could not afford such newfangled things as telephones, electric lights, or automobiles, they were no different than most Anglo farmers in north Louisiana, throughout the South, or in other parts of the nation. Yet, the essential points are that neither geographical nor social barriers prevented the diffusion of the latest technological innovations throughout the towns and villages of the Cajun homeland and that these inventions began to affect the Cajun culture not after World War II but before the turn of the 20th century. Indeed, times of great innovation—mechanized agriculture, oil and sulfur booms, electricity, and telephones—badly blurred the most sacrosanct icons of the Cajuns during the last decades of the 19th century.

But the most significant change in Cajun culture in the 19th century was the tremendous erosion of its language. The demise of French political influence critically affected the essence of the Cajun culture, its language. As early as the Reconstruction Constitution of 1864, the Louisiana legislature stridently required that only English could be used in the state's public schools. Not only did the use of French erode significantly during the 19th century, but the language itself changed markedly. The unique patois of south Louisiana evolved from different "gumbos," each based on a French "roux," of several languages. The introduction of English, however, had the greatest effect in corrupting the French spoken in the Cajun homeland. Scholars blame this historical corruption on an educational process that was permeated with English words, ideas, and viewpoints and that had restricted contact with French culture, especially French literature. In 1900, more than three-quarters of the residents of all but three Louisiana parishes claimed they could speak English. Only in St. Martin (60 percent English-speaking), Lafayette (61 percent), and Vermilion (62 percent) parishes did more than a quarter of the population tenaciously refuse to speak anything other than their local French patois.

In the 20th century, freedom brought by the automobile and information beamed by radio, movies, and television captured the Cajuns and ensured the Gallic cultural dissolution. Epitomizing such disintegration, *L'Abeille*, Louisiana's last important French-language newspaper, suspended publication in 1923, following the moribund path of 26 other French-language and 21 bilingual newspapers that had ceased publishing between 1860 and 1900.

Today, the more than one-half million people of Cajun ancestry make up about 12 percent of Louisiana's population. Cajuns are still married to their automobiles, watch CNN and MTV on cable television, hold critical state political clout called "Cajun Power," live in three-bedroom, two-bath brick homes, program computers, use their cellular phones and electronic mail to communicate globally, have been swept up in the current "gambling craze," and, although their spicy foods remain hot commercial "properties" that have won over the nation, eat more Big Macs than boudin. Cajuns have thus become mainstream urban Americans.

It seems that today America wants to know more about the Cajun homeland, a region that has been dramatically portrayed either as sinister swamps filled with reptiles or as picturesque bayous draped with moss and magnolias. Centered in Lafayette, the nascent Cajun renaissance still faces the test of time. Yet the ironies are many. As the Cajuns anxiously try to regain their identity from the secure embrace of a national culture, myopic perceptions of their heritage become media events.

LAWRENCE E. ESTAVILLE
Texas State University

Barry Jean Ancelet, Jay Edwards, and Glen Pitre, *Cajun Country* (1991); Carl A. Brasseaux, *Acadien to Cajun: Transformation of a People, 1803–1877* (1992); Lawrence E. Estaville, in *Homelands: A Geography of Culture and Place across America*, ed. Richard L. Norstrand and Lawrence E. Estaville (2001); Nicholas R. Spitzer, in *Louisiana Folklife: A Guide to the State*, ed. Nicholas R. Spitzer (1985).

Atlanta

Atlanta today is part aging southern gentlewoman, part hip-hop princess, and part Yankee. The city has not a single identity but three major strands derived from historical experiences and recent aspirations. For many, the image of Atlanta is linked to the Old South, depicted in Margaret Mitchell's *Gone with the Wind*. The imprint of this Atlanta is still visible, though the long-abandoned textile mills are being converted to in-town loft housing, and even Margaret Mitchell's house has burned twice and now is only a reconstruction. The traditional downtown, with its stately gold-domed capital, is still the seat of political power, but it has been eclipsed by the newer northern downtown of Buckhead, the economic heart of the city.

Many Atlantans are recent arrivals from various points in the North and overseas. Atlanta natives, those born in the city, are rare. The 20-county Atlanta region experienced tremendous growth, up 39 percent since 1990; 4.1 million Atlantans were counted in the 2000 census. Drawn by jobs in the new economy and corporate headquarters, including United Parcel Service, Philips, Home Depot, Allis-Siemens, and Simmons, these 921,431 (1990–99) new residents have driven Atlanta's notorious urban sprawl, especially to the city's north. For them, the Buckhead area, as well as other points along the I-285 ring road, is Atlanta's downtown; their connection to the older South is through the occasional consumption of southern food or subscription to *Southern Living*. Some have adopted usage of "y'all."

Atlanta has long been a major national center of black life, even though many blacks are not native southern-

Centennial Olympic Park, Atlanta, Ga., 2004
(Centennial Olympic Park, Atlanta Convention and Visitors Bureau)

ers but the returning descendants of blacks who moved north in the early 20th century. While Ku Klux Klan members were initiated atop nearby Stone Mountain, Martin Luther King Jr. and his associates grew and nurtured the civil rights movement in the Sweet Auburn district downtown. Though the average income of blacks still lags behind that of whites, metropolitan Atlanta is home to a strong black elite and professional class. A new elite of professional athletes and musicians has replaced the scions of the civil rights movement and their descendants atop the social hierarchy. Atlanta is the national center for hip-hop and is home to major recording studios (such as So So Def), as well as performers, including Outkast, Ludakris, Usher, Goody Mob, Missy Misdemeanor, 2-6 Mafia, and Babyface. Michael Jackson, Whitney Houston, the Rolling Stones, and others have recorded all or parts of records at the local studios. This group is claiming its own space in Atlanta's landscape, creating multimillion-dollar mansions in traditionally poor southwest Atlanta (known as SWATS among the hip-hop crowd), as well as in the traditional wealthy enclaves of the northern suburbs. In predominantly white Buckhead, new clubs (such as 112, Worldbar, and Carnival) draw the city's African American youth, creating unease among many of its residents.

Like much of the South, Atlanta continues to have a high level of voluntary segregation. Blacks and whites largely worship in different churches, play in different clubs, and live in different neighborhoods. School and work continues to be the main arena for racial integration. However, the economic underpinnings of segregation cannot be ignored. Although the poverty rate for the metropolitan area overall is quite low (10 percent), the poverty rate within the city of Atlanta is much higher at 27.3 percent. The overwhelming majority of residents within the city limits are black (73.1 percent), and the city's traditional core remains home to a significant poor black population.

Contemporary Atlanta thrives partly because it continues to be a key transportation link. Atlanta was at the heart of the South's railroad network in the 19th century, and automobile and truck traffic have flourished more recently, with the city serving as an interstate highway hub.

Today Atlanta sees itself as a model for a new South in a new millennium and its regional leader. It is a place where the traditional South, African American culture, and northern influences intermingle to create a southern-defined national culture that is neither truly national nor truly southern but a mix of many of the best elements of both. There is occasional cultural conflict, as most anywhere, but it has taken on a new character as the cultural influences have intermixed more than any of the current residents' grandparents could ever have imagined.

DONA STEWART
Georgia State University

Ronald H. Bayor, *Race and the Shaping of Twentieth-Century Atlanta* (1996); Karen J. Ferguson, *Black Politics in New Deal Atlanta*

(2002); Larry Keating, *Atlanta: Race, Class, and Urban Expansion* (2001); Joseph F. Thompson and Robert Isbell, *Atlanta: A City of Neighborhoods* (1993).

Birmingham

Sited in the last vestige of the Ridge and Valley Province of the Appalachian mountain system, Birmingham, Ala., is situated in Jones Valley between Red Mountain to the south and Sand Mountain to the north. The valley is named after John Jones, a rough character of some notoriety, who established the first settlement in 1815. Between 1815 and 1820, numerous families made their way into the valley between Red and Sand mountains, many giving their names to settlements that now form a number of the independent municipalities making up the Birmingham Metropolitan Standard Area (MSA)—McAdory, Tarrant, Roebuck, Wood (Woodlawn), Truss (Trussville), and others. Farming was the chief occupation of early settlers, but the area was rich in industrial raw materials, principally coal, iron ore, and limestone—the trio of essential ingredients for an iron and steel industrial base. The beginning of Birmingham's iron and steel legacy started in Roupes Valley in 1830. Developed by Ninion Tannehill into a prospering business, it was a critical industrial component of the Civil War era in the state.

The city owes its birth, however, to the advent of the railroad. A consortium of planters and industrialists prior to the Civil War realized the necessity of a railroad to open the area to markets. Following the war, the promoters and capitalists behind the South and North Railroad met in December 1870 and formed the Elyton Land Company. Starting with a tract of approximately 4,100 acres, the city was incorporated on 19 December 1871 and named after the famous iron manufacturing center in England. By the turn of the century, the city had become a major industrial complex for the Deep South, taking the nickname "the Magic City" as a measure of its meteoric rise to prominence. By 1903 the city had created a visual symbol to go along with its name. The Italian sculptor Giuseppe Moretti fashioned a cast iron statue of Vulcan, Roman god of fire and metalworking, for the Commercial Club. The statue, second in height in the United States to the Statue of Liberty and the tallest cast iron statue in the world (at 55 feet), was exhibited at the Louisiana Purchase Exhibition in St. Louis in 1904, taking the Grand Award for the entire fair. It has been the city's symbol ever since.

Birmingham's industrial infrastructure continued to expand through the first half of the 20th century, but changes were coming. By the 1960s and 1970s, changing market conditions, environmental pollution regulations, and the inroads of the petrochemical industries in making substitution products destroyed the market for much of Birmingham's iron manufacturing. By the end of the 1970s, it had ceased to be a force in national iron and steel manufacturing, shifting from primary manufacturing to a focus on service industries—education, health care, banking, and insurance. In the process of change from industrial to service economy, Birmingham became the international symbol of the struggle for black civil rights in America. Police commissioner Eugene "Bull" Connor and police dogs attacking civil rights demonstrators in 1963 made Birmingham a symbol of white resistance to social change. Today, the Birmingham MSA is a thriving urban community with a population of slightly less than 901,000 in 32 independent municipalities, of which the city of Birmingham is the largest. Not unlike Pittsburgh, to which it was likened in its industrial heyday, Birmingham is a transformed urban landscape that exemplifies the model of the New South city.

D. GREGORY JEANE
Samford University

Leah Rawls Atkins, *The Valley and the Hills: An Illustrated History of Birmingham and Jefferson County* (1981); Lynne B. Feldman, *A Sense of Place: Birmingham's Black Middle-Class Community, 1890–1930* (1999); John C. Henley, *This Is Birmingham: The Story of the Founding and Growth of an American City* (1963); Marjorie Longenecker White, *The Birmingham District: An Industrial History and Guide* (1981); Bobby M. Wilson, *America's Johannesburg: Industrialization and Racial Transformation in Birmingham* (2000), *Race and Place in Birmingham: The Civil Rights and Neighborhood Movements* (2000).

Black Belt

The Black Belt region, also called the Black Prairie, extends 300 miles across central Alabama and northeast Mississippi and into Tennessee. It is flat land, 20 to 25 miles wide, and lies within the Gulf South's Coastal Plains, from 200 to 300 feet below the uplands that are north and south of the region. The dark soil for which the Black Belt was named was once famous for its richness and the abundant cotton produced in it. Cotton was, in fact, the main cash crop from the 1820s until early in the 20th century, when losses from the boll weevil forced agricultural diversification. Some geographers speculate that the region, drained by the Alabama and Tombigbee river systems, was originally a grassland. The unusually fertile soils resulted from the weathering of the Selma Chalk, a limestone layer that was the remains of an ocean floor.

Social scientists sometimes use the term "Black Belt" to refer to those parts of the South dominated by cotton plantations and having a high proportion of blacks in the population. Howard W. Odum, for example, in *Southern Regions of the United States* (1936), defined the Black Belt as extending into Georgia, the Carolinas, and western Mississippi. The culture of the poor who live in these areas has been the topic of several major studies, beginning with Odum's and including Charles S. Johnson's *Growing Up in the Black Belt* (1941) and Arthur F. Raper's *Tenants of the Almighty* (1943). These accounts give an insight into the lives of tenant-farm families and portray the changes that they experienced as tenancy collapsed. Johnson's description of the lives of rural black youths in several southern counties, based largely on interviews, gives details of their home lives, education, aspirations, and attitudes toward whites. The Black Belt has been the incubator for much black culture, probably because of the concentration of population. Raper's study of Greene County, Ga., examines the benefits brought to the area by New Deal programs designed to alleviate the poverty of tenancy and to improve living conditions in the area. Other observers have noted the insularity of the region. The Communist Party in the 1930s called for a "Black Belt Nation," wherein majority black areas could achieve self-rule.

In the post–World War II era, the Black Belt became a major battleground for the civil rights movement. In the 1950s, Rosa Parks and Martin Luther King Jr. made Montgomery the site for a new phase of the black freedom struggle. In the 1960s, the Black Belt town of Selma became one of the bloodiest spots of the civil rights struggle, with the Selma to Montgomery March leading to passage of the seminal Voting Rights Act of 1965. In the late 1960s, voters elected blacks to town and county offices, making the Black Belt the center of black elected officials in the nation.

The region's white tenant-farm families had been the subjects of James Agee and Walker Evans's *Let Us Now Praise Famous Men* (1936). Their blend of compassion and objectivity in photographs and text gives an intimate portrait of the lives of poor whites in Hale County, Ala., and includes vivid details of clothing, education, housing, and work. The book inspired William Christenberry, a Hale County native, to photograph the rural southern landscape, preserving the icons of that culture. Christenberry's artwork has at-

tracted further attention to the unique Black Belt area and its people. The Black Belt Folk Roots Festival in Eutaw, Ala., celebrates the culture of western Alabama and eastern Mississippi each August. Civil War reenactors celebrate the battle of Selma, and civil rights pilgrims visit the Edmund Pettus Bridge, beginning point of the Selma to Montgomery March, both cultural tourism sites now.

KAREN M. MCDEARMAN
University of Mississippi

L. J. Chestnut Jr. and Julia Cass, *Black in Selma* (1990); William Christenberry, *Southern Photographs* (1983); Allen Tullos, in *The New Regionalism*, ed. Charles Reagan Wilson (1998); Ronald C. Wimberley and Libby V. Morris, *The Southern Black Belt* (1997).

Carolina Lowcountry

The southeastern coast from North Carolina to Georgia rises barely above sea level. Often land's edge is identified by a narrow sandbar that may be miles from the mainland; in other places, such as Myrtle Beach, that sandbar is pushed up against the mainland. Near or far, the southeastern Atlantic littoral is a zone of sand and water in motion, constantly being carried south by the coastal countercurrent but settling and resettling between the sandbars and rivers draining the interior. The larger sandbars, the barrier islands, are unstable, sliced by inlets, and prone to radical changes during major storms. Marshland, Sidney Lanier's Sea of Grass, fills much of the intervening space between barrier islands, stranded beach ridges, and the mainland.

Ocean access to this coast is difficult because of shallow, shifting sandbars at most inlets. Good harbors are found at the mouths of the largest rivers: St. Mary's (Kings Bay) and the lower Savannah (Savannah) rivers in Georgia; the Cooper/Ashley (Charleston) and Waccamaw/Peedee (Georgetown) rivers in South Carolina; and, to a lesser extent, the Cape Fear (Wilmington) River in North Carolina. Not surprisingly, the coast's three largest cities — Charleston, Savannah, and Wilmington — are located on these superior locations for transfer between ocean and land, and Charleston and Savannah are among the top 10 ports in volume in the United States today.

In this coastal swampland, a rice-oriented plantation economy was established at the end of the 1600s and flourished until the eve of the Civil War. Planters, seeking greater opportunity after leaving the densely crowded British sugar islands, especially Barbados, began arriving in South Carolina shortly after 1650. They spent several decades searching for the right crop for the Carolina coast before finding rice. The complex technology needed to turn the marshes and cypress swamps into productive rice paddies was probably introduced by slaves originally from the Senagambia Coast, where rice had been cultivated for over a thousand years. It also appears that the slaves used their understanding of this technology to negotiate a task labor system of laboring, rather than the gang system used in the interior. The task system assigned workers a job to do each day. The day's work was done when the job

was finished, giving time for fishing, tending one's own garden or rice plot, or just sitting and talking about times past.

Labor demands for growing rice were huge, the work was demanding, and the profits were great. The result was a plantation region characterized by an overwhelmingly African American population with a small and often absent planter class by the time of the Civil War. As few Europeans understood the intricacies of rice cultivation, labor management and assignment was usually overseen by the slaves themselves. The result was that much of the numerically dominant African American population often went for long periods without contact with whites. English or French need not be spoken. Allowances for ancient traditions were made automatically. Life went on as it had for centuries as many African elements of everyday life continued and the African-origin population created its own distinctive regional culture, today called Gullah in South Carolina and Geechee elsewhere. Rural portions of this rice coast are still characterized by a population that is overwhelmingly African American, where people still speak with a rich West African lilt and rice is sold in 50-pound bags in country stores and suburban supermarkets.

The decades following the Civil War, difficult for much of the South, were especially hard on the Carolina Lowcountry. Rice production dwindled, disappearing entirely around the turn of the 20th century, and no financially rewarding alternative was found. The region slid into a deep, abiding poverty.

Out-migration dominated population change.

Lowcountry cities, especially Charleston, were extraordinarily diverse ethnically at the end of the American Revolution. Substantial numbers of Germans, French Huguenots, Sephardic Jews, Irish, and others migrated directly from Europe or came south from Boston, New York, and Philadelphia, along with nearly as many New Englanders and others, looking for new opportunities. Charleston hosts the oldest synagogue in continuous use in the United States, and Savannah hosts the second-largest St. Patrick's Day celebration.

Little was added to this rich mix in the century following the Civil War. While coastal cities to the north thrived, Charleston, among the largest (and richest) cities in the country at the time of the Revolution, was not in the top 200 by 1940. Most rice plantations returned to marshland. One consequence of this long period of quiet was that the Gullah/Geechee culture survived in isolated areas all along the coast with little encroachment from the broader American culture.

Change began to arrive along the rice coast after the end of World War II. That change has been largely concentrated in a narrow belt near the coast. Inland, the Lowcountry is an area of often very large pine tree plantations, cut largely for pulp and paper, scattered among large sections of marginally used land. Change near the shore has taken a number of different forms. Carolinians, and then people from across the eastern third of the country,

began to discover the joys of the coast's endless sand beaches. Small oceanfront recreation and second-home communities, mostly visited by folks from the nearby Piedmont, had long been part of a relaxing summer. These numbers exploded during the last half of the 20th century as Americans celebrated their wealth. The Grand Strand, the coast centered on Myrtle Beach, now has more than 300,000 visitors during a busy summer week. The Grand Strand appealed to the "normal" visitor, and other places reached out to the wealthy. Places like Jekyll and St. Simons islands, in Georgia, began attracting wealthy winter visitors by train late in the 1800s. Today places such as Figure Eight Island and Bald Head in North Carolina and Kiawah Island and Hilton Head in South Carolina continue the tradition of second, and increasingly year-round retirement, homes for the very well-to-do. Between the Myrtle Beaches and the Hilton Heads, nearly all accessible places with sand and beach access along the entire coast, unless set aside for preservation or alternative use, are now crowded with second-home "beach cottages" rented by the week during the summer season. The only extensive portions of the barrier islands preserved through the National Park System are on the Outer Banks of North Carolina and on Cumberland Island, Ga.

The military has also played a major role in these changing economic fortunes. The Department of Defense located two of its largest marine training facilities here—Camp Lejeune in North Carolina and Parris Island in

South Carolina—taking advantage of a diversity of land/water environments and a long warm season. The role of the navy has diminished considerably in recent years, but for a while the Charleston area had one of the largest concentrations of naval facilities in the country.

The Lowcountry's three major urban areas have followed rather similar trajectories in recent decades. All are growing in population. Charleston and Savannah have become the fourth and fifth largest ports in the nation, respectively, exceeding New Orleans in total annual tonnage because of their massive container facilities. They have been surrounded on their inland sides by processing industries, traditionally in chemicals and wood products. Today high-tech plants service the growth of automobile and other industry on the Piedmont. All have encouraged tourism based on their old, water-oriented city centers. Housing values around Savannah's city squares, or south of Broad in Charleston, have exploded in value as outsiders buy into these now highly desirable locations. One result is an urban core area of often dramatic contradictions. Districts of multimillion-dollar 18th- and early 19th-century mansions located just blocks from seemingly endless public housing projects are the norm. Indeed, this massive disparity in wealth, with most of the poor African American, typifies the Lowcountry.

The current status of the Gullah/Geechee culture is a measure of some of the consequence of this shift in regional fortunes. The culture has become a vital component of the Low-country's attractions for tourists. The coast highway, U.S. 17, north from Charleston is lined with Gullah women selling baskets made of woven sea grass. Gullah festivals attract large crowds. The enterprising visitor can take Gullah tours, eat restaurant Gullah meals, listen to Gullah music, and purchase volumes of Gullah tales. Yet, change is erasing much of the Gullah/Geechee culture. Coastal development often comes at the expense of once-isolated Gullah communities. The media, public education, visitors in huge numbers, Gullah migration, and numerous other influences have brought massive change to the everyday life of the Gullah/Geechee. Traditional family values and life are increasingly threatened. The person selling the grass baskets is increasingly likely to have learned her skill in basketry classes rather than by watching her granny. As is common with other Americans whose cultures once were maintained by isolation, many in the community are struggling to find ways to preserve this rich cultural heritage. This task is not an easy one.

JOHN FLORIN
University of North Carolina at Chapel Hill

Stephen Birdsall and John Florin, *Regional Landscapes of the United States and Canada* (1999).

Cherokee Settlement

The Cherokee nation, located in eastern Tennessee, the western Carolinas, northeastern Alabama, and northern

Georgia, was one of the last important American Indian strongholds in the eastern United States in the early 19th century. The direct impact of its historical presence is confined to a few historic sites and buildings scattered throughout its home region and the small Qualla Reservation in North Carolina. Its influence on contemporary rural Appalachian settlement landscape, however, continues. Cherokee settlement patterns provide a case study of Indian influence on the South.

The Cherokee were divided into four culturally distinct communities on both sides of the Great Smoky Mountains at the time of European contact in the 18th century: the Valley, Overhill, Middle, and Lower Towns. The core of Cherokee settlement was in the Middle Towns along the upper reaches of the Little Tennessee River in the western Carolinas. This period's settlement landscape featured large palisaded villages of 350 to 600 persons located in the major stream valleys of the region.

On his visit to the Cherokee country during the 1770s, William Bartram found villages clustered around roundish council houses located on an artificial hill or rise, as well as some scattered dwellings. The palisades around the villages disappeared during the relatively peaceful mid-18th century, and a more dispersed settlement pattern soon followed.

The four most common Cherokee building types during the 18th century were the council house, the summer and winter residential houses, and storage buildings. The council house was a large domed post-and-beam structure

designed so that each of the Cherokee clans present in the village would have equal access to the center during community meetings. Its size varied depending upon the population of the village. The summer house was a three-roomed, raised, rectangular, post-and-beam house with woven reed or wicker walls. A long porch was built across the facade for use during the muggy summers. The adjacent winter house was often occupied by more than one family. It was built of poles in a domed shape with heavy walls, no windows, a small door, and an upper air hole for a chimney. A fire burned continually during the winter. Beds were located around the sides of the single room. The corn storage sheds were small post-and-beam structures raised four to five feet off the ground.

The Cherokee settlement landscape was greatly altered after the incursion of white influences into the region. Population pressures and conflict along the eastern and northern borders moved the focal point of power from the western Carolinas first to Tennessee and later to northern Georgia. The Cherokee settlement pattern at the time of removal was also almost totally transformed. Clustered village settlements were replaced by isolated farmsteads. The traditional domed council house vanished. The summer and winter houses were replaced by small, single-pen, hewn-log, one-story, puncheon-floored, wooden-end chimney cottages. These log houses were occasionally enlarged to dogtrot, saddlebag, and I-house forms, but more often a second or third structure was built when additional space was needed. The outbuildings were also patterned on the white frontiersman's buildings and included, in declining order of frequency, corncribs, smokehouses, potato houses, and stables. The remainder of the farmstead consisted of a small truck garden near the house and one or more 5- to 20-acre cornfields.

The impact of Cherokee settlement upon both initial white settlement and the current landscape has been greater than generally believed. The Cherokee were removed from their traditional lands in the 1830s, and the vacated areas were distributed among white settlers. White settlement of the region, therefore, was essentially a continuation of the previous Indian patterns of field- and house-site selections. The vacated Cherokee housing generally was occupied by the new white owners; many such houses are still used today. Indian agricultural methods, especially in the house gardens and the crop complexes and in the philosophies of field selection, also continued to be important in the white landscape. Indian paths and roads became white wagon roads and were eventually preserved in the state and county highway systems.

The principal differences between the two landscapes have been in the growth of towns. There were no true European-style Cherokee towns in northern Georgia at the time of removal. The Cherokee capital of New Echota, for example, never had more than a handful of houses occupied at any one time, most of those by whites. At the time of removal, Cherokee towns were social and economic communities whose residents were widely dispersed. Thus, at the time of removal the Indian "town" of Hightower had more than 100 residents scattered along 30 miles of the Ellijay River valley, whereas the white town of Ellijay founded in the same location had only about 50 residents clustered around the courthouse within three years of its occupation.

RICHARD PILLSBURY
Folly Beach, South Carolina

Gary C. Goodwin, *Cherokees in Transition: A Study of Changing Culture and Environment Prior to 1775* (1977); Henry T. Malone, *Cherokees of the Old South* (1956); Richard Pillsbury, *Geoscience and Man*, vol. 23 (1983).

Cotton Gins

Cotton gins once were common features on the landscape across much of the Lowland South. The demise of cotton in areas where it was king and the replacement of many small gin plants by a few large ones in areas where cotton continues to be an important crop have resulted in the dramatic decrease in the number of cotton gins in the South. The number declined from 30,000 in 1900 to less than 10,000 in 1945. In 2002 only 739 active cotton gins remained in the southern states. However, the average number of bales processed per cotton gin increased from less than 500 in 1900 to nearly 21,000 in 2002.

During the early part of the 20th century, larger, centrally located plants employing what was termed a "ginning system" replaced small, labor-intensive, antebellum-type ginning facilities. The type of ginning facility that developed prior to the Civil War consisted of a

Cotton gin, Mississippi, no date (Ann Rayburn Paper Americana Collection, Archives and Special Collections, University of Mississippi Library, Oxford)

ginhouse in which the removal of seed from the lint, or ginning, took place. In the ginhouse, the seed cotton was fed into a gin stand powered by horses or mules. The lint cotton was carried in baskets from the ginhouse to a horse- or mule-powered press. Most of the cotton plantations had such a facility, and it could process three or four bales of cotton in a day.

The ginning system was developed during the 1880s. A steam-powered plant integrated the ginning with the baling and automated the movement of cotton through the facility. A ginning system contained several gin stands and could process three or four bales of cotton per hour. The term "cotton gin" came to refer to such plants, whereas in its original usage the term had referred to just the gin stand.

The introduction of mechanical

harvesters following World War II initiated another period of dramatic change in cotton ginning. Because mechanically harvested cotton contains more trash and moisture than cotton picked by hand, seed-cotton dryers and lint-cleaning devices had to be added to gin plants, and whereas handpicking commenced in late summer and frequently continued into December, mechanical pickers compressed the harvest season into a period of approximately six weeks. High-capacity gin plants with larger gin stands were introduced to handle the increased flow of cotton from the fields. Recent innovations include module storage of cotton prior to ginning and the use of universal density presses that produce bales ready for shipment to distant markets without further compressing.

A modern cotton gin represents a

substantial capital investment and is capable of ginning 10 or more bales of machine-harvested cotton per hour. Antebellum-type ginning facilities were within 2 to 4 miles of one another, and plants employing ginning systems were 3 to 12 miles apart. Modern cotton gins may draw cotton from a 30-mile radius.

CHARLES S. AIKEN
University of Tennessee

Charles S. Aiken, *Geographical Review* (April 1973); Charles A. Bennett, *Cotton Ginning Systems in the United States and Auxiliary Development* (1962), *Saw and Toothed Ginning Developments* (1960); USDA-NASS, *Cotton Ginning 2002 Summary* (2003).

Courthouse Square

Comparatively few towns developed in the South, because from the days of earliest settlement the region's largely rural residents traditionally resented towns and those living in them. Southerners believed that local government should be local, and southern states have the smallest counties in the nation. The establishment of a seat of local government thus became the single most important force in town creation in the region prior to the railroad era. Founding new communities at sites near the access center of the counties as they formed further allowed local officials to sell building lots to raise funds for the construction of the courthouse, jail, and other necessary government buildings. It also allowed them to create street layouts that enhanced the visual and psychological impact of the new center. Situating the town on the highest point in the surrounding area and

locating the courthouse on an enlarged lot, often in the center of the street or at a point with high visibility, guaranteed that the courthouse and its square would project the authority of the community, the surrounding businesses as the power behind that authority, and the adjacent jail as the unspoken fate of those who questioned either.

Four basic courthouse square and associated street designs were used in laying out county seats in the South. The oldest is the widened-street design dating from 17th-century Virginia. It consists of an enlarged courthouse lot on one side of the main street. The plan is most common in Tidewater Virginia, although examples are occasionally found in other early settled areas. The second design is a geometric version of the widened-street plan called a secant square. It was created by incising the four corners of the main intersection to leave an open space in the street for the courthouse building. The design was first used in 1681 in America to create space for the Philadelphia city hall. This plan was widely used in other large Pennsylvania towns and was often carried to the southern Appalachians by westward-moving farmers from Pennsylvania. In the South it is almost always found in communities on or along the fringes of the Appalachians. Today this open public space often is occupied by a war memorial, statue, or a bit of grass because replacement courthouses built after the mid-19th century typically needed more space and were located on an adjacent traditional building lot or two.

The third design, the central square,

Courthouse, Monticello, Fla., 1939 (Marion Post Wolcott, photographer,
Library of Congress [LC-USF-34-51787-D], Washington, D.C.)

is considered to be the regional arche-
type. It consists of a full-city-block
square at the intersection of the two
main through roads with traffic circling
the square. This is the most common
courthouse square pattern in county
seats founded after about 1830, and its
distribution parallels the founding of
new counties in the South after that
date. Courthouses occupying these
spaces often appear to be situated on an
artificially higher site, but this usually
was a result of erosion lowering the
surrounding streets before they were
paved.

The fourth design is the offset
central-square subform created when
the courthouse block is set astride the
main through road. This design, with
obvious ancillary antecedents in the

secant design, has the advantage of
placing the courthouse in a position of
increased physical, visual, and psychological dominance within the town
plan. Used primarily after 1820, the
off-set square design was most common in more westerly areas, although it
was also sometimes used when eastern
counties were split during the late 19th
century and new seats of government
were created.

County courthouses from the 19th
century almost always were located on
the square. Other typical structures on
the early 19th-century square included
wells, cisterns, and occasionally the jail
and lawyers' offices. Jails tended to be
relocated to less prominent locations in
the late 19th century as a reflection of
increasing demands on their facilities

and the changing character of those who were to be incarcerated in them.

Through the middle of the 20th century, most businesses in town were located facing the courthouse square. An analysis of late 19th-century activities in county seats in Georgia found that the general merchandise store was the single most common business located on the building lots surrounding the square, followed, in order of declining frequency, by offices, grocery stores, dry-goods stores, millineries, drugstores, hotels, lodge halls, and saloons. The second most common land use on the blocks facing the square was residential: typically about 20 percent of this space was devoted to dwellings located along one side and at the back of other blocks.

The courthouse square of the early 21st century has undergone a metamorphosis since its heyday in the 19th century. The original courthouse has frequently been replaced with a new building on a nearby site, though the original might remain as a museum or offices. Increased consumer mobility has brought competitive shopping to even the most isolated community. The expansion of national retailers, Wal-Mart being the most prominent, which locate in only selected communities, has provided incentives for consumers to travel out of town to shop. Coupled with the general population decline of the rural South over the past 40 years, this reduction in consumer demand has closed most of the traditional businesses around the square. The remaining stores often have an air of decay. The smaller county seats typi-

A Georgia courthouse
(Richard Pillsbury, photographer)

cally have as many boarded-up store buildings as open ones; the larger ones are little better off because the surviving businesses have often fled to the automobile-friendly shopping strips at the edge of town. Indeed, if it were not for the florist shops serving the local funeral homes and churches, antique stores serving the occasional urban forager, and vestige family businesses kept open more from tradition than profitability, there would be no commercial activity whatsoever along the margins of most of these squares today. A few attempts at historic preservation and downtown revival have slowed this trend in some communities, but even these activities often do little more than highlight their decline rather than halt the process.

Nonetheless, the courthouse has long been identified as the geographical center of southern communities. In *Requiem for a Nun*, William Faulkner wrote of Jefferson, Miss.: "But above all, the courthouse: the center, the focus, the hub . . . looming in the center of the county's circumference . . . laying its vast shadow to the uttermost rim of the horizon . . . ; dominating all: protector of the weak, judicate and curb of the passions and lust."

RICHARD PILLSBURY
Folly Beach, South Carolina

SUZANNE ANDRES
Georgia State University

Richard Francaviglia, *Geographical Survey* (1973); Richard Pillsbury, *Southeastern Geographer*, vol. 18 (1978); Edward T. Price, *Geographical Review* (January 1968).

Cuban Settlement

Cuban Americans represent the third largest group of Latin American origin living in the United States, being exceeded in number only by Mexican Americans and Puerto Ricans. Currently, about 1.2 million Cubans live in the United States, 67 percent of whom are in the state of Florida. Very few Cubans live in other southern states (even in Florida they account for only about 5 percent of the state's population), but their importance is magnified because they are heavily concentrated in the metropolitan area of Miami, where over 650,000 persons of Cuban descent live. In Dade County (metropolitan Miami), about 60 percent of the population consists of persons of Hispanic origin, about 50 percent of whom

are either first- or second-generation Cubans. The Cubans have had a major impact on the cultural landscape and economy of Miami, so much so that their major area of concentration is called "Little Havana."

Cubans came as permanent settlers to Key West as far back as 1831, but immigration to Florida, and especially to Tampa, increased in the 1870s. These early Cuban Americans came to the United States for a variety of reasons. Many were simply unemployed or looking for better jobs; others in the 20th century were politically alienated from right-wing Cuban regimes. The number of emigrants from Cuba rose sharply after the 1959 Castro Revolution. The Cubans who have moved to the United States have not, until recently, been representative of the population left behind in Cuba.

The earliest significant wave of Cuban immigrants after 1959 contained many professionals and entrepreneurs and thus created a serious "brain drain" in Cuba. As a result of this selection, a social and economic base was established in Miami that would help ease the adjustments of future immigrants. Today, Cuban Americans generally enjoy high levels of socioeconomic status compared to most other groups of Latin American descent.

Without warning, in April 1980, Fidel Castro suddenly allowed a massive exodus to the United States through the Cuban port of Mariel. Over the next six months, approximately 125,000 Cubans immigrated to this country, with about 80 percent settling in south Florida. The "Marielitos" come closest as a group to representing the population in Cuba. Although the Cuban government included in this group about 5,000 prisoners from Cuban jails and patients from mental institutions, the vast majority (perhaps 95 percent) were not criminals or misfits. The collective wisdom of most who have studied them is that the Mariel immigrants will quickly and effectively accommodate themselves to life in the United States.

Cuban Americans attempted to preserve parts of their island culture after moving to Florida. The refugees from the 1959 revolution especially worked at this goal. The widespread use in south Florida of Spanish in shops, restaurants, banks, churches, and government offices is the most visible evidence of their success in maintaining cultural forms. Spanish language bookstores stock writings of Cuban expatriates, Cuban-born artists perform in ethnic theater and dance groups, and neighborhood grocery stores in Miami stock fruits and vegetables traditional to the Cuban diet. Spanish-language television and radio stations broadcast programs for Cuban Americans, and a daily newspaper — owned, like the broadcast facilities, by Cuban Americans — publishes stories of interest to the community. Latin rhythms are heard in the nightclubs in Little Havana.

THOMAS D. BOSWELL
University of Miami

María Cristina García, *Havana USA: Cuban Exiles and Cuban Americans in South Florida, 1959–1994* (1996); Guillermo Grenier and Lisandro Pérez, *The Legacy of Exile: Cubans in the United States* (2003); Félix Masud-Piloto, *From Welcomed Exiles to Illegal Immigrants: Cuban Migration to the United States, 1959–1995* (1996).

Delta

The Yazoo Mississippi Delta is not the true delta of the Mississippi River, but the fertile alluvial plain shared by the Mississippi and Yazoo rivers. It is 160 miles long and 50 miles wide at its widest and encompasses all of 10 Mississippi counties and parts of 8 more. Distinguished by its flatness and its fertility, the Delta was even better defined by its late-developing plantation economy and the distinctive society that that economy nurtured.

Destined to become the richest agricultural region in the South, the Delta was only sparsely settled in 1860 and still not far removed from the frontier in 1880. During the next two decades a new network of levees and a modern railway system opened the plantation South's last frontier for full-scale settlement and development.

The fertile Delta drew not only ambitious whites but also blacks, who saw it as the best place to test their newly won freedom and climb the agricultural ladder to become independent landowners. For many whites, the Delta became a land of wildest fantasies fulfilled, but for thousands of blacks the Delta that had promised them the rural South's best chance for upward mobility became the burial ground for hopes and dreams. In reality the Delta proved to be little more than a stopover for many southern blacks on their way (via the conveniently located Illinois Central Railroad that bisected the area) to the North. The Delta experienced

A crew of 200 black hoers, many of them ex-tenant farmers, on the Aldridge Plantation, hoeing cotton for one dollar a day, near Leland, Miss., 1937 (Dorothea Lange, photographer, Library of Congress Prints and Photographs Division [LC-USF-34-017135-C], Washington, D.C.)

a massive out-migration of blacks in the years after World War I. During the same period the region was emerging as the birthplace of the blues. This new musical idiom explored the shared experiences of southern blacks who had tested the economic, social, and political parameters of their freedom, as defined by a rigidly enforced system of caste, and discovered that, for them, the American Dream was little more than a cruel myth.

Meanwhile, despite their constant fears over labor shortages, Delta planters thrived on the annual gamble on the price of cotton, living lavishly and laughing at debt. Even the onslaught of the boll weevil did the Delta relatively little harm. Meanwhile, by channeling

all of its acreage reduction and related payments through the planter and looking the other way as these same planters illegally evicted now-superfluous sharecroppers, the Agricultural Adjustment Administration (AAA) further entrenched the large landholder in the region. In 1934, 44 percent of all AAA payments in excess of $10,000 nationwide went to 10 counties in the Delta. This largesse facilitated mechanization and consolidation of agriculture, and as federal farm programs continued, the money kept rolling in. In 1967 Delta planter and U.S. senator James Eastland received $167,000 in federal payments. The Delta's poor blacks were not nearly so fortunate, as a power structure dominated by lavishly subsidized planters declared war on the War on Poverty.

Many Delta planters finally met their day of reckoning in the farm crisis of the 1980s, and, although the Delta was the birthplace of the Citizens' Council and a bastion of white resistance to racial equality, the black-majority area finally elected a black congressman, Mike Espy, in 1986. The region's history had been one of tension and struggle — between the races, against the poorer hill counties, against the impenetrable swampy wilderness and the ravages of flood, pestilence, and disease, and finally, against the intrusions of civil rights activists and federal civil rights policies.

Out of this tangle of tension and paradox came a remarkable outpouring of creativity, one that made the Delta's artistic climate arguably as rich as its agricultural one. Greenville alone produced writers William Alexander Percy, Walker Percy, Shelby Foote, Ellen Douglas, Hodding Carter II, Hodding Carter III, David Cohn, and Beverly Lowry. Classical composer Kenneth Haxton is from the Greenville area, as are sculptor Leon Koury and artist Valerie Jaudon. The Delta has produced a host of entertainers, including Jim Henson, creator of the Muppets, country singers Charley Pride and Conway Twitty, and an especially large number of blues singers past and present, from the legendary Charley Patton to contemporary artists like B. B. King and James "Son" Thomas. Sometimes appalling, always fascinating, the Delta's historical and cultural experience often seemed that of an entire region in

microcosm. It richly deserved the title, given by writer Richard Ford, of "the South's South."

JAMES C. COBB
University of Georgia

Robert L. Brandfon, *Cotton Kingdom of the New South: A History of the Yazoo Mississippi Delta from Reconstruction to the 20th Century* (1967); James C. Cobb, *The Most Southern Place on Earth: The Mississippi Delta and the Roots of Regional Identity* (1992); David L. Cohn, *Where I Was Born and Raised* (1967); Tony Dunbar, *Delta Time* (1990); John C. Willis, *Forgotten Time: The Yazoo-Mississippi Delta after the Civil War* (2000).

Faulkner's Geography

Most of William Faulkner's works are set in Yoknapatawpha County. Yoknapatawpha is a fictional place inhabited by fictional persons, but Faulkner integrated it into a geographical setting that included prominent actual places. Yoknapatawpha County is in north-central Mississippi, 70 miles south of Memphis, Tenn. Faulkner thought of Yoknapatawpha as having the same geographical position as the real Lafayette County, Miss., and the geography of the fictional place is based heavily on the geography of that county. Like Lafayette County, Yoknapatawpha County is drained in the north by the Tallahatchie River and in the south by the Yoknapatawpha, the fictional name of the Yocona River. Jefferson, the political seat of Yoknapatawpha County, has many geographical similarities to Oxford, the political seat of Lafayette County.

Despite similarities between Yok-

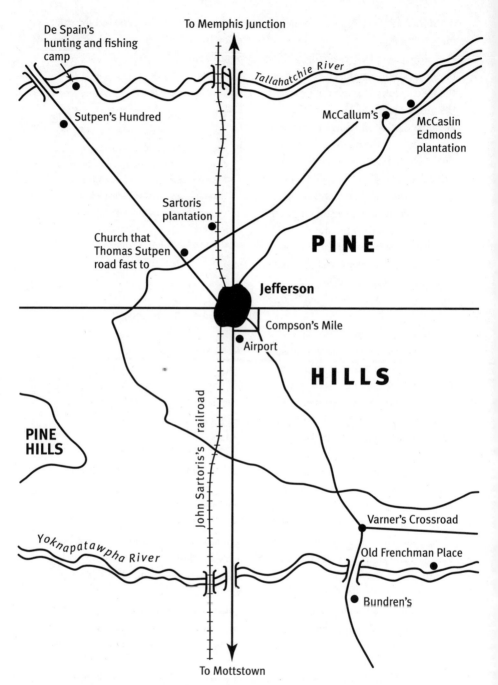

MAP 14. *Yoknapatawpha County (Source: Charles S. Aiken, "Faulkner's Yoknapatawpha County: Geographical Fact into Fiction," Geographical Review* [1977])

napatawpha County and Lafayette County, many differences exist. Faulkner created Yoknapatawpha by combining the real, the modified, and the imaginary. The geography of Lafayette County and Oxford were changed in four principal ways—locations were shifted, place names were changed, components were omitted, and reality was blended with fabrication. Shifts in locations of objects, places, and events were sometimes intercounty and involved temporal as well as geographical changes. In addition to Lafayette County, Faulkner also drew from Marshall, Tippah, and Panola counties, Miss., in creating Yoknapatawpha.

In developing his model for Yoknapatawpha County, Faulkner neither intended it as Lafayette County thinly disguised nor, at the other extreme, as the entire South in microcosm. Rather he viewed it as a place that, though located in the South, was one in which he could describe the universal experience of humankind.

CHARLES S. AIKEN
University of Tennessee

Charles S. Aiken, *Geographical Review* (January 1977 and July 1979); Calvin S. Brown, *A Glossary of Faulkner's South* (1976).

Georgia Land Lottery

The land-lottery system used to distribute Georgia public lands to citizens of the state after 1803 was unique and, although little known outside the state, brought about considerable change in the method of land occupation and settlement. Instead of pioneers moving into former Indian territories and claiming vacant land almost at random, orderly land acquisition was achieved after 1803. The new lands were systematically surveyed and mapped by the state prior to their occupation by settlers.

The Headright Land Act of 1783 proved to be a reasonable method of dispensing public lands to Georgia's citizens until 1789. From 1789 to 1802, however, the state became entangled in a series of land frauds concerning land within the present state limits as well as a vast territory extending west from the Chattahoochee River to the Mississippi River.

The radical new system of distribution adopted in response to this situation was a public land lottery controlled and conducted by state officials. Six lotteries were held between 1805 and 1836. Each area of the public land to be opened for settlement was created as a county unit and then divided by survey into large numbered land districts. Each district was then subdivided into numbered land lots. The size and area of both land districts and individual land lots in each lottery were determined by the specific legislative acts authorizing each of the six lotteries. Land-district and land-lot lines were generally aligned with the four principal compass points—north, south, east, and west—with the exception of the lotteries of 1805 and 1807 and a portion of the 1820 lottery. Fragments of land lots in the various lotteries were retained by the state and, after each lottery, sold at public auction.

After the lottery was authorized, qualified citizens of the state registered for it in their respective counties. The list of registrants was then sent to the capital, where each name was placed on an individual lottery ticket and put into a drum. Each land lot offered in the lottery was identified by county, land district, and land-lot number on another ticket (for example, "District 2, Lot 27, Baldwin County"), and each of these was placed in a second drum. Winners were required to pay a small grant fee. Upon payment, the land won became theirs. Lots that were not claimed reverted to the state and were sold later. Once a person received land by lottery draw, there were no requirements for improvements or even residence on the land in order to maintain possession. Essentially, all of the territory west of the Oconee-Altamaha rivers was distributed by means of public lottery.

GERALD L. HOLDER
Sam Houston State University

James E. Callaway, *The Early Settlement of Georgia* (1948); Georgia Secretary of State, Surveyor General Department, *Land Lotteries* (1966); S. G. McLendon, *History of the Public Domain of Georgia* (1924).

Little Dixie

The establishment of "dixies" beyond the boundaries of the South itself in the 19th century was a phenomenon rich with meaning. The idea of a "Little Dixie" located outside the geophysical South echoes important themes in cultural history. Although there are "dixies" in Utah, Wyoming, Oklahoma, southern Illinois, and Indiana, and probably elsewhere, the best known of these islands of southern culture is Missouri's "Little Dixie" folk region.

Little Dixie is a cultural region in northern Missouri (significantly not in the Ozarks in the southern part of the state) composed of eight counties and a vague zone of transition in surrounding counties. The principal counties are Howard, Boone, Callaway, Audrain, Randolph, Monroe, Pike, and Ralls. The main towns are Fayette, Keytesville, Salisbury, Marshall, Columbia, Fulton, Mexico, Huntsville, Moberly, Paris, Monroe City, Bowling Green, New London, Hannibal, and Palmyra. The region was settled in the early 19th century by emigrants from the Tidewater and Piedmont areas of Virginia, Maryland, the Carolinas, Kentucky, and Tennessee, with Virginia and Kentucky the most important sources. The settlers were largely of British Protestant stock and transplanted their cultural traditions alongside crops of burley tobacco and hemp. These pioneers were well suited to the new environment, and many chose this area because it so closely resembled their home territories.

The region, which comprises forest, prairie, and rich bottomland, is bounded by major rivers—the Missouri on the south and the Mississippi on the east. The deep loess soils of the river hills along the Missouri River were particularly inviting for tobacco growing. The northern border of Little Dixie coincides with later settlement by northerners and easterners. The western border is vague and meanders along the Missouri River toward Kansas City. The region lies culturally and physiographically between the Ozark Highlands and the Corn Belt.

Upland South traditions of fiddle playing, social dance, basket making, the preservation of meat, religious practices, dialect and speech, attitudes toward social organization, and most eloquently, perhaps, traditions of vernacular architecture and political behavior demonstrate the linkages between the people of Little Dixie and the home regions of the Piedmont, the Tidewater, and the Bluegrass. The "old southern mansions" that mark the rural landscape and the persistent devotion to "the Democrat Party" are reminders of a way of life now nearly lost because of the Civil War (and particularly the memory of Reconstruction), settlement by "Yankees," and simply the passage of time. Material culture—architecture, diet, farmstead site arrangement, craft traditions, agricultural economic practices—can still, however, provide a tangible nexus for regional feeling. The region's most famous writer, Samuel Langhorne Clemens (Mark Twain), born to a slaveholding family in Monroe County, first learned about life and human behavior at his Uncle John Quarles's farm in Little Dixie.

Disfranchised by Reconstruction administrators and left with a meager remnant of the prewar way of life, white southerners after the Civil War began to create a psychological space for themselves, a region thought of as Little Dixie, in which old ways and old things retained and regained meaning in the face of change and loss. For older white southerners, the postwar events that upset the economy and altered

hierarchical social patterns, and the coming of northerners and German-speaking immigrants able to purchase the lands of the impoverished settlers, represented the close of an era that would later be thought of by some as a golden age of early Missouri.

The idea of Little Dixie evolved in the 1870s and 1880s in response to the malaise and loss experienced by those who had originally created much of Missouri society. A feeling of continuity and order was achieved through evolution of a memory culture that respected and lauded selected elements of past ways of life and work. The vision of Little Dixie's residents is largely based on a "southern" past (which some call "the old slave days") of log houses, tobacco fields, country ham, foxhunts, rail fences, and what they imagine to have been a more genteel lifestyle, and on the dominance of the Democratic Party in political life.

Today, media attention and numerous local businesses with "Little Dixie" in their name help keep the vision of Little Dixie alive in Missouri and in other areas.

HOWARD WIGHT MARSHALL
University of Missouri–Columbia

Robert M. Crisler, *Journal of Geography* (November 1950), *Missouri Historical Review* (October 1947 and July 1948); Howard Wight Marshall, *Barns of Missouri: Storehouses of History* (2003), *Folk Architecture in Little Dixie: A Regional Culture in Missouri* (1981), *Journal of American Folklore* (October–December 1979), in *Readings in American Folklore*, ed. Jan Harold Brunvand (1979).

Mason-Dixon Line

"An artificial line . . . and yet more unalterable than if nature had made it for it limits the sovereignty of four states, each of whom is tenacious of its particular systems of law as of its soil. It is the boundary of empire." Writing his history of the Mason-Dixon line in 1857, James Veech portrayed the well-founded anxiety of the day: the fear that the horizontal fault between slave and free territory was about to become an open breach. Although the Mason-Dixon line was long associated with the division between free and slave states, slavery existed on both sides when it was first drawn. To settle a long-standing boundary dispute arising from ambiguous colonial charters, the Calvert and Penn families chose English astronomers Charles Mason and Jeremiah Dixon to survey the territory. After four years of work (1763–67), they fixed the common boundaries of Maryland and Pennsylvania at 39°43′17.6″ north latitude, marking their line at every fifth mile with stones bearing the arms of the Penn family on one side and the Calvert crest on the other. Halted in their westward survey by the presence of hostile Indians, their work was concluded in 1784 by a new team that included David Rittenhouse, Andrew Ellicott, and Benjamin Banneker.

In 1820 the Missouri Compromise temporarily readjusted the fragile tacit balance between slave and free territory and extended the Mason-Dixon line to include the 36th parallel. By that date, all states north of the line had abolished slavery, and the acceptance of the line as the symbolic division both politically and socially between North and South was firmly established.

The Mason-Dixon line has been a source of many idiomatic expressions and popular images. Slogans ("Hang your wash to dry on the Mason-Dixon line") originated with early antislavery agitation; variations on the theme (Smith and Wesson line) and novel applications (the logo for a cross-country trucking firm) are contemporary phenomena. A popular shorthand for a sometimes mythic, sometimes very real, regional distinction, the term Mason-Dixon line continues to be used, and its meaning is immediately comprehended.

ELIZABETH M. MAKOWSKI
University of Mississippi

Journals of Charles Mason and Jeremiah Dixon (1969); John H. B. Latrobe, *History of Mason and Dixon's Line* (1855); James Veech, ed., *Mason and Dixon's Line: A History* (1857).

Memphis

Overlooking the Mississippi River, Memphis, Tenn., is located on the Fourth Chickasaw Bluff, some 60 feet above the river, and occupies one of only a few sites in the lower Mississippi Valley where the meandering Mississippi abuts a bluff. This site offered protection from flooding and was good for trade and defense. From the mid-16th century until the late 18th century the site was periodically occupied by the Spanish, the French, and the British. Despite these intrusions, the area was effectively within the domain of the Chickasaw Indians until cession to the United States in 1818. Founded in 1819, Memphis has grown to a population that numbered 650,100 in 2000 and a five-county metropolitan area that contained 1,135,614 inhabitants. The city's growth has been predicated upon nearby resources and centrality within the nation. The area's humid subtropical climate and fertile soils make it one the country's prime areas for cotton, rice, and soybeans. Early commerce in Memphis was closely tied to the hardwood lumber industry and cotton brokerage, both of which remain important, but more recent growth is based upon connectivity and centrality. Memphis is the country's third-largest rail center, fourth-largest inland port, and has the world's largest air cargo airport. Centrality and multimodal transportation has enabled Memphis to become a major distribution center, attracting national and global industries such as Auto Zone, Federal Express, and International Paper. The city also is home to St. Jude's Children's Research Hospital, an internationally known hospital for cancer research.

The initial settlers of Memphis were of English, Scots-Irish, and African stock. However, Germans, Irish, and Italians, Protestant, Roman Catholic, and Jewish, all settled in the city, creating a diversity not found in other inland cities of the South during the late 1800s and early 1900s. In 2000 the metropolitan area was predominantly white and the majority population of the city was African American. The Euro-African culture of Memphis is expressed in two festivals that are rooted in the agricultural crop calendar (planting and harvesting of cotton). The city is known for its barbecue restaurants

B. B. King's Blues Club, on Beale Street, Memphis, Tenn., 2004 (Tennessee Department of Tourist Development)

and annual international barbecue competition. The origins and diffusion of black gospel, blues, and rockabilly music are closely associated with Memphis, where the careers of W. C. Handy, Elvis Presley, Carl Perkins, Johnny Cash, Rufus Thomas, and B. B. King began. Attesting to this musical heritage are the Beale Street entertainment district; Graceland, the home of Elvis Presley; the Stax Recording Studio; and the Gibson Guitar museum. The National Civil Rights Museum, located on the site of the assassination of Dr. Martin Luther King Jr., is a testament to the significance of that movement.

Although terminology such as "Mid-South" and "Mid-America" are attributed to Memphis's locational image, the city has more recently sought to identify itself with the aura of Memphis, Egypt, and the Nile River. This connection is emphasized through museum exhibitions and the name of the city's largest public arena, the Pyramid. The city is home to the National Basketball Association's Grizzlies, a AAA baseball team, a minor league hockey team, a motor sports race track, professional golf and tennis tournaments, and the Liberty Bowl.

W. THEODORE MEALOR JR.
University of Memphis

Gerald M. Capers Jr., *The Biography of a River Town: Memphis, Its Heroic Age* (1966); John E. Harkins, *Metropolis of the American Nile: An Illustrated History of Memphis and Shelby County* (1982); R. W. Johnson, *Journal of Geography* (March 1928); Memphis Chamber of Commerce, <http://www.memphischamber.com>; Robert A. Sigafoos, *Cotton Row to Beale Street: A Business History of Memphis* (1979).

Mills and Milling

Southern gristmills were generally small, custom-grinding operations scattered liberally across the landscape. Their service area was small, and frequently they were built where water could easily be diverted or impounded to power a water wheel.

The southern mill was usually a frame structure of one or two stories and had one or two runs of stones (a pair of grinding stones). Some of the larger mills that ground both corn and wheat had three runs, with one devoted to grinding wheat for flour. The earliest mills were occasionally log and closely resembled the Norse mill of central and northern Europe. Water was directed against the vanes of a horizontal wheel attached to a vertical shaft. The shaft passed through a stationary bedder stone and balanced a runner stone that turned at the same speed as the wheel. Found mostly in Appalachia, this horizontal mill quickly gave way to the vertical mill. Horizontal mills have no gearing, and grinding speed is directly controlled by the volume of water allowed to flow against the wheel. Vertical mills have gears that transmit the power from the wheel to the stone; gearing schemes ranged from simple to complex, depending on the number of runs of stones.

Southern mills were neither as mechanically sophisticated nor as structurally well built as those encountered in other parts of the eastern United States. They also differ in that southern millers persisted in the use of vertical, water-powered wheels long after the turbine was commonly accepted as the power standard. Rather than changing to turbines as soon as possible as a matter of efficiency, the change and the requisite regearing occurred when the old wooden or iron wheels required replacement. As a result, mills in other regions of the east modernized more rapidly, increasing in size and dramatically outstripping southern grinding capacity.

In addition, southern gristmills focused almost exclusively upon the production of cornmeal. Wheat was a secondary crop, especially in the Deep South, and other cereals were even rarer. Wheat milling, or merchant

Gristmill, on the way to Skyline Drive, in Virginia, 1938 (Russell Lee, photographer, Library of Congress [LC-USF-33-11410-MS], Washington, D.C.)

milling as it was known to the trade, was restricted to urban areas and their hinterlands where populations were larger, food preferences were more diverse and with a specific demand for bread flour, and capitalization for the necessary additional equipment was more readily available. The smaller frame mill of the South continued to meet private needs or the limited demands of local farmers.

Milling was one of the earliest economic activities in the South. Although European technological antecedents are undisputed, the southern miller and millwright were quite flexible in adapting mills to meet local demands. Commonly held opinions that mills acted as magnets drawing settlers to the frontier, and that mill sites served frequently as centers for town development, cannot be supported by the data. The rise of merchant milling and changes in southern dietary preferences brought on by national marketing, electricity, and the advent of the blacktop road and automobile all had an impact on the decline of water-powered milling in the South. This decline was evident in the 1930s and accelerated by the end of World War II to the point that southern gristmilling ceased to be a viable economic activity. *Waterground* (Appalshop Film, Frances Morton, director, 1977) is a film study of one of the last southern water-powered gristmills.

In spite of the decline of gristmilling as an industry, and the exacting toll of the southern environment on wooden structures, mills surviving with enough integrity to be restored have benefited from the general surge of America's nostalgia for and interest in restoring its heritage, especially over the last 20 years. Few mills have been restored to full operating capacity, but it is not uncommon to find restored structures in local parks or scattered here and there across the landscape, operating on fair days or selected weekends in the warmer months of the year. On the upper end of the spectrum, a few have been adaptively restored to serve as bed-and-breakfast operations and to produce meal for sale to guests and locals. In rare instances an old mill has been converted into a private residence, but this is usually a larger structure from the late 19th or early 20th centuries and is the exception rather than the rule in adaptive restoration.

D. GREGORY JEANE
Samford University

Elieser S. Posner and Arthur N. Hibbs, *Wheat Flour Milling* (2d ed., 2004); C. Wayne Smith, *Crop Production: Evolution, History, and Technology* (1995); John Storck and Walter Dorwin Teague, *Flour for Man's Bread: A History of Milling* (1952).

Nashville

Halfway between Memphis and the Smoky Mountains, Nashville, Tenn., has historically exhibited characteristics of both the Lowland and the Upland South. The city is situated on the banks of the Cumberland River and emerged like many other frontier cities as a trading post but also as the urban focal point of the agriculturally fertile Nashville Basin. The city did not lose centrality with changing modes of transportation; instead, it became a hub of the Louisville and Nashville Railroad, a company that wielded enormous in-

fluence in the city at the turn of the 20th century.

The favorable location spurred further economic activities such as printing, publishing (especially of a religious nature), finance, and shoe and apparel manufacturing. Several educational institutions, including Vanderbilt University and African American Fisk University, lent some credence to Nashville's aspiration to be the "Athens of the South," complete with its replica of the Parthenon in Centennial Park. In the 1930s the locally owned National Life Insurance Company started a symbiotic relationship with the fledgling music industry, which initiated a new era for the city. The WSM ("We Shield Millions") radio station and the Grand Ole Opry became advertising opportunities for the insurance industry, as well as a successful medium for popularizing country music nationwide.

The music industry has even created its own corporate neighborhood, Music Row, located within sight of downtown Nashville but largely separate from the city's more traditional business community, which has always regarded "Music City USA" as a mixed blessing. Even if the Nashville area's economy today is distinctly postindustrial, some of the most high-profile recent economic expansions in the region have been in the manufacturing industry: Dell Computers and the Saturn and Nissan automobile assembly plants. However, the most important segment of the economy is probably the health care industry. Centered around the country's largest hospital owner, Columbia/HCA and its numerous spin-

Nashville, Tenn., skyline, 2004 (Tennessee Department of Tourist Development)

off companies, the industry forms an agglomeration of national prominence in health care management.

Nashville today is the center of a sprawling eight-county metropolitan area with a population exceeding 1.2 million, 570,000 of whom live in Nashville–Davidson County (a unified city-county government since 1962). Nashville follows the path of dispersed urban form and low-density residential development. The affluent Brentwood/Franklin area south of Nashville has experienced rapid office, retail, and residential growth, emerging as a so-called edge city. At the same time, Nashville's skyline has been altered by booming real estate and downtown revitalization. A new entertainment district emerged in the 1990s at lower Broadway and historic Second Avenue. The music industry has invested in tourism-related development downtown, and, spearheaded by entrepreneurial "Yankee" mayor Phil Bredesen, Nashville now has two major league sports teams (the National Football League's Tennessee Titans and the National Hockey League's Nashville Predators) entertaining enthusiastic crowds in downtown venues.

Nashville's place in the urban hierarchy is more prominent than ever before as the 39th-largest metropolitan area in the nation. It is increasingly affluent, with a diverse economic base and a population from various cultural and geographical backgrounds. Significant Sunbelt migration, with an increasing "foreign-born" component, has altered the traditional southern demographic structure. Longtime residents often remark that Nashville is physically, politically, culturally, and economically quite a different city than it was only a generation before.

OLA B. JOHANSSON
THOMAS L. BELL
University of Tennessee

James F. Blumenstein and Benjamin Walter, *Growing Metropolis: Aspects of Development in Nashville* (1976); Bill Carey, *Fortunes, Fiddles, and Fried Chicken: A Nashville Business History* (2000); Dan Daley, *Nashville's Unwritten Rules: Inside the Business of Country Music* (1998); Don Doyle, *Nashville since the 1920s* (1985); David Halberstam, *The Children* (1998); Robert G. Spinney, *World War II in Nashville: Transformation of the Homefront* (1998); James D. Squires, *The Secrets of the Hopewell Box: Stolen Elections, Southern Politics, and a City's Coming of Age* (1996).

New Orleans

French colonists founded New Orleans in 1718 as a key link in a vast territorial arc stretching from the St. Lawrence River to the Gulf of Mexico. The city defended against English intrusions and controlled resource exploitation throughout its hinterland. Despite situational advantages, the city occupied an inhospitable floodplain site.

Regularly washed by high waters, the nascent colonial entrepôt gradually filled its grid street pattern following construction of protective levees.

Lacking precious minerals, the colony had an ample quantity of pest-resistant cypress timber that emerged as the first important export commodity. During the French and Spanish periods (1699–1803), rice and sugar became key staples supporting riparian plantations that depended on the city's port. When the United States acquired the Louisiana Territory in 1803, New Orleans's commercial interests dominated the cotton trade within the interior valley, particularly with the widespread use of steamboats after 1820. In 1860 New Orleans had become the country's sixth-largest city. Eastbound railroads intercepted much of the downstream commerce, reducing the city's effective hinterland by the 1870s. With its upstream economic base captured, postbellum cotton production in disarray, and only a modest manufacturing sector, the city fell to 15th position by 1900.

New Orleans retained a strong French influence and by southern standards attracted an ethnically diverse population. In the mid-1800s French speakers lived in the downstream faubourgs; the "American Sector" stretched upriver around a giant crescent-shaped meander. African Americans were a sizable population. Many were slaves, but New Orleans had a considerable free-black population. Both freed slaves and free people of color who immigrated constituted an important group of craftspeople and

Above-ground cemetery in New Orleans, 2004 (<www.neworleansonline.com>, Michael Terranova, photographer)

merchants. Irish, German, and Italian immigrants flocked to the city in the 19th century. Most European newcomers lived near the docks or in the swampy rear districts and were particularly susceptible to diseases, such as yellow fever, which was a persistent scourge in the 19th century. In the late 20th century, Vietnamese exiles created a major ethnic enclave, and white flight has produced an African American majority.

With its strong Catholic tradition, New Orleans stands in sharp contrast to southern Protestant cities. The famous Mardi Gras festival is a great citywide celebration with religious roots. As a port city, it developed bawdy entertainment districts in which African Americans gave rise to jazz. Its ethnically complex population produced "creole" building forms, and African

American builders developed the shotgun house type. Entertainment and historic architecture have been cornerstones for a thriving tourist industry. Spicy creole cuisine is another savory attraction.

Coping with site limitations remains a critical concern. A massive levee system had protected New Orleans from river and lakefront flooding. Within the barrier ring, wetland drainage enabled postwar suburban sprawl but caused extensive subsidence of formerly water-laden soils. Pumps had to lift all rainfall out of the giant impoundment. The local economy in the 1990s suffered the exodus of oil company offices, and the city struggled to maintain its costly drainage works.

Hurricane Katrina devastated New Orleans and its surroundings in August 2005. The hurricane hit land east of the

city, bringing catastrophic damage to
St. Bernard Parish and Jefferson Parish,
and the city itself flooded when the 17th
Street Canal levee broke. The following
days left much of New Orleans under
water, destroyed historic neighborhoods, brought thousands of deaths,
led to images of social breakdown, fos-
tered environmental contamination
and destruction, and made refugees of
hundreds of thousands of people. City,
state, and national relief efforts were
slow in the face of the enormity of the
crisis, bringing criticism of the political
and bureaucratic response. The storm
also hit south Mississippi hard, leaving
the future of these areas of the Gulf
Coast in question.

CRAIG E. COLTEN
Louisiana State University

Craig E. Colten, *An Unnatural Metropolis:
Wresting New Orleans from Nature* (2005);
David Goldfield, *Region, Race, and Cities*
(1997); Arnold R. Hirsch and Joseph Logs-
don, eds., *Creole New Orleans: Race and
Americanization* (1992); Peirce Lewis, *New
Orleans: The Making of an Urban Landscape*
(2003).

Northern Cities, Blacks in

The most distinctive feature of black life
in the South in the first half of the 20th
century was the crystallization of a distinct African American nationality. The
sense of identity among the masses of
black people based on a shared culture
and common experiences in institutions such as churches provided the
matrix sustaining life in the South and
laying a foundation that was later trans-
ferred to newer settings in the North
and West.

Pushed by the ravages of the boll
weevil, floods, unemployment after
the collapse of an exploitative tenancy-
sharecropping system, and surging
racism, black people were eager to escape the South. But not until these
factors were combined with the pull of
better jobs and a better life, especially
in the war-stimulated, labor-starved
industries of northern cities, did a
mass migration begin. The move was
facilitated by black newspapers like the
Chicago Defender, by labor recruiters
offering free train tickets, and by word
of mouth.

The African American move from
the South to the North, from country
to city, and from farm to factory is one
of the most significant social transformations in the history of the United
States. No aspect of the lives of black
people was left unchanged. The dynamic interaction of a southern-based,
rural African American nationality and
northern, urban experiences is key to
understanding this process.

In 1900, 9 of every 10 black people
lived in the South and about 8 of every
10 lived in rural areas. Although only
170,000 blacks migrated from the South
in the first decade of the 20th century,
that number increased to 454,000 between 1910 and 1920 and to 749,000
between 1920 and 1930. Between 1930
and 1950 black out-migrants from the
South, mainly to the North and to
cities, totaled 1.9 million. As a result,
the percentage of blacks living in the
North in 1950 increased to 34 percent,
and the percentage living in cities had
increased to 62 percent.

In 1940 over a million of the 3 million black people in the North lived in four cities—New York, Chicago, Philadelphia, and Detroit—increasing their black populations 7- to 30-fold. Between 1910 and 1940, for example, New York's black population increased from 91,709 to 458,444; Chicago's population grew from 44,103 to 277,731 during the same period.

A definite pattern existed to black migration, with proximity to settlement sites and established transportation routes playing important roles. In 1930, 22 percent of Cleveland's blacks had been born in Ohio but 36 percent had come from Georgia and Alabama. In Detroit, more blacks came from Georgia (21 percent) and Alabama (about 14 percent) than were born in Michigan (14 percent). For Philadelphia, 32 percent were born in Virginia and South Carolina, and only 30 percent were natives of the state. Finally, almost as many black Chicagoans had been born in Mississippi (17 percent) as in Illinois. Moreover, there was a distinct age and gender selectivity to the migrations: between 1920 and 1930, 45 of every 100 black males between 15 and 34 left Georgia, and between 1940 and 1950, Mississippi lost almost one-half of its young black adults.

The settlement patterns of southern blacks, especially the compactness and segregation of the black community, encouraged the survival of southern culture. Racial segregation existed in the North as well as in the South. A 1940 study of 109 cities using a residential segregation index with 100 as a maximum score revealed a score of 83.2 for the Northeast (e.g., New York) and 88.4 for the North Central region (e.g., Chicago), as compared to 89.9 for the South. More specifically, the concentration of blacks increased between 1910 and 1950—from 66.8 to 79.7 in Chicago, from 46.0 to 74.0 in Philadelphia, from 64.1 to 80.9 in Boston, and from 60.6 to 86.6 in Cleveland. The result of this concentration was to promote the retention of older southern habits and customs.

The most profound change was in the world of work. In 1910, 60 percent of black men worked in agriculture, but by 1950 only 18.4 percent of blacks were employed as farmworkers. By 1950 also, 38 percent of blacks in general were employed as blue-collar workers in the factories and 34 percent were service workers such as maids and janitors. Although blacks were still on the lowest rungs of the northern economic ladder and constrained by racially discriminatory "job ceilings," which confined them to "Negro jobs," these low-status jobs were usually higher than those on the upper rungs of southern sharecropping tenancy. They brought higher pay, new skills, greater association with whites, and new organizational participation such as in unions.

In addition, a cultural transformation occurred, necessitated by new conditions and the pace of urban life with its greater freedom. Although racial segregation existed, black life in northern cities was less isolated and intimate than in the rural South. Soul food was commercial and available in numerous restaurants, and, as poet Sterling Brown said, "leisurely yarn-spinning" and "slowpaced aphoristic conversation became lost arts."

Religious life underwent profound changes. The rise of the "storefront" church in the city represented the adaptation of the small rural church to city life. In Chicago in the 1940s, 75 percent of the 500 churches in the black community were storefronts. These churches were clustered in the poorer areas of the black community in which migrants were concentrated. Storefronts provided a more intimate context for self-expression and social contacts than the larger, more bureaucratized city churches.

Holiness and spiritualist sects helped solve personal crises and facilitated the adjustment to disruption in family life, loss of social status, and other changes resulting from the transition. Practices such as faith healing were common in some of these churches and similar to practices found in the South. Among the most widely known were the Father Divine Peace Mission Movement and the Moorish Science Temple of America, a forerunner of the Nation of Islam.

Although black membership in churches decreased in the urban North and although the significance of the church as a center of social life declined as it competed with other institutions, including movies, concerts, and other forms of recreation, the church nevertheless remained a key institution in the social life of black people in northern cities and provided a context for sustaining other aspects of rural southern life.

Urban life influenced the form, tempo, and lyrics of black music. The blues had long dealt exclusively with "despair and sadness" over wretched rural conditions, both natural and social: "Don't you see how them creatures, now have done me wrong? Boll weevil's got my cotton and the merchant's got my corn." Mirroring the urban reality of Motown (Detroit), the form remained, but the words were appropriately refocused: "Please Mr. Foreman, slow down your assembly line. I don't mind working, but I do mind dying."

The disruptive impact of the migrations and the harshness of the post–World War I and Depression era caused the producers of the new gospel music to consciously incorporate into black church music the sounds and the forms of earlier black musical traditions, including blues and jazz. According to the "Father of Gospel," Thomas A. Dorsey, the music helped "to give [black people] something to lift them out of that Depression . . . out of the muck and mire of poverty and loneliness, of being broke." In the face of dispersal from the Black Belt South, integration into the urban industrial economy, and racism, black migrants from the South "could go back home" through the blues and other southern musical traditions.

Black family life was affected by the trek north. Initially, urban families retained many of the basic characteristics of their rural counterparts—a larger proportion of children (relative to whites) and more grandchildren living with grandparents (the extended family). Since 1950, however, the number of husband-wife families has declined and the number of divorces has increased. The number of female-headed households and the number of black children living in these households has increased dramatically. Whether these developments represent the "disorganization" of the black family or show its strength in adapting to a hostile environment is much debated. In moving from the South to the North, the black family clearly, in any event, changed in both form and function. Compounded by other developments, such as high unemployment among black youth, the problems created by this shift remain unsolved.

One issue that has not been sufficiently researched is the vibrant interchange that goes on between black people in the North and their southern kin. Black newspapers report on visits and reunions in almost every issue.

Social movements among black people in northern cities showed their southern roots. The Universal Negro Improvement Association of Marcus Garvey, one of the largest, is said to have been successful in large measure because of its appeal to newly arrived black southerners who were won over by the movement's emphasis on independent landownership and institutional development, reflecting their nationlike aspirations. Similarly, the increased popularity of the newly organized Communist Party in the 1930s was related to its claims that the Black Belt region of the South was a

black homeland and that blacks had the right to national self-determination and a government of their own choosing. More importantly, Communists were active organizers of several key campaigns, which appealed to the sentiments of transplanted black southerners. One example was the international defense of the Scottsboro (Ala.) boys, nine black youths unjustly accused and given the death sentence for allegedly raping two white women who later admitted to false testimony. The appeal of such later leaders as Martin Luther King Jr., Malcolm X, and other civil rights activists also reflected the sustained interest of northern blacks in conditions in the South — a region defined by Malcolm X as "everything below Canada."

RONALD BAILEY
Northeastern University

Abdul Alkalimat, *Introduction to Afro-American Studies: A Peoples College Primer* (1986); St. Clair Drake and Horace Cayton, *Black Metropolis: A Study of Negro Life in a Northern City* (1945); Arnold R. Hirsch, *Making the Second Ghetto: Race and Housing in Chicago, 1940–1960* (1998); Donald L. Miller, *City of the Century: The Epic of Chicago and the Making of America* (1996); Joe William Trotter Jr., *Black Milwaukee: The Making of an Industrial Proletariat, 1915–1945* (1984).

Northern Cities, Whites in

During the decade following World War II, social scientists in the North Central Census states became aware of the numbers of working-class white southerners who had migrated to northern cities during the war. Studies of this migrant stream revealed many similarities to earlier immigrants from Europe who had become ethnic minorities. People from particular states or counties often moved to certain cities such as Detroit, Flint, and Chicago. They concentrated in low-rent areas accessible to factories or transportation lines, developing neighborhood institutions and networks.

In such locales, "southern culture," derogatory labels — "hillbillies" and "rednecks" — and unfavorable stereotypes were most evident. Clannishness, a proclivity to violence, a love of country music, and low standards of sexual morality have been part of the stereotype. White southerners have also been accused of bringing hostility toward blacks to these northern regions.

Although appearing to be ethnically distinct because of differences in language, food preferences, and music, such culture was ethnic only by coincidence. The overlay of southern ethnic differences on working-class culture was seen most clearly in the "hillbilly taverns" found in sections of some northern cities.

The distinctive accent, regional food preferences, and evangelical Protestant Christianity are enduring traits retained by white southern migrants, but even these are modified within a generation or two. New migrants are a countervailing influence in keeping their culture alive. Since 1980, however, the volume of migration has decreased even though white migrants from the South to the North Central states still outnumber black migrants.

LEWIS M. KILLIAN
University of West Florida

Chad Berry, *Southern Migrants, Northern Exiles* (2000); Kathryn Borman and Phillip Obermiller, eds., *From Mountain to Metropolis* (1994); Phillip Obermiller, Thomas Wagner, and Bruce Tucker, eds., *Appalachian Odyssey: Historical Perspectives on the Great Migration* (2000).

Ouachitas

The Ouachitas, also called the Ouachita Mountains, are a region in west-central Arkansas and east-central Oklahoma. A part of the Central Uplands physiographic region, the Ouachitas are one of the few east-west–aligned upland areas in the United States. Formed by tremendous pressure as the Llanoria plate pushed north against the horizontal layers of sedimentary rocks, the Ouachitas were raised into folded ridges alternating with long valleys.

The Ouachitas have several subdivisions, including the Fourche Mountains, the Central Ouachitas, and the Athens Piedmont Plateau in Arkansas. The San Bois, Windy Stair, and Kiamichi mountain subdivisions are found in Oklahoma. The Ouachitas are covered with a temperate deciduous and coniferous forest, including scrubby post oak, black hickory, and shortleaf pine. Both natural and artificial surface water bodies are found in the Ouachitas. Although major streams such as the Ouachita, Saline, Cossatot, and Kiamichi originate in the Ouachitas, natural lakes are rare. Today, all of the lakes are man-made. Some serve also as flood control and navigation lakes, but their primary purpose

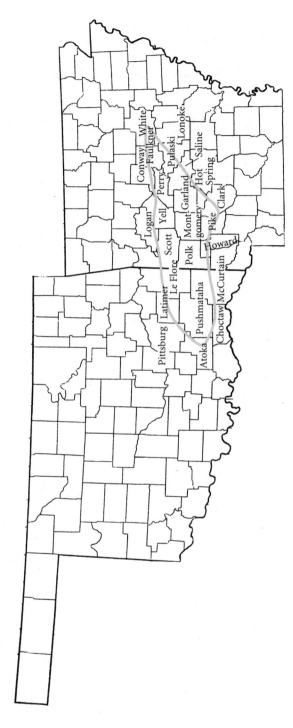

MAP 15. The Ouachita Region

is recreation. These large lakes, including Lake Ouachita, DeGray Lake, Lake Greeson, and Eufaula Reservoir, attract thousands of recreational visitors each year.

The Arkansas portion of the Ouachitas experienced immigration in the antebellum period, primarily white settlers coming from Tennessee, Missouri, and the lower southern states. The Civil War disrupted this immigration. In the postbellum decade the majority of immigrants in the Arkansas Ouachitas came from Texas and Missouri. Non–Native American immigrants were excluded from Oklahoma until after 1889. Slow population growth characterized the region after 1880. Total population grew at a rate of 3 to 5 percent until 1900. Growth halted between 1900 and 1940 as out-migration exceeded in-migration. World War I, the Depression, rural-to-urban migration, and loss of returning veterans all contributed to this decline. Although total population has increased since 1940, rural densities continue to decline throughout the region. Today the region boasts only a few urban places of over 10,000 in population.

Railroad development in the 1880s and timber companies harvesting the forest resources spurred population growth in the region. Timber companies leased large tracts of land to cut timber. The Ouachita National Forest was established in 1907. It covers more than 1.8 million acres, some of which continue to be leased for timber cutting.

Outdoor recreation is important to the Ouachitas. Its forests, hilly terrain, rivers, and lakes offer significant camping, hunting, boating, and fishing opportunities for residents and nonresidents alike. Hot Springs National Park in Arkansas is a national tourist destination for its lakes, thermal springs, historic heritage, and horse racing.

GERALD T. HANSON
University of Arkansas at Little Rock

Gerald T. Hanson and Carl H. Moneyhon, *Historical Atlas of Arkansas* (1992); Robert Walz, "Migration into Arkansas, 1834–1880" (Ph.D. dissertation, University of Texas, 1958).

Ozarks

The Ozarks region is a mid-continent upland region noted for its physical beauty and often associated with stereotypical images of hillbillies and poverty-induced backwardness, on the one hand, and rugged, frontierlike individualism, on the other.

Spanning an area of about 40,000 square miles (roughly the size of Ohio), the Ozarks cover most of the southern half of Missouri and northwestern and north-central Arkansas, as well as much smaller portions of northeastern Oklahoma and southeastern Kansas. Geographers divide the region into four major subdivisions—the Boston Mountains, the St. Francois Mountains, the Springfield Plain, and the Salem Plateau—along with a number of smaller subdivisions. Rivers mark the boundaries of the Ozarks on three sides—the Missouri on the north, the Mississippi and the Black on the east, and the Arkansas on the south. On its western edge, the Ozark region tends to fade imperceptibly into the Great Plains.

In spite of the frequent references to mountains in the Ozarks, the region is not technically mountainous but rather a severely eroded plateau. The highest elevations, found in the Boston Mountains of northwestern Arkansas, exceed 2,500 feet above sea level.

Physically, the Ozarks region is noted for its abundance of water resources and karst features (sinks, underground streams, and caverns) and for its steep and rugged terrain, although large swaths of the region contain rolling hills of minimal relief. The region bears striking geologic and geomorphic similarities to Appalachia and the Cumberland Plateau. These similarities, combined with the commonalities of the Upland South folk cultures found in each region, have led some scholars to describe the Ozarks as a smaller version of Appalachia.

The Ozark region has long been characterized as a rural region peopled by isolated inhabitants. Although this is a relatively modern characterization, archaeologists have unearthed evidence that suggests a tradition of Ozark isolation and sparse population, a tradition with ancient roots that owes much to the region's geography. It appears that the prehistoric residents of the region participated only in a peripheral manner in the developments of the Mississippi River valley. By the time of European settlement along the Mississippi in the 17th century, the Ozarks region was the realm of the Osage, though the Ozark fringes provided homes and territories to other tribes such as the Illinois, Caddo, and Quapaw.

The earliest white settlements in the region date from the early 18th century, when French and French Canadian settlers established Ste. Genevieve and other outposts along the northeastern Ozark fringe. These French settlements would exercise little long-term effect on Ozark history, however, as the region was overrun by American settlers who began trickling into the region in the 1790s and flooding the area after the War of 1812. The vast majority of these settlers came to the Ozarks from the Upper South states of Tennessee, Kentucky, North Carolina, and Virginia and in the process transported the society and culture of the Upland South, and largely Appalachia, to this trans-Mississippi highland. Although slavery existed in the region, the Ozarks' isolation and ruggedness prevented the development of plantation-style agriculture. One result was a much smaller slave population than in most areas of the South, which, combined with sporadic race-related violence and subsequent black flight in the years around the turn of the 20th century, translated into a modern Ozark region that is home to very few blacks. Because of the Ozarks' straddling of the Arkansas-Missouri border, the region was particularly and tragically affected by the Civil War era's bushwhacker-jayhawker conflicts caused by divided loyalties.

In the late 19th and early 20th centuries, railroads and timber companies penetrated the Ozark interior, providing new market opportunities for farmers but stripping the region of its grand virgin forests of pine and hardwoods. Mining for lead, iron, zinc, manganese, and other minerals also became a profitable concern in some Ozark areas. Nevertheless, the vast majority of Ozarkers continued to eke out livings on hillside and creek bottom farms, where general, semisubsistence activities such as dairying, livestock raising, and corn growing were supplemented by cotton raising, fruit raising, or truck farming. By the middle of the 20th century, poultry farming and livestock raising had become the most common agricultural activities in the region.

The Ozark region—or at least most of it—has undergone tremendous change since the 1950s. Out-migration sparked by agricultural transformation and poverty took tens of thousands of Ozarkers out of the region in the quarter century beginning with World War II, and beginning in the 1960s tens of thousands of retirees, back-to-the-landers, and more recently Hispanic workers rushed into the hills to replace them. And in many Ozark areas, tourism has replaced farming, timbering, or low-wage manufacturing as the economic linchpin. Nevertheless, in many ways the image of the Ozarks remains unchanged—a backward, or bucolic, land of innocent hillbillies or rustic frontiersmen. The Ozark region continues, in fact, to rank as one of the nation's most rural regions. Beyond the metropolitan areas (at least by U.S. Census Bureau standards) of the Fayetteville-Springdale-Bentonville area in northwestern Arkansas and Springfield, Mo., the region's largest

city, the Ozarks remains the domain of the small town and rural community. Environmental advantages, both physical and social, largely drive the Ozark tourism industry and fuel the modern fascination with the region.

BROOKS BLEVINS
Lyon College

Brooks Blevins, *Hill Folks: A History of Arkansas Ozarkers and Their Image* (2002); W. K. McNeil, *Ozark Country* (1995); Milton D. Rafferty, *The Ozarks: Land and Life* (2001); Vance Randolph, *The Ozarks: An American Survival of Primitive Society* (1931); Carol O. Sauer, *The Geography of the Ozark Highland of Missouri* (1971).

Piedmont

The Piedmont region extends from the Hudson River to central Alabama, bordering on the Blue Ridge and Appalachian mountains, and ranges from 10 to 125 miles in width. Although it is part of the Appalachian highlands, the Piedmont landscape is rolling but not mountainous. Its relatively infertile soil discouraged settlers until the late 18th and early 19th centuries. The region has been known predominantly as an agricultural region, although it developed industries such as textiles and furniture making in the 19th century. The development of the southern Piedmont (extending to Birmingham, Ala.) has been shaped by the iron and coal industries.

The term "Piedmont" refers to the North and South Carolina Piedmont "crescent," which includes parts of Georgia and Alabama. The Carolina Piedmont has been characterized since the mid- to late-20th century by urban growth. Its cities are headquarters for various large business enterprises, including R. J. Reynolds tobacco company in Winston-Salem, N.C., and Burlington Industries in Greensboro, N.C.

The textile industry was the first industry to develop in the Piedmont. Numerous small streams attracted power spinning (built on waterwheels) as early as 1790 in several South Carolina communities. The first mill was built in North Carolina in 1813, and, after the Civil War and Reconstruction, abundant cheap labor gave the area's textile industry an enormous boost. The low humidity of the region was originally thought to be an obstacle to the operation of the mills, but artificial humidity was developed to create the necessary atmosphere.

Tobacco is one of the most important crops in the northern Piedmont area. The attendant tobacco industry, the manufacture of cigarettes and chewing and smoking tobacco, is concentrated in a few centers in Virginia, Kentucky, and Tennessee but is centered in North Carolina. James B. Duke's use of the first cigarette-rolling machine in the 1880s catapulted the region into its prominent (and, at one point, dominant) role in the industry.

The Piedmont region has been the source of and the setting for some important southern literature. *The Mind of the South* (1941) was written by W. J. Cash from Gaffney, S.C., whose father was an employee of a textile mill. His interpretation of the nature of south-

erners rests largely on his treatment of his native Carolina Piedmont region. Cash focused much of his study on the rise of the upland cotton planter in the early 19th century and the later growth of the textile mill and mill village. The fiction of Reynolds Price, from Macon, N.C., is set in the rural Piedmont South. His works, such as *A Long and Happy Life*, his first novel, and *The Names and Faces of Heroes*, a collection of stories, use regional syntax and colorful description to evoke the setting. Other writers who were influenced by their roots and study in the Piedmont region are Thomas Wolfe, born in Asheville, N.C., and Erskine Caldwell, whose *Tobacco Road* (1932) is set in Wrens County, Ga.

KAREN M. MCDEARMAN
University of Mississippi

Jacquelyn Dowd Hall et al., *Like a Family: The Making of a Southern Cotton Mill World* (1987); Thomas W. Hanchett, *Sorting out the New South City* (1998); Louis D. Rubin Jr., *William Elliott Shoots a Bear: Essays on the Southern Literary Imagination* (1975); Anthony M. Tang, *Economic Development in the Southern Piedmont, 1860–1950: Its Impact on Agriculture* (1958); Allen Tullos, *Habits of Industry: White Culture and the Transformation of the Carolina Piedmont* (1989).

Piney Woods

The piney woods, or Pine Belt, of the Southeast is a vast region of forestland stretching through nine southern states from the Carolinas through Georgia and into Texas. The land of the "pine barrens" is not particularly well suited for agriculture, but the heavy rain-fall and long, warm, sunny summers provide ideal conditions for the rapid growth of pines. The most important species of pine found in the region are the shortleaf, longleaf, loblolly, and slash. The heaviest and strongest of these, the southern longleaf yellow pine, is the most popular among timber growers.

The piney woods has been the victim of human settlement and exploitation. Pioneers used burning techniques they learned from the Indians to clear the land for cultivation and building. Industries later developed markets for pine products and methods for extracting resins and producing turpentine. Beginning in the 20th century, pine was used for a variety of timber products, including pulpwood for paper. The free grazing of livestock also took its toll on the piney woods region.

During the antebellum period the national government first attempted to preserve and protect forests. At the turn of the century the government began the development of policies that recognized that forests are not only commodities to be exploited but also renewable resources. During the New Deal era, state and national conservation efforts were given a boost by the Civilian Conservation Corps, which planted acres of worn-out farmland with trees.

Geographers and historians have studied the way people have adapted to the southern forests. The region has been characterized by poverty and relatively sparse population because of the dense woods. Frank L. Owsley showed

in the early 1950s that classification of antebellum Pine Belt inhabitants as agricultural poor whites was misleading. Actually, the primary occupation of the people of the piney woods was grazing cattle and hogs. They also hunted and trapped for food—true to their character as frontiersmen, according to Owsley.

Developments in the south Mississippi area drained by the Pearl River are indicative of 20th-century trends in the piney woods region. The Pearl River, positioned halfway between the Mississippi River and the Alabama and Tombigbee river systems, runs through the heart of the Pine Belt. The Pearl River bottomlands were uncharacteristically fertile for the pine lands, and some cotton plantations were developed there. Migrants eventually set up communities along the river, and the land was cleared, using the river to transport pine and cypress logs to the sawmills downriver. Railroads eventually changed the landscape further, and the timber industry flourished. By the 1930s, however, the pine supply had been devastated and the cutover soil depleted of nutrients, forcing the region to turn to alternate sources of income. Initially, the lower Pearl River residents planted the Chinese tung tree for its nuts, from which oils were extracted for sale to varnish and paint companies. Hurricane Camille in 1969 destroyed the troubled tung industry. At the same time, a National Aeronautics and Space Administration (NASA) rocket test facility in the area also gave economic hope to the piney woods people, but the NASA program fell short of expectations and once again the region was left in poverty.

KAREN M. MCDEARMAN
University of Mississippi

Samuel C. Hyde Jr., ed., *Plain Folk of the South Revisited* (1997); John Hawkins Napier III, *Lower Pearl River's Piney Woods* (1986); Howard W. Odum, *Southern Regions of the United States* (1936); Frank L. Owsley, *Plain Folk of the Old South* (1949); Noel Polk, ed., *Mississippi's Piney Woods: A Human Perspective* (1986); Rupert B. Vance, *Human Geography of the South: A Study in Regional Resources and Human Adequacy* (1932).

Primogeniture

Legally defined, primogeniture means the right of the eldest son to inherit, to the exclusion of younger sons, the estate of his family because of his seniority of birth. In Europe the practice was long included in so-called entail laws, which limit the inheritance of property. These ancient European practices had virtually no impact on the landholding patterns that emerged in the South. Although southern colonial history dates back to Jamestown, the medieval concept of one great landed aristocracy in the southern colonies passing down vast domains to their eldest son is false. In fact, ambitious sons interested in land, agriculture, and profit moved south into the Carolinas and Georgia and later westward as far as coastal Texas. These locations offered an abundance of land superior in quality to much of that found in Tidewater Virginia.

Primogeniture had a formidable and unrelenting foe in the person of Thomas Jefferson of Virginia. For him, these practices represented an evil that must not be allowed to exist in the American colonies. Through the efforts of Jefferson and many other southern patriots, primogeniture was abolished and legally prohibited throughout the South by 1791.

Therefore, if primogeniture was ever important in the South, it was short-lived and was implemented in a rather restricted geographical region. Although the concept appeared in regional folklore and in earlier historical accounts, in fact the law did not shape the landholding systems of the early South.

GERALD L. HOLDER
Sam Houston State University

John R. Alden, *The South in the Revolution, 1763–1789* (1957); Julian P. Boyd, *William and Mary Quarterly* (October 1955); Walter Clark, ed., *The State Records of North Carolina* (1895–1905); Thomas Jefferson, *Notes on the State of Virginia*, ed. William Peden (1955); C. Ray Keim, "Primogeniture and Entail" (Ph.D. dissertation, University of Chicago, 1926), *William and Mary Quarterly* (October 1968); Richard B. Morris, *Columbia Law Review* (1927).

Richmond

Richmond began as a small trading port in colonial Virginia and evolved into the state capital, a major industrial city, the second capital of the Confederate States of America, and eventually a modern city in the New South. The settlement arose in the falls region of the James River, once a borderland between the Tidewater's Powhatan Confederation and the Monacan Indians to the west. Virginia's Indians shared the resources of the falls, mining the rock outcroppings for tools and harvesting the runs of migrating shad. An inland trade developed first with native groups and eventually with European and enslaved African settlers. The colonial settlement was chartered in 1742 and supposedly named for Richmond upon Thames in England. As with many such settlements, growth occurred slowly because of the dominance of plantation-based tobacco agriculture.

The successful conclusion of the Revolutionary War brought new life to the city, which grew from 3,761 residents in 1790 to 9,735 in 1810, when it was the 12th-largest city in the United States. A rising industrial center and now state capital, the city saw an influx of merchants, government functionaries, enslaved workers, free blacks, and craftsmen, many working on Richmond's first building of major architectural significance—the Virginia State Capitol, designed by Thomas Jefferson.

The Richmond economy faltered in the 1820s and 1830s, exacerbated by the national economic downturn of 1837. The 1840s saw renewed activity, and late antebellum industrial leaders included the Tredegar Iron Works, the Gallego Flour Mills, and a number of major factories in the suitably named town of Manchester directly across the James River from Richmond. Major canal projects and five railroads converged on the city by 1861. The domestic slave trade became one of the most dynamic sectors of the city's economy, as the Upper South exported many thousands of men, women, and

children into the bourgeoning Cotton South.

After Virginia's secession, the Confederate capital was moved from Montgomery, Ala., to Richmond in May 1861, placing it only about 100 miles from the federal seat of government. Despite proximity to Union lines and arms, the city offered the Confederacy a substantial railroad network, a powerful arms-making industry, and a venerable political heritage that helped legitimate its claim as the true heir of the American Revolution. It is estimated that the city tripled in population as workers, government functionaries, soldiers, and often their families converged on the new capital. The social disruption wrought by war led to dramatic scenes: a bread riot led by the city's women in 1863, an explosion in the Confederate cartridge-making shops that killed many women workers, and high mortality among Union prisoners confined to the Belle Isle Prison in the James River. The Evacuation Fire (2–3 April 1865) brought widespread destruction to Richmond at war's end.

Virginia's Reconstruction lasted until 1870, when a new state constitution was adopted. From 1871 to 1902, 33 African Americans served Jackson Ward on Richmond's city council. In 1902 the new state constitution effectively disfranchised most African Americans. The post–Civil War period also saw the development of Confederate memorial movements and the rise of the Lost Cause ideology, as seen in the Hollywood Memorial Association's monument to the Confederate dead at Hollywood Cemetery and in equestrian statues of Robert E. Lee (1890), James Ewell Brown ("Jeb") Stuart (1907), and Stonewall Jackson (1919) on Richmond's Monument Avenue.

The 1902 state constitution disfranchised most blacks, and de facto separation in some public accommodations was quickly replaced by de jure segregation in almost all aspects of life. The segregation of streetcars inspired a boycott by African American residents in 1904 that failed after a protracted battle, and soon neighborhoods and all public facilities were strictly segregated. Exacerbating this trend was the determined exodus of white middle-class residents outward from the central city, aided by the introduction of electric streetcars in 1888, the first operational system in the United States. Developers soon recognized the potential of the lines and began building new suburbs, such as Ginter Park, Lakeside, and Woodland Heights, and also created popular amusement centers such as Forest Hill Park, which featured a midway, carousel, and popular rides. Most black residents remained in segregated downtown communities such as Randolph and Jackson Ward.

Challenges faced Richmond's economy in the early 20th century. The grain-milling business, long a mainstay, waned because of the opening up of the American Midwest and competition from abroad. Richmond's port could not accommodate the larger draught of newer ships, and oceangoing trade shifted toward the Hampton Roads area. The largest metal-working firms did not inaugurate the production of steel on a large basis and decreased in

significance. One continued area of growth was the manufacturing of tobacco, especially cigarettes. The American Tobacco Company, Liggett and Myers, Larus Brothers, Lorrillard, and latecomer Philip Morris all had plants in the city.

Major changes in post–World War II Richmond resulted from the Bartholomew Plan in 1946, which advocated zoning enforcement, housing rehabilitation, and other measures to stem flight from the city center. Unfortunately, the city seemed to favor demolition rather than rehabilitation, knocking down many downtown neighborhoods that provided homes for low-income people. Likewise, new interstate and expressway projects ripped through black and white working-class communities. These actions stirred a nascent historic preservation movement, and activists such as Mary Wingfield Scott of the William Byrd Chapter of the Association for the Preservation of Virginia Antiquities made common cause with neighborhood associations.

Economic transformation also affected the city landscape in major ways. Richmond's famed Tobacco Row of major manufacturers stood empty by the late 1980s — the neighborhood now contains downtown apartments for young urban professionals. The move from manufacturing to a knowledge and service economy saw the dramatic growth of Virginia Commonwealth University (1969) and of the private University of Richmond. Other Richmond institutions of higher learning include Virginia Union University

(1865), a historically black Baptist school, Union Theological Seminary in Virginia (1812), and the Presbyterian School of Christian Education (1914). Richmond also has a strong banking and financial services community, anchored by the Federal Reserve Bank of Richmond, founded as one of twelve regional centers by the Federal Reserve Act of 1913.

Postwar reform changed the face of city government. A modified city charter abolished the elected mayor and bicameral city council in favor of a city manager and nine-member council, with a relatively weak mayor elected from within the council. The policy of massive resistance to integration in the 1950s followed by state leaders and some local officials prevented any meaningful integration of Richmond schools until the late 1960s. By that time flight to the suburbs had largely resegregated the schools. In 1960 the major downtown department stores, Miller and Rhoads and Thalhimers, and other Broad Street accommodations were integrated through sit-ins. Richmond annexed a large swath of Chesterfield County in 1970 after lengthy litigation, again greatly expanding the city and bringing in white suburbanites as well as their taxes and votes. More recently, Richmond's population has declined from a high of 249,621 in 1970 to less than 200,000 in 2005, as the city continues to lose population to the growing suburbs of the surrounding counties.

Richmond struggles with the legacy of Jim Crow segregation and urban decline. The failure of major downtown projects such as Sixth Street Marketplace and the flight of retail to suburban malls, a high per-capita murder rate, a declining population, and constant battles over historical memory have plagued the city. The placing of a statue of tennis legend and author Arthur Ashe on Richmond's Monument Avenue drew a wide range of reactions. Some African Americans expressed dismay that a black hero would share space with Confederate traitors, and Confederate heritage groups protested what they saw as the defiling of their sacred avenue. The majority, especially most of the many newcomers to the city, voiced embarrassment at the negative national press coverage and wondered why so many natives could not get over a war that occurred more than 130 years ago. Only time will tell if changes in governance, attempts at racial reconciliation, and recent public projects, such as the new convention center, the redevelopment of the city's riverfront, and a proposed performing arts center, can revitalize downtown and unify the city.

GREGG KIMBALL
Library of Virginia

Gregg D. Kimball, *American City, Southern Place: A Cultural History of Antebellum Richmond* (2000); John T. O'Brien, *From Bondage to Citizenship: The Richmond Black Community, 1865–1867* (1990); Robert A. Pratt, *The Color of Their Skin: Education and Race in Richmond, Virginia, 1954–1989* (1992); Christopher Silver, *Twentieth Century Richmond: Planning, Politics, and Race* (1984); Emory M. Thomas, *The Confederate State of Richmond: A Biography of the Capital* (1971); Marie Tyler-McGraw, *At the Falls:*

Richmond, Virginia, and Its People (1994);
Marie Tyler-McGraw and Gregg D. Kimball,
In Bondage and Freedom: Antebellum Black
Life in Richmond, Virginia (1988).

Sea Islands

The area known as the Sea Islands, or the Lowcountry, includes the entire southeastern coastal region together with the adjacent islands extending from southern North Carolina to Florida. Apart from the inhabited and arable lands, the islands consist of brackish and salt marshes, beaches, and wooded areas. Some of the better-known islands are Johns, James, and Wadmalaw (the so-called Bible Islands) near Charleston, S.C.; Edisto, where there is a palm-lined beach; and Ladies and St. Helena islands near Beaufort, S.C., where Penn Center, founded as a school for the islanders near the end of the Civil War, is located. Daufuskie—known through the photographic work of Jean Moutassamy-Ashe—Sapelo, and St. Mary's in Georgia are three islands still reachable only by boat. Jekyll has been developed into a conference center; Ossabaw is a privately owned writers' colony. St. Simons has been suburbanized since the 1950s, and Sea Island, developed as a luxury resort, has been in and out of the news as various prominent people have honeymooned there.

The three main ethnic groups are African American, European American, and a triethnic (Native American, African American, and European American) mixed group known as "Brass Ankles." Until the 1930s the Sea Islands were accessible only by boat. Causeways and bridges, which now connect some of the islands to the mainland, have had a major impact on the life of the islanders. Inhabited originally by Yamassee and other Native Americans, the area was invaded, explored, marched through, settled on, and written about successively by the Spanish, the English, and the French. Africans were brought to work the land, making possible large single-crop economies such as the pre-Revolutionary indigo, rice, and cotton and in later years potatoes, tomatoes, soybeans, and cabbage.

During the mosquito season, the islands' European American residents moved away to escape malaria, leaving behind the enslaved Africans, many of whom had the sickle-cell gene that protected them from the disease. Because of their isolation, African Americans preserved many of their African customs in their material folk culture and life, as evident in the distinctive patterning of their quilts, the construction of baskets, women's modes of hair tying, cookery, the making of fishnets, and the practice of fishing. The African influence persists, too, in the Sea Islanders' insurance and burial societies, praying bands, and lodges. The Sea Island creole language (also known as Gullah or Geechee), like the folklore, exudes Africanness, as Lorenzo Dow Turner demonstrated in an epochal study. Much of Turner's work was based on naming customs, some of which are still practiced today.

Books have been written about the area—travel accounts, novels, folklore collections, explorers' journals, educational and religious missionaries' diaries, military records, and studies in history, language, and sociology. Charlotte Forten Grimké, W. F. Allen, Lucy McKim Garrison, Thomas Wentworth Higginson, William Gilmore Simms, Abigail Christensen, Charles Colcock Jones, Pat Conroy, Elsie Clews Parsons, Julia Peterkin, Guy B. and Guion Griffis Johnson, Guy and Candie Carawan, and many others have produced fascinating works about the area and its people, whose folkways command attention and respect.

The formerly high concentration of African American residents has changed in recent years for two main reasons: northward migration of the African American islanders in search of better economic opportunity and the influx of European Americans through suburban, resort, and commercial developments. Recent developments on Kiawah, Hilton Head, and Daufuskie islands (S.C.) threaten the serene beauty of the islands as well as the cultural integrity of their African American folkways, which have few defenses against the advance of mainland-originated technology.

MARY ANN TWINING
Buffalo, New York

Edith McBride Dabbs, *Sea Island Diary: A History of St. Helena Island* (1983); Charles Joyner, *Down by the Riverside: A South Carolina Slave Community* (1985); Elsie Clews Parsons, *Folk-Lore of the Sea Islands, South Carolina* (1923); Lorenzo Dow Turner, *Africanisms in the Gullah Dialect* (1949); Mary Ann Twining and Keith E. Baird, eds., *Sea Island Roots: African Presence in the Carolinas and Georgia* (1991).

Sugar Plantations

Traditionally large agricultural enterprises with landholdings ranging from 200 to 8,000 acres, sugar plantations are devoted to the planting, cultivation, and harvesting of sugar cane and the processing of cane juice into brown sugar and molasses. Sugar plantations have been a distinctive part of the southern landscape since the mid-18th century. They originated in New Orleans in 1742. By 1806, 75 enterprises were dispersed along the Mississippi River to Baton Rouge. By 1844 some 464 French- and Anglo-American–owned sugar plantations of 200 acres or more had made appearances along the Mississippi River and westward into south-central Louisiana along the alluvial natural levees of Bayou Lafourche, Bayou Teche, and the bayous of Terebonne Parish.

Sugar mills numbered 1,240 in 1845, and by 1849 there were 1,536 sugar mills on the Louisiana landscape. The Civil War, cane diseases, and the incorporation and consolidation of enterprises brought the number of mills to 50 on 190 plantations by 1970. Recently, depressed sugar prices, rising fuel and machinery costs, environmental regulations, and the urbanization and industrialization of cane lands have reduced the Louisiana sugar industry to 21 mills.

Elsewhere in the South, small numbers of antebellum sugar plantations once occupied parts of coastal South Carolina, Georgia, Florida, and southeastern Texas. Louisiana, however, dominated the sugar industry with 95 percent of the total antebellum production and continued to be the leader in the southern sugar industry until 1973. Today, a modern sugar industry in Florida typically leads the South with half of the cane acreage and two-thirds of production from seven high-capacity mills. By comparison, Louisiana now has 39 percent of the acreage and 29 percent of the production from 21 mills. In the lower Rio Grande Valley of Texas, a single new mill accounts for the remaining 6 percent of the southern sugar crop.

Source areas from the 18th and 19th centuries for sugar plantation traits in Louisiana were principally the French Caribbean and Anglo-American areas of the Upland and Tidewater South. The French Caribbean contributed (1) the initial sugarcane plants and the cultivation techniques of the Jesuits in 1742 from Santo Domingo (Haiti); (2) an early but specialized sugar technology brought by skilled Caribbean sugar makers; (3) a cultural mix of French Caribbean settlers, planters, and slaves; (4) architectural traits, most notably the hip roof and galleries (wide porches) for plantation mansions, half-timbered construction (a trait that also came directly from France), and quite possibly the shotgun house type initially used for slave quarters. Furthermore, from France, the arpent survey system of linear measure (192 feet per arpent) produced long, narrow landholdings 40 arpents deep, which led to linear settlement patterns among French plantations.

The Anglo-American source areas of the Upland South and the Atlantic Tidewater region supplied the sugar plantation system with (1) landscape traits of block-shaped or gridded settlement patterns; (2) Tidewater architectural traits in plantation mansions with front-facing gables, porticos, pediments, and Georgian symmetry in floor plans; (3) architectural traits from the Upland South's houses of the pen tradition with paired rooms, central hallways, and exterior chimneys; and (4) a significant cultural mix of culture-bearing planters and settlers from the English-speaking South.

JOHN B. REHDER
University of Tennessee

Bob Angers, *Acadian Profile* (April 1982); John B. Rehder, *Delta Sugar: Louisiana's Vanishing Plantation Landscape* (1999); J. Carlyle Sitterson, *Sugar Country* (1953); U.S. Department of Agriculture, *Sugar and Sweetener Report*, vol. 5 (February 1980).

Tidewater

The Tidewater coastal region extends from Delaware to northeastern Florida and from northwestern Florida to the Mississippi Delta. It is a low, flat, sandy or swampy area that enjoys abundant rainfall and a long, warm growing season. The Tidewater is known particularly for its agriculture, forest industries, commercial fishing and oystering, and military installations. It is also attractive to millions of tourists. The Outer Banks, a chain of islands off the North Carolina coast, is the site of a rapidly developing tourist industry that features the Wright Brothers National Memorial and many public recreational areas.

The term "Tidewater" is often used to refer only to the coastal area of Virginia, stretching some 100 miles inland from the sea and southward to the North Carolina border. Tidewater Virginia has been called "a blend of romance and fact." It is in the Virginia area that historic preservation efforts have successfully restored and promoted the region's history as tourist attractions. Beachfront tourist sites and recreational facilities have been developed, and each year thousands of people visit the Tidewater's historic areas, including Jamestown, Williamsburg, and the Yorktown battlefield. The popular Assateague Island nature preserve and the seashore town at Chincoteague testify to the natural beauty of the region. The southern Tidewater in Virginia contains the important seaport of Hampton Roads and the center of the region's sea industry. The densely populated area is the headquarters for the U.S. Navy's Atlantic fleet and contains one of the biggest shipyards in the world. Norfolk, Va., the largest city in this branch of the Tidewater, was renewed during the mid-20th century and today boasts new downtown and waterfront developments, as well as a convention center and the East Virginia Medical School.

Some of the swampy areas of the Tidewater have recently been drained in an effort to reclaim the rich soil for agriculture. New crops, such as soybeans, have proved successful on some of this reclaimed land. Two of the area's famed swamps are protected as wildlife refuges and state park areas. Okefenokee Swamp, which lies mostly in Georgia, is the third-largest swamp in the South. Legendary Dismal Swamp in Virginia is the home of a variety of unique wildlife and species of plants, and since the 1960s it has been the focus of concerted preservation efforts.

KAREN M. MCDEARMAN
University of Mississippi

T. H. Breen, *Tobacco Culture: The Mentality of the Great Tidewater Planters on the Eve of Revolution* (2001); Neal R. Peirce and Jerry Hagstrom, *The Book of America: Inside 50 States Today* (1983); William Styron, *A Tidewater Morning* (1994); Paul Wilstach, *Tidewater Virginia* (1929).

INDEX OF CONTRIBUTORS

INDEX

Page numbers in boldface refer to articles.

87; wages of, 185; religious lives of, 186; family life of, 186; children and youth, 186, 187; female, 187; unemployment of, 188

Black Thunder (Bontemps), 65

Blue Ridge Mountains, 4, 8, 95, 144

Blues music, 7, 177, 178, 186

Bob Wills and His Texas Playboys, 137

Boll weevil, 6, 21, 35, 93, 106, 157, 170

Bontemps, Arna, 65

Bootlegging, 53

Bostonians, The (James), 62

Brammer, Bill, 138

Brazil, 40, 63, 86; Americana, 63; Campo, 63; Iguape ("Lizzieland"), 63; Retiro, 63; Rio Doce, 63; Santeram, 63; São Paulo, 63

Brazil, the Home for Southerners (Dunn), 63

Bread, 12, 69, 71; corn, 69, 78; spoon, 69; wheat, 78

"Breadbasket" region, 134

Breckinridge, John C., 63

Breseden, Phil, 181

Brown, Sterling, 65, 185

Buildings, 4, 9; commercial, 4, 17; designs of, 4; public, 16, 64; prefabricated, 17; barns, 19; European log, 28; facades of, 46, 48; Indian, 58

Businesses and businessmen, 62, 64, 65, 68; Pulte Homes, 23; Centex Homes, 23; Perdue Farms, 39; Pillsbury, 39; Tyson Farms, 39, 75; Manpower Development Corporation, 82; Mammy's Cupboard, 130; Dell Computers, 139; Texas Instruments, 139; Allis-Siemens, 153; Home Depot, 153; Simmons corporation, 153; United Parcel Service, 153; Elyton Land Company, 156; Auto Zone, 177; Federal Express, 177; International Paper, 177; Columbia/HCA, 180; National Life Insurance Company, 180; Burlington Industries, 193; R. J. Reynolds Company, 193; Gallego Flour Mills, 196; Tredgar Iron Works, 196;

American Tobacco Company, 197; Liggett and Myers, 197; Lorrillard, 197; Philip Morris, 197

Cajuns, 6, 28, 55, 108; language of, 29; foodways of, 71

Caldwell, Irskine, 193

California, 64, 72; San Francisco, 66; Los Angeles, 76, 109

Calvert family, 176

Camp meetings, 32, 118

Canada, 6, 28, 63

Cane (Toomer), 65

Carawan, Guy and Candice, 200

Caribbean, 6, 22, 24, 58; planters from, 25; drug trafficking from, 52; slaves from, 60; Jamaica, 63

Carter, Hodding, II, 171

Carter, Hodding, III, 171

Carter, Jimmy, 71, 139

Cash, Johnny, 177

Cash, W. J., 183

Casinos, 75

Castro, Fidel, 168

Catfish, 5, 7, 24, 38, 70

Catslide, 22, 23

Cattle, 9, 26, 38, 40, 64, 136

Caudill, Harry M., 42

Central America, 58, 63, 73; Honduras, 63; El Salvador, 73; Guatemala, 73; Nicaragua, 73

Charleston, S.C., 2, 6, 9, 24, 53, 59, 108, 125, 143; housing of, 11, 25; diversity of, 25; freedmen in, 25; Germans in, 25; Huguenots in, 25, 59; Irish in, 25; Jews in, 25, 59, 86, 87; slaves in, 25; mansions of, 124; South of Broad district of, 124

Chemical plants, 26, 43

Cherokee Indians, 24, 26, 76, 108; settlement of, **161–63**; influence of whites on, 162; migration of, 162; removal of, 162; traditional houses and buildings of, 162, 163; agricultural methods of, 163; farmsteads of, 163; roads of, 163; towns of, 163

square, 165, 166; widened-street design, 165; war memorials in, 165; central-square subform, 166; jails of, 166; offices facing, 166; businesses around, 167; historic preservation of, 167; in Faulkner novels, 168

Cowboys, 64, 136

Crafts and craftspeople, 2, 31, 123

Creoles, 6, 25

Crime, 12, **49–55**; drug-related, 12, 51, 52; violent, 49; ancillary, 52; burglary, 52; robbery, 52; among poor, 53; teen, 53; urban, 53

Crockett, Davy, 135

Crops, 4, 25, 35, 76; cotton, 1, 5, 6, 7, 14, 15, 87; tobacco, 1, 5, 7, 10, 15, 20, 35, 60; of Arkansas River valley, 5; soybeans, 5, 35, 92; tomatoes, 12, 20; of Atlantic Coastal Plain, 24; Indigo, 24, 111; hay, 27, 38; peanuts, 31, 36, 92; modern, 35; winter wheat, 35; animal fodder, 39; apple products, 39, 40; fruit, 39, 40; citrus, 40; indigenous, 58; pecans, 63, 89; peaches, 89; loss of, 93; alternate, 93; irrigation of, 93; lien on, 136

Crossroads, 17, 46, 142, 143

Cuba and Cubans, 30, 56, 61, 63, 73; attitudes of, 30; clothing of, 30; in Florida, 30, 55, 168; foodways and diet of, 30, 71; lifestyles of, 30; population of, 30, 168; as entrepreneurs, 168; and exodus of 1980, 168; in Key West, 168; in Miami, 168; and post-Castro Revolution, 168; professional, 168; settlement in United States, **168–71**; activities of, 169; assimilation of, 169; language of, 169; refugee, 169

Cumberland Gap, 95

Cumberland Valley, 8

Dairies, 27

Daniels, Charlie, 137

Daniels, Jonathan, 130

Davidson, Donald, 129

Davis, Jefferson, 65

Death rate, 114

Dedalus, Stephen, 67

Deep South, 70, 79, 104, 135, 156

Delaware, 109

Deliverance (film), 42

Delta, Mississippi, 6, 7, 10, 92, 95, 169–71; cotton resurgence in, 36; alluvial plain of, 169; emancipated slaves in, 169; fertility of, 169; levees of, 169; plantation economy of, 169, 170; society of, 169; and blues music, 170, 171; cotton in, 170; mechanization of farms of, 170; out-migration of blacks from, 170; poor blacks of, 170; sharecroppers in, 170; artists of, 171; civil rights activities within, 171; literature of, 171; musicians of, 171; racial tensions of, 171

Democratic Party, 44, 175

Design, "new urban," 48

Dialect, 13; loss of, 14

Diplomats, 68

Disease, 58

Districts, historic, 31

Diversity, 55, 57; of foodways, 69; religious, 118

"Dixie" region, 134, 174, 175

Dixon, Jeremiah, 176

Dobie, J. Frank, 137

Doctors, 16, 64, 68

Dorsey, Thomas A., 186

Douglas, Ellen, 171

Drug Enforcement Administration, 53

Drugs, 12, 51; cocaine, 51, 52, 53; designer, 51; ecstasy, 51; illegal, 51; methamphetamines, 51, 52; and violence, 51, 53; heroin, 52; marijuana, 52, 53; trafficking, 52, 53; on interstates, 53; seizures of, 53; smugglers, 53; and inner city, 53

Duke, James B., 193

Dunn, Ballard S., 63

Early, Jubal, 63

Eastland, James, 170

Ecology, 69, 71

Economy, southern, 2, 4, 89; in Appalachia, 5, 42, 44; in central Florida, 47; post-Reconstruction, 61; backwardness of, 68; revolution of, 94

Edmund Pettus Bridge (Selma, Ala.), 158

Education, 2, 12, 51, 64, 66, 116; schools, 10, 123, 142; clerical, 12; in Appalachia, 44; colleges, 64, 66, 89; lack of resources for, 65; graduate and professional, 69

Eggleston, George C., 64

Ehrlich, Benjamin, 89

Elazar, Daniel, 134

Elderly, the, 109

Ellicott, Andrew, 176

Ellison, Ralph, 68

Emigrants, 62; Mexican, 61; Vietnamese, 61; Korean, 61; Indian, 61; from Eritrea, 61; from Nigeria, 61; from the Arabian Gulf, 61; from the Ukraine, 61; from Poland, 61; white, middle class, 62; black, 62, 65, 66; communities of, 62; customs of, 62; professional, 62; émigrés, 63; Confederate, 63; to Central America, 63. *See also* Exiles and expatriates; Immigrants

Employment, 10, 56; outside South, 68; of Hispanics, 75; manufacturing, 78, 81; of blacks, 106, 185

England, 18, 59, 60, 66; settlers from, 58; exiles to, 63; London, 86

Ennui, 2, 33

Espy, Mike, 171

Ethnic groups, 55, 56, 58, 62; geography of, **55–58**; impact of, 55; origins of, 55; traits of, 55; indicators of, 56; black, 57; exclusiveness of, 57; European, 57; Hispanic, 58; patterns of, **58–62**

Europe and Europeans, 1, 3, 24, 26, 32, 59; immigrants from, 7, 56; farms of, 10; English, 18, 59, 60, 66; and Creole culture, 25; Irish, 25, 60, 61, 67; Scotch-Irish, 28, 57, 108; Polish, 61; Italy, 66; Hungarian, 57; habitation, 58; Germanic, 59; Iberia, 59; Salzburg,

Austria, 59; Rhineland, 60; Scotland, 60; Ukraine, 61; exiles to, 63; Portuguese, 64; foodways of, 69

Evans, Eli, 88

Evans, Walker, 158

Exiles and expatriates, 2, **62–69**; black, 62, 65, 64, 65, 66; Confederate, 62, 63; political, 62; post-Reconstruction, 62; reasons for being, 62, 63, 64, 66, 68; white, 62, 64; assimilation of, 63; in Caribbean, 63; in Central America, 63; in Europe, 63, 66; graves of, 63; in Mexico, 63, 66; return of, 63; in South America, 63; descendants of, 64; numbers of, 64; in New York City, 64; societies of, 64, 68; within United States, 64; of Agrarians, 66, 67; intellectuals as, 66, 67, 68; in North, 66, 67, 68; alienation of, 67; return of, 67; myth of, 68

Expansion, regional, 31; of Northeast, 31; of northern Virginia, 31

Expressways, 45

Fabric, synthetic, 43

Factories, 10, 26, 79

Family, 121; values, 11, 32, 57; breakdown of, 12, 51; ties, 57; traditional, 122; of blacks, 186

Farms and farmers, 5, 9, 10, 16, 143; of Ozarks, 5; European, 10; mechanization of, 10, 27, 35; small, 10, 14, 61; tenant, 10, 32, 35; of Lowlands, 14, 19, 35, 61; colonial, 15; markets for, 16, 31; housing on, 18, 19, 26; of Gulf Coastal Lowlands, 20; catfish, 24; corporate, 26, 27; Upland, 26, 27, 38, 39, 92; dairy, 27; poultry, 27; peanut, 36; hobby/part-time, 38, 39; poor, 38; thoroughbred horse, 38, 39; fruit, 39, 40; citrus, 40; irrigation on, 40; nursery/floriculture, 40

Fast food, 13, 32, 129

Father Divine Peace Mission Movement, 186

Faulkner, William, 66, 67, 138, 168; geography of, **171–73**; and Jefferson, Miss., 171, 173; Yoknapatawpha, 171, 172

Feedlots, 39, 40

Ferguson, James, 136

Festivals, 31, 57, 71, 123; International Barbecue (Owensboro, Ky.), 71; Black Belt Folk Roots, 158

Fields, W. C., 63

Fireplaces, 11, 25, 29

First Amendment, 132

Fish and fishing, 6, 12, 24, 25, 70; camps, 13

Fisk University (Nashville, Tenn.), 180

Flagler, Henry, 7

Floods, 106

Florida, 2, 5, 7, 28, 30, 31, 44; Centennial, 2; Seaside, 2; retirees in, 3, 122; geology of, 7; Ocala, 7, 124; population of, 29, 30, 40, 45, 109, 113; railroads in, 29; settlement of, 29; southern, 29–31; tourism in, 29, 30; township-and-range land division, 29; architecture of, 30; beaches of, 30; immigrants in, 30; Cape Kennedy, 30; Cubans in, 30, 55, 71; landscape of, 30; manufacturing in, 30; towns in, 30; as vacation destination, 30; technological industry in, 31, 83; cattle production of, 40; commercial agriculture of, 40, 41; crops of, 40, 41; and floriculture, 40; sugar production of, 40, 41; immigrants to, 41, 58; Lake Okeechobee, 41, 77, 122; Miami, 41, 53, 61, 73, 76, 87; rural life of, 41; central, 45; Disneyfication of, **45–49**; Brevard County, 47; Celebration City, 47, 48, 49; Eatonville, 47, 48; economy of, 47; Lake County, 47; Orange County, 47; Osceola County, 47, 48; Polk County, 47; Seminole County, 47; workforce of, 47; foodways of, 69, 71; Hispanics in, 72; Tampa, 83; Fort Lauderdale, 87; Jews in, 87, 88; Palm Beach, 87; land surveying of, 91; slavery in, 104; Catholics in, 119; churches in, 119; Gainesville, 122, 141; Dade County, 168; Key West, 168. *See also* Orlando, Fla.

Folkways, 2, 31, 42, 56, 200

Foodways and diet, 1, 2, 4, 9, 31, 56, **69–72**; traditional, 2, 12, 32; catfish, 5, 7, 24, 38, 70; corn, 5, 12, 20, 21, 24, 27, 35, 39, 43, 69, 78, 92; barbecue, 7, 13, 20, 24, 31, 70, 71, 138, 177; hoecakes, 7, 78; biscuits, 12, 63, 71, 138; black-eyed peas, 12, 68; butter beans, 12; greens, 12, 24, 138; iced tea, 12, 24; okra, 12, 148; peas, 12, 24; quick breads, 12; sweet potatoes (yams), 12; buttermilk, 13, 24; fast food, 13, 32, 71; plate meals, 13; of Atlantic Lowland, 20; Brunswick stew, 20; chicken, 20, 24, 38, 39, 63, 71, 138; Hoppin' John, 20; lima beans, 20; of Gulf Coastal Lowlands, 24; hush puppies, 24, 70, 78; seafood, 24, 29; of Gullah people, 25; of Acadians, 29, 71; chickory, 29; coffee, 29, 71; Moon Pies, 32; junk, 36; food conglomerates, 39; salt, 43; of ethnic groups, 57; watermelon, 63; collards, 68; ham, 68, 70, 138; as ritual, 68; breads, 69, 71, 78; Conch salad, 69; diversity of, 69; marketing of, 69; of original settlers, 69; bourbon, 70, 78; curing, 70; flitters, 71; mutton, 71; battercakes, 71; beef, 71, 138; coleslaw, 71; of Cubans, 71; nationalization of, 71; pancakes, 71; peppers, 71; pickles, 71; sausage, 71, 138; Tex-Mex, 71; vocabulary of, 71; of Indians, 77, 78; Coca-Cola, 89; chitlins, 123; of Southwest, 134, 138; chicken-fried steak, 138; Chili Appreciation Society International, 138; National Blackeyed Pea Association, 138; redeye gravy, 138; gumbo, 149; boudin, 153; soul food, 185

Football, 139; college, 139, 141; high school, 141; professional, 139

Foote, Shelby, 171

Ford, Richard, 171

Forests, 5, 9, 10, 15, 20, 21, 79, 92, 93;
  cypress, 6, 24; clearing of, 93
Frank, Leo, 88
Fraternity of American Descendants, 63
Freedman's Bureau, 25, 105

Gaines, Ernest J., 104
Gangs, 53
Gardens, 21, 24, 25, 27
Garreau, Joel, 134
Garrison, Lucy McKim, 200
Gaunse, Joachim, 86
Gentry, 15, 16
Georgia, 2, 3, 4, 6, 7, 17, 38, 39, 59, 66, 90;
  Savannah, 2, 9, 24, 59, 86, 143; Kenne-
  saw Mountain, 5; Stone Mountain,
  5, 155; Augusta, 6, 143; Columbus, 6;
  counties of, 12; Madison, 17; housing
  in, 23; peanut farming in, 36; Hispanics
  in, 58, 72, 73, 75; plantations of, 58, 112;
  Ebenezer colony, 59; Plains, 71; Cobb
  County, 75; Dekalb County, 75; Fulton
  County, 75; Gwinnett County, 75; Jews
  in, 86, 88; land-lotteries of, 90; forests
  of, 93; slave trade of, 104; population
  of, 113; Big Canoe, 123; sea islands of,
  123; Eastman, 131; Marietta, 132; Athens,
  141; Macon, 143; Greene County, 158;
  Cumberland Island, 160; Ellijay, 163;
  Hightower, 163; New Echota, 163; Bald-
  win County, 174. *See also* Atlanta, Ga.
Germans, 25, 57, 59, 71, 108; Jewish, 87
Ghost Riders (McCrumb), 42
Gillespie, Dizzy, 65
Globalization, 81
Golden Apples, The, (Welty) 66
Gone with the Wind (Mitchell), 153
Government, 12; county, 12; in northern
  Virginia, 31
Goyen, William, 138
Graves, John, 138
Great Awakening, 118
Great Depression, 1, 10, 23, 106
Great Migration, 8, 106, 107
Great Plains, 136

Great Plains, The (Webb), 135
Great Smoky Mountains National Park,
  44
Great Wagon Road, 60
Greenbelt, 48
Grimké, Charlotte Forten, 200
Grits, 12, 31, 52, 78, 123, 138; "grits belt," 71
Growing up in the Black Belt (Johnson),
  157
Gulf Coastal Lowland, 7, 8, 9, 21; houses
  of, 18, 20, 21, 22, 23, 24; farms of, 20;
  landscape of, 20; migration to, 20; ten-
  ant farms of, 21, 23; foodways of, 24;
  petroleum industry of, 79; manufactur-
  ing industry of, 81; land surveying of,
  90; land use in, 92
Gulf of Mexico, 2, 7, 52, 75
Gullah people, 25, 128, 159, 160, 161, 199
Guns, 49, 51, 53

Hale, Ruth F., 134
Handy, W. C., 177
Harlem Renaissance, 65, 68
Haxton, Kenneth, 171
Hayes, Roland, 65
Headright Act of 1783, 173
Health care, 44, 156
Henderson, Fletcher, 65
Herbert, Paul, 151
Higginson, Thomas Wentworth, 200
Highlands, southern, 42, 95
Hill, Samuel S., 132
Hillbillies, 188
Hindman, Thomas C., 63
Hip-hop, 153, 155
Hispanics, 2, 30, 58, **72–76**; immigration
  of, 2, 41; in Southwest, 2, 135; churches
  of, 72; grocery stores of, 72; language
  of, 72; in Mexican border states, 72;
  of Mexican descent, 72; newspapers
  of, 72; populations of, 72, 74, 75, 76,
  116; radio of, 72; of Central and South
  America, descent, 73; in Florida, 73;
  soccer leagues of, 74; employment of,
  75; in metro Atlanta, 75; tension be-

tween, 75; from other parts of United States, 76

Hogs, 9, 38, 69

Hold Autumn in Your Hand (Perry), 136

Homelessness, 67

Homesickness, 62, 68

Homicide, 49; by juveniles, 53; rates, 53

Homogenization, 32

Hopkins, Lightnin', 137

Horses, thoroughbred, 27; farms of, 38, 39

Hospitality, 68

Hotels, 16, 75

Hot Springs National Park, 190

House of Burgesses, 15

Housing, 1, 9, 10, 11, 17, 27, 31, 32; colonial, 1, 11; manufactured, 2, 22; floor plans, 4, 11, 25; builders of, 11; construction preferences for, 11; in towns, 17, 26; cottages, 18; farmstead, 18, 26; Greek Revival, 18, 21, 22; hall-and-parlor, 18, 21, 22; halls, 18, 21, 25, 29; I houses, 18, 21, 22, 25, 26; kitchens, 18, 21, 29; slave quarters, 18, 23; of upper middle class, 18, 23; in Carolinas, 19; in Virginia, 19, 21; dogtrot, 21, 22, 31, 101; of Gulf Coastal Lowlands, 21–24; doublewides, 22; kits, 22; log, 22, 23, 24, 27, **100–103**; Louisiana bungalow, 22; modular, 22; of New Orleans, 22; plantation, 22, 29; pyramidal, 22, 23; of river towns, 22, 23; saddlebag, 22, 23, 26, 32; shotgun, 22; of Upland South, 22, 26, 27; prefabricated, 23; of tenant farmers, 23; African, 25; Charleston singles, 25; Lowcountry, 25; mansions, 25, 27, 111; city, 26; in West Virginia, 26, 27; horse, 27; house raisings, 28; Acadian, 29; Georgian, 29; art deco, 30; condominiums, 30; in Florida, 30; Spanish stucco rococo, 30; in Appalachia, 44; of retirees, 44, 124; summer, 44; costs of, 48; Ghettos, 61; restoring of, 122, 124

Houston, Sam, 135

Hughes, Langston, 66

Huguenots, French, 25, 59

Humphrey, William, 138

Hunting, 6, 25; fox, 27

Huntington, W.Va., 43

Hurricanes: Katrina, 183, 184; Camille, 194

Hurston, Nora Zeale, 65

Hydroelectric power, 44

Identity, sense of, 55, 62

Illinois, 6, 174; Chicago, 6, 13, 31, 49, 109, 185, 187

Illinois Central Railroad, 6, 39, 169

I'll Take My Stand (Agrarians), 66

Imagineers, 46, 47, 48, 49

Immigrants, 2, 30, 33, 55, 56, 95; Hispanic, 2, 30, 58, 72, 73, 75, 76; Acadian, 6; Caribbean, 6, 30, 41; European, 7, 119; Cuban, 30, 61, 71; in Florida, 30, 41; in Northeast, 30; Chinese, 33; Mexican, 33, 58, 61; Southeast Asian, 33; Latino, 41; lack of, 57; Asian Indian, 61; Koreans, 61; during World War I, 106; German, 108, 119; Scotch-Irish, 108; Catholic, 118; Scandinavian, 119. *See also* Emmigrants

Income, 2, 51, 117

Indiana, 174; Gary, 109; Muncie, 109

Indians, American, 6, 24, 33, 56, 58, **76–78**; Cherokee, 24, 26, 76, 108; Creek, 24, 108; Choctaw, 29, 76, 108; removal of, 58, 76, 77, 108; Algonquin, 76; Caddoan, 76; Catawba, 76; Chitimacha, 76; decimation of, 76; Iroquois, 76; languages of, 76, 77; Muskogean, 76; Natchez, 76; Natchitoches, 76; Powhatan, 76; Seminole, 76, 108; Shawnee, 76; Siouan, 76; Tunica, 76; Tuscarora, 76; Yuchi, 76; foodways of, 77, 78; monuments of, 77; place names of, 77, 78; population of, 77; roads of, 77; and attraction to nature, 78; beliefs of, 78; crafts of, 78; impact of, 78; landmarks of, 78; Chickasaw, 108; relocation to Indian Territory, 108; southwestern, 135; Micmac, 147; Attakapas, 148; Houma, 148; Opelousa, 148; Qualla Reservation, 162

Magruder, John B., 63
Maine, 95
Malaria, 11, 128
Malcom X, 187
Manufacturing, 43, 79, 92; changes in,
  79; cigarette, 79, 81; furniture, 79, 81;
  growth and decline of, 79, 82; iron and
  steel, 79, 81; paper, 79, 81; petroleum
  products, 79, 80, 81; textile, 79, 80, 82;
  apparel, 80, 81, 82; on Coastal Plain, 80,
  81; machinery, 80; electronics, 80, 82;
  of Piedmont, 80; post–World War II,
  80; employment, 81, 84; decline of, 81;
  food, 81; automobile, 81, 82; foreign
  competition of, 81; mergers within, 81;
  wood, 81; employees, 82, 84; hi-tech
  equipment, 82, 84, 85; pharmaceuticals,
  82; software, 82; telecommunications,
  82; higher-skill, 84; in metro areas, 84;
  in small cities and towns, 94
Mardi Gras, 183
Marielitos, 168
Marketplaces, 46, 48
Maryland, 6, 8, 10, 19, 22; Baltimore, 6, 87,
  88; barns of, 20; Jews in, 87; Catholics
  in, 119
Mason, Charles, 176
Mason-Dixon line, 95, **176**
Massachusetts, 64; Boston, 64, 185; Cam-
  bridge, 66, 68
Materialism, 67
Mathews, Little Jimmy, 20
Maury, Matthew Fontaine, 63
McCrumb, Sharyn, 42
McDonald's, 2
McMurtry, Larry, 137, 138
Meatpacking, 40, 75
Mechanization, farm, 35
Media, 28, 32
Meinig, D. W., 134
Memorials, public, 16, 196, 197
Memory, 62, 67
Memphis, Tenn., 13, 109, **176–78**; activi-
  ties in, 177; Beale Street, Memphis, 177;

blacks in, 177; churches of, 177; climate,
  177; corporate headquarters within, 177;
  diversity of, 177; food of, 177; Gibson
  Guitar Museum, 177; Graceland, 177;
  music of, 177; National Civil Rights
  Museum, 177; population of, 177; St.
  Jude Children's Hospital, 177; Stax
  Recording Studio, 177; Grizzlies, 178;
  Liberty Bowl, 178; Methodists, 11, 12,
  28, 117, 119; clergy of, 12; growth of, 118
Metropolitan Statistical Areas, 84
MexAmerica, 134
Mexican Americans, 55, 56, 61, 75
Mexico, 33, 52, 53, 58, 63, 66; Ciudad
  Juarez, 53; Confederate émigrés in, 63;
  Carlota, 63; Cordova, 63
Michigan, 31; Detroit, 31, 49, 185, 187;
  Flint, 187
Midwest, 2, 5, 29, 43, 72, 76
Migration, 4, 32, 56, 61, 63, 64, 95, 125;
  patterns of, 4, 7–9, **108–11**, 185, 187;
  routes, 8; out, 17, 61, 71, 88, 105; to Gulf
  Coastal Lowlands, 20; of Pennsylvanians, 26; black, 49, 65, 66, 71, **104–8**, 109,
  110, 184; of Industrial Revolution, 61;
  international, 61; Mexican, 61; Middle
  American, 61; of Jews, 86, 87, 88; during
  Civil War, 104; forced, 104; of freedmen and women, 104; to Northern
  cities, 104; restriction of black, 104; of
  slaveowners, 104; trans-Appalachian,
  104; to countryside, 105; during Reconstruction, 105; during World War I, 105,
  109; to Midwest, 105; along railroads,
  106; during Great Depression, 106; during World War II, 106, 109, 121; Great,
  106, 107; reasons for, 106, 184; Western, 106; blame for, 107; reverse, 108; of
  elderly, 109; to Florida, 109, 111; from
  Carolinas to New York City, 109; from
  Kentucky to Hamilton, Ohio, 109; from
  Louisiana to Los Angeles, 109; from
  Mississippi to Chicago, 109; from West
  Virginia to Cleveland, 109; of immi-

New Mexico, 72, 133

New Orleans, La., 2, 9, 53, 58, 63, 143, 152, **182–84**; housing of, 22; Jews in, 86; black population of, 182; floodplain of, 182; French influence on, 182; levees of, 182; port of, 182; food of, 183; and Hurricane Katrina, 183, 184; and jazz, 183; and Mardi Gras, 183; tourism of, 183

New South, 51, 65, 157, 195

New urbanism, 48

New York City, N.Y., 20, 31, 49, 53, 62, 67; émigrés to, 64, 65, 67; prosouthern sentiment of, 64; New York Southern Society, 65; Hispanics from, 76; migration to, 109; blacks in, 185

New York Days (Morris), 67

New York Times, 132

Newspapers, 72, 106, 184

"New urban" design, 48

Night Comes to the Cumberland (Caudill), 42

Nine Nations of North America, The (Garreau), 134

North, 2, 17, 51, 61, 104; immigrants in, 30; expansion of, 31; southern distrust of, 51; southerners in, 64; Jews in, 86; black migration to, 106; conditions in, 106; blacks in, 184–87; cities of, 184–88; whites in, 187, 188

North Carolina, 3, 4, 6, 9, 38, 44, 59, 79; Durham, 3, 6, 79; Raleigh, 3, 74, 143; Wilmington, 6, 9, 24, 59; migration from, 8; housing of, 11, 18; tobacco farms of, 19; peanut farming in, 36; chicken production of, 38; Lumbees in, 57; Hispanics in, 58, 73, 74; Asheville, 66, 83, 123, 144; barbecue of, 70, 71; Charlotte, 74, 109; Duplin County, 74; Fayetteville, 74; Sampson County, 74; Winston-Salem, 74, 79, 100; Hickory, 76; manufacturing industry of, 81; Research Triangle Park, 83; Roanoke Island, 86; land surveying of, 91; slave trade of, 104; plantations in, 111; Cashiers, 123; Pinehurst, 123; High-lands, 144; Bald Head Island, 160; Camp Lejune, 160; Figure Eight Island, 160; Outer Banks, 160; Greensboro, 193; Macon, 193

North toward Home (Morris), 67

Oaks, live, 21, 24

Oceanographers, 63

O'Connor, Flannery, 132

O'Daniel, W. Lee "Pappy," 136

O'Donovan, William R., 64

Odum, Howard W., 133, 157

Oglethorpe, James, 86

Ohio, 7, 66, 91; Hamilton, 109; Cleveland, 109, 185; Youngstown, 109

Oil, 6, 28, 79; refineries, 79, 80; embargo, 81

Okeefenokee Swamp, 77

Oklahoma, 36, 53, 74, 133, 174

Old South, 65

Oranges, 40

Orlando, Fla., 3, 45, 46, 53, 83; Disney-fication of, 45–49; Black Zone of, 47; polarization of, 47; as the urban future, 47

Ouachita Mountains, 5, **188–90**; Highlands of, 92; soil quality of, 92; retirees in, 123; streams of, 188; subdivisions of, 188; vegetation of, 188; population of, 190; railroads in, 190; recreation in, 190

Ouachita National Forest, 190

Out-migration, 6, 17, 61, 71, 107

Outsiders, 33, 42; suspicion of, 51, 57

Owsley, Frank L., 194

Ozark Mountains, 5, 110, **190–92**; Germans in, 57; Highlands of, 92; soil quality of, 92; retirees in, 123; stereotypes in, 190; subdivisions of, 190, 191; agriculture of, 191, 192; cities of, 191; forests of, 191; Indians of, 191; settlement of, 191; industries of, 192

Pacific Ocean, 23

Paris, France, 63, 174

Parks, Rosa, 158

Railroads, 6, 7, 17, 32, 43, 142, 156; towns along, 17; in Florida, 29, 40; Chesapeake and Ohio Railway, 43; segregated cars of, 65; black workers on, 106; South and North Railroad, 156; Louisville and Nashville Railroad, 180

Rainey, Ma, 65

Raleigh, Sir Walter, 86

Ranchers, 135

Raper, Arthur F., 157, 158

Reconstruction, 23, 51; economy after, 61; exiles after, 62

Recreation, 94

Redbones, 6

Rednecks, 188

Red River Valley, 91

Reed, John Shelton, 67, 68

Refugees, 63

Regions, 14; agricultural, **35–41**; Lowland, 35–38; Upland, 38–40; Florida industrial, 40–41; industrial, **79–86**; language, **94–100**; religious, **117–21**; retirement, **121–25**

Religion, 9, 11, 12, 56, 57; fundamentalist, 11, 88, 120; Jewish, 25, 86–90; serpent handling, 28, 42; programs, 28; Upland, 28; of Acadians, 29; Appalachian, 42, 120; Protestantism, 57, 117, 119, 120; Christian, 117–21; regions of, 117–21; white, 117; Catholic, 118, 119; diversity of, 118; Evangelicals, 118, 119, 120; on northern borders, 121; southwestern, 134; black, 186; Nation of Islam, 186

Requiem for a Nun (Faulkner), 168

Restaurants, 13, 32; cafeterias, 13; cafés, 13, 138; family-style, 13; fast food, 13, 32, 129; fish-camp, 13; soul food, 185

Retailers, national, 32

Retirees, 2, 33, 44; in Florida, 3, 122; in Appalachia, 44; affluent, 121; population of, 121; regions of, 121–25; activities of, 123; food and diet of, 123, 124; impact of, 123; midwestern, 123; housing of, 124; preferences of, 124

Revolutionary War, 59, 100, 104

Rice, 1, 5, 6, 24, 25, 29, 58, 129; coast, 22, 60; African, 60; consumption of, 125; economy, 125, 126; cultivation of, 125, 126; introduction of to South Carolina, 125; Madagascar, 125; milling of, 125; slaves, 125, 126, 127; workers, 125; plantations, 125–29; export of, 126; in Georgia, 126; growing season of, 126; mills, 126; in North Carolina, 126; prosperity of, 126; and task system, 126; planters of, 127, 128; in Arkansas, 128; collapse of, 128; competition, 128; European markets of, 128; and Gullah culture, 128; in Louisiana, 128; mechanization of, 128

Richmond, Va., 6, 43, 44, 79, 143, **195–98**; blacks in, 196, 197; during Reconstruction, 196; economy of, 196; Indians near, 196; and Lost Cause, 196; population of, 196; settlement of, 196; slave trade of, 196; women in, 196; cigarette manufacturers in, 197; historic preservation of, 197; Memorial Avenue in, 197; neighborhoods of, 197; streetcars in, 197; universities of, 197; banks of, 198; during Jim Crow, 198; murder rate of, 198; white flight from, 198

Ridge and Valley Province, 8, 26, 27

Rittenhouse, David, 176

Rivers, 5, 6, 15, 24; Ohio, 2, 7, 26, 43; Potomac, 2, 26, 60; Arkansas, 5; Mississippi, 5, 9, 22, 26, 58, 148; Little Tennessee, 8, 26, 60; Pee Dee, 9; Connecticut, 20; Savannah, 20, 22; Tennessee, 22, 43; towns along, 22, 23; James, 26, 60, 195; tributaries of, 58; Atchafalaya, 77, 91; Monongahela, 77; Oconee, 90, 174; Cape Fear, 125; Satilla, 125; Alabama, 157; Tombigbee, 157; Ellijay, 163; Tallahatchie, 171; Yocona, 171; Chattahoochee, 173; Cumberland, 180

Roads, 7, 15, 28; paved, 10, 17; macadam, 21; highways, 44, 45; interstates, 45, 53, 79, 80, 82, 84, 130; Indian, 58, 77; building of, 130

Roadside, **129–33**; historical markers along, 129, 130; monuments along, 129; natural attractions of, 129; pilgrimages of, 129; reshaping of, 129; signs, 129, 130, 132; Texan, 130; tourist traps, 130, 131; trees, 130; wildflowers, 130; billboards on, 130; interstate, 130, 132; businesses, 131; souvenirs, 131; churches, 132; crosses, 132; folk art, 132; fireworks, 132; Appalachian, 132; religious signs, 132

Rock and roll, 7

Rodgers, Jimmie, 137

Rouss, Charles B., 64

Rubber, synthetic, 43

Rubin, Louis D. Jr., 66, 67

Rumrunners, 53

Ryan, Thomas, 64

Salvador, Frances, 88

Schmidt, William E., 132

Scholars, 62; black, 65

Schools, 10, 123, 142; black, 13; medical, 64; northern, 64; University of Tennessee (Knoxville), 141; University of Texas (Austin), 141; Vanderbilt University (Nashville, Tenn.), 180; University of Richmond, 197; Presbyterian School of Christian Education (Richmond, Va.), 198; Union Theological Seminary in Virginia (Richmond), 198

Sea islands, 3, 24, **199–201**; agriculture of, 199; cotton on, 199; Gullah people of, 199; Indians of, 199; landscape of, 199; location of, 199; names of, 199; population of, 199; rice plantations of, 199; settlement of, 199; writers of, 200; writing on, 199; blacks in, 200; folkways, 200

Sea World, 45

Sedimentary rocks, 4

Segregation, 57, 65, 185

Selma Chalk, 157

Selma to Montgomery March, 158

Servants, indentured, 15

Settlement patterns, 10, 56, 57, 94, 95, 108; phases of, 10; in Appalachia, 42

Settlers, 69; French, 6, 58; European, 7, 10, 58, 60, 108; English, 15, 25, 58, 60; German, 25, 60; Irish, 25; Carolinian, 26; of Upland South, 26; Scotch-Irish, 28; Pennsylvanian, 60; Welsh, 60; foodways of, 69; in Chesapeake region, 108

Sharecropping, 1, 10, 112, 135, 170

Shenandoah Valley, 8, 10, 27, 39, 42, 77

Ships and shipping, 15

Sibley, Henry W., 63

Sick of Shadows (McCrumb), 42

Simms, William Gilmore, 200

Slaves and slavery, 10, 15, 59, 60, 125; quarters, 12, 22, 23, 111, 112; in Atlantic Lowland, 19; in Piedmont, 19; activities of, 25; churches of, 25; foodways, 25, 69; impact of, 59; gang system, 25; Gullah, 25; Lowcountry, 25; music of, 25; personal histories of, 25; task work system, 25, 125; Caribbean, 60; on rice coast, 60, 125, 126, 127; revolts of, 65; emancipation of, 104; escape of, 104; migration of, 104; trade of, 104, 108; West Indian, 108; ancestors of, 125; Liberian, 125; and knowledge of rice culture, 125; Senegalese, 125; Upper Guinean, 125; overseers, 127; freedoms of, 128; health of, 128

Slidell, John, 63

Smith, Bessie, 65

Smith, Landgrave, 125

Smokehouses, 21, 27, 102

Smoky Mountains, 3, 4, 8, 44, 123

Snowbelt, 72, 110

Social activities, 10, 17

Sociologists, 49, 67

Soft drinks, 12, 24, 32

Soil, 4; quality of, 5, 92; of Appalachia, 5; of Lowland South, 5; of Ozarks, 5; of Atlantic Coastal Plain, 24; of Upland South, 92

Soldiers, 32; Confederate, 62; exile of, 62

Sommers, Sam, 89

Urbanization, 51, 93, 94
Urban life, 2, 9, 95, 107; bias of, 11; and crime, 51, 52
Utah, 174

Vandiver, Frank, 135
Veech, James, 176
Vegetables, 12, 20, 24, 40
Vera Cruz, Mexico, 63
Villa America, Brazil, 63
Villages, 20, 29
Violence, 12, **49–55**; among children and youth, 51, 53; drug-related, 51, 53; inner-city, 51, 53; patterns of, 51; rural, 51; white, 51, 188; gang, 53; in suburbs, 53; toward blacks, 188
Virginia, 2, 6, 7, 26, 27, 39, 40, 42, 60, 92; Williamsburg, 2; Northern, 3, 10, 31; Chesapeake, 7; migration from, 8, 60; housing of, 11, 19, 21; Tidewater region, 15, 69; tobacco of, 19; Charlottesville, 27, 123; Middleburg, 27; peanut farming in, 36; Winchester, 39; Newport News, 43; Valley of, 60, 100, 108; Smith-field, 70; Hispanics in, 72, 73; computer industry of, 83; telecommunications industry of, 83; Jews in, 87, 88; plantations of, 111; Petersburg, 143; Roanoke, 144. *See also* Richmond, Va.
Virginian, The (Wister), 136
Vocabulary, 69, 71; American Indian, 77
Voting Rights Act of 1965, 158

Wal-Mart, 89
Walt Disney Company, 45
Walt Disney World, 30, 45
Ward, Joshua, 127
War on Poverty, 170
Warren, Robert Penn, 66
Washington, D.C., 3, 6, 31, 44, 49, 61; Jews in, 87; churches of, 119
Washington, George, 65
Waterground (film), 179

Wealth, 44, 47
Weaver, Richard M., 67
Web and the Rock, The (Wolfe), 66
Webb, Walter Prescott, 135
Webster, Merriam, 62
Welty, Eudora, 66, 67
West Virginia, 5, 7, 26, 43, 61; Charleston, 43; Parkersburg, 43
Wharves, 46, 48
Whites, 6; and homicide, 49; migration of, 187; in northern cities, **187–88**; food preference of, 188; language of, 188; religions of, 188
Who's Who in America, 68
Widows, 64
Winn, Mary, 129
Wisconsin, 20
Wise Blood (O'Connor), 132
Wister, Owen, 136
Wolfe, Thomas, 62, 66, 67, 193
Women, 61, 64, 187, 196
Woodlands, 35
Woodson, Carter, 65
Workers, 47; religious, 68; domestic, 75; service-sector, 75; manufacturing, 79, 80, 82, 84; wages of, 80; educated, 84; black, 106, 185
World War I, 22, 32, 66, 105, 106
World War II, 1, 6, 7, 10, 13, 29, 32, 36, 39, 40, 43, 61, 65, 79, 87, 88, 112
Wright, Richard, 65, 107
Writers, 62, 64; black, 65, 66; of Southwest, 137, 138; Delta, 171
Wyoming, 174

Yankees, 65
Yellow fever, 128
Yoknapatawpha, 171, 172
Young, Lester, 65
Youth, 7, 53, 138, 155, 188
Yulee, David Levy, 88

Zelinsky, Wilbur, 134